Russia Survival Guide. Business & Travel

Russia Survival Guide is a cogent and comprehensive briefing and reference tool for persons traveling on business and/or pleasure to Russia. No other guide is more up-to-date. No other guide covers more of Russia.

Russia Survival Guide provides contact information for 77 of Russia's largest cities, most of which were closed to foreigners just six months ago. But that is only one part of this travel and business resource, which includes everything from how to get cash in a crunch in Yekaterinburg, to how to avoid committing cultural *faux pas*, to how to register your business in Russia, to how to select a partner or management personnel. *Russia Survival Guide* will tell you where to get government funding for an investment project, where to get medical aid in Omsk, and where to look for the best books, maps and periodicals on Russia. And much, much more.

This guide is the product of many person's unflagging efforts, including Stephanie Ratmeyer, S. Todd Weinberg, Bella Gubnitskaya, Yuri Pankratov, Jennifer Krebs, Clare Kimmel, Scott D. McDonald, Patrick Ryan, Glenn Holstein, Ken Pafford, Nina Goryachyova, Tatyana Subbotina, Julia Gubnitskaya, Marina Gershtein, Anna Subbotina, Galina Levina, Katya Alekseyeva, Irina Petrova and Dmitri Katsyzny.

Corrections and comments are enthusiastically encouraged. Please contact Russian Information Services at either of the addresses on the page facing.

Russia Survival Guide is just one of a series of publications of Russian Information Services. Other publications include:

Where in Moscow (4th ed.)
Where in St. Petersburg (2nd ed.)
Russian Travel Monthly
The New Moscow: City Map and Guide (2nd ed.)
The New St. Petersburg: City Map and Guide (1st ed.)
Business Russian
Business Legal Materials: Russia
Russian News Abstracts

All information in this guide is the most authoritative information available at the time of printing.

The Publisher
March 1994

For Stephanie, Christopher and Sarah

Table of Contents

I. Facts & Reference   I

2.Preparations & Visas   58

3. Travel & Accommodations   79

4. Russian City Guide   98

5. Money & Crime   127

6. Food & Health 138

7. Communication & Shipping 147

8. Doing Business 158

9. Russian Business Law 169

Tables, Graphs & Illustrations

1

Facts & Reference

Russia Facts*

Number of accredited foreign journalists in Moscow: 1,556

Percent of Moscow businesses with offices in residential buildings: 25%

Russian hard currency revenues hidden abroad each year (est.): $4.2 bn

Cost of a minute of prime time advertising on Russian TV: $12,500

Percent of Russian homes with a VCR: 8%

Number of Mercedes' registered in Moscow: 5,021

Of which are new: 967

Average number of car thefts in Moscow, per month: 675

Average number of car thefts in Los Angeles, per month: 5,800

Rank of the US among sources of foreign investment in Russia: 1

Percent of Russians 'affiliated' with the Russian Orthodox Church: 33%

Soviet military spending in 1985: $241 bn

Russian military spending in 1992: $39.6 bn

Tons of poison gas in Russia's chemical weapons arsenal: 40,000

Soviet oil production in 1988 (mn barrels/day): 11.4

Russian oil production in 1993 (mn barrels/day): 7.2

Percent of Russians working in privatized companies: 20%

Number of murders in Moscow, per day: 3

Number of murders in New York, per day: 6

Number of major crimes in Moscow in 1993: 19,000

Number of major crimes in Los Angeles in 1993: 302,000

Number of times Moscow police officers used their guns in 1993: 1,358

Number of times L.A. police officers used their guns in 1993: 144

Number of Russian troops based outside Russia: 200,000

See first page of index for sources

Russia and the Independent States

✪ National capital	—— International Boundary
Izhevsk • City	- - - - Time zone Boundary
Latvia Country	
🕐 Local time when 12:00 in Moscow	0 — Miles — 800

94, Russian Information Services, Inc.

Average Year-Round Temperatures in Russia (°C)

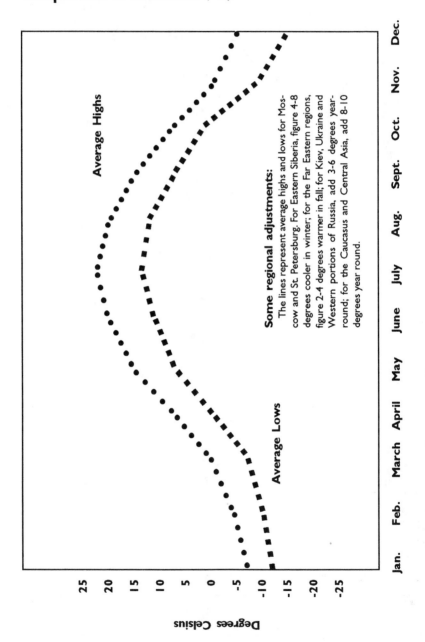

Average Highs

Average Lows

Some regional adjustments:

The lines represent average highs and lows for Moscow and St. Petersburg. For Eastern Siberia, figure 4-8 degrees cooler in winter; for the Far Eastern regions, figure 2-4 degrees warmer in fall; for Kiev, Ukraine and Western portions of Russia, add 3-6 degrees year-round; for the Caucasus and Central Asia, add 8-10 degrees year round.

Jan.   Feb.   March   April   May   June   July   Aug.   Sept.   Oct.   Nov.   Dec.

25   20   15   10   5   0   -5   -10   -15   -20   -25

Degrees Celsius

City Codes Within the CIS

To direct-dial long distance within the Commonwealth of Independent States, dial 8, wait for a dial tone, then dial the city code as listed below and then the local number. You will need to add zeroes or twos between the city code and the local number to make a total of 10 digits if the number of digits do not already equal ten.

City	Code	City	Code
Almaty	327	Kursk	07100
Arkhangelsk	818	Lipetsk	0740
Ashkabad	363	Lvov	0322
Astrakhan	85100	Magadan	41300
Baku	8922	Magnitogorsk	35137
Barnaul	3952	Minsk	0172
Bishkek	331	Moscow	095
Blagoveshensk	41622	Mozhaisk	238
Borodino	39168	Murmansk	815
Bratsk	39531	Nikolaev	0510
Brest	01622	Nizhny Novgorod	8312
Bryansk	08322	Noginsk	251
Bukhara	365	Novgorod	8160
Cheboksari	8350	Novosibirsk	3832
Chelyabinsk	351	Odessa	048
Cherkassy	0472	Omsk	38122
Chita	30222	Orel	0860
Dagomys	8620	Orenburg	35300
Dnepropetrovsk	0562	Pavlodar	3182
Donetsk	0622	Penza	8412
Dushanbe	3772	Perm	3422
Fergana	373	Petropavlovsk	3150
Gomel	02322	Petrozavodsk	81400
Grozny	8712	Pinsk	01653
Irkutsk	3952	Poltava	05322
Ivanovo	09322	Pskov	81122
Izhevsk	3412	Rostov	08536
Kaliningrad	01122	Rostov-on-Don	8632
Kaluga	08422	Rovno	0360
Karaganda	3210	Ryazan	0912
Kaunas	0127	St. Petersburg	812
Kazan	8432	Samarkand	366
Kemerovo	38422	Saransk	8342
Khabarovsk	4210	Saratov	8452
Kharkov	0572	Semipalatinsk	3222
Kiev	044	Sergeyev Posad	254
Kirov	833	Sevastopol	0690
Kostroma	09422	Simferopol	06522
Krasnodar	8612	Smolensk	08100
Krasnoyarsk	3912	Sochi	8620
Kuybyshev	8462	Stavropol	86522
Kurgan	35222	Sukhumi	88122

Sumgait	89264
Suzdal	09231
Syktyvkar	82122
Taganrog	86344
Tambov	07522
Tashkent	3712
Tbilisi	8832
Termez	37622
Tomsk	38222
Tula	0872
Tver	08222
Tyumen	3452
Ufa	3472
Ulan-Ude	30122
Ulyanovsk	84222
Uralsk	31122
Vitebsk	02122
Vladimir	09222
Volgograd	8442
Vologda	81722
Volokolamsk	236
Voronezh	0732
Vyborg	278
Yakutsk	41122
Yalta	0600
Yaroslavl	0852
Yekaterinburg	3432
Yerevan	8852
Zaporozhe	0612
Zhitomir	041

☑ For other cities, or if you have difficulties with dialing, or if you want the number for directory assistance for a certain city (some are listed in Chapter 4), call 07.

☑ Note that Moldova, Estonia, Lithuania and Latvia now have their own country dialing codes (see chart on the following page).

International Country and City Codes

To dial an international call from Russia, first dial 8, wait for a dial tone, then 10, then the country code, then the city code and local number.

Algeria	213	Georgia	7	Korea, South	82	
Argentina	54	Germany	49	Seoul	2	
Buenos Aires	1	Berlin	30	Kuwait	965	
Armenia	7	Bonn	228	Latvia	371	
Australia	61	Dusseldorf	211	Riga	2	
Melbourne	3	Frankfurt	69	Liberia	231	
Sydney	2	Munich	89	Libya	218	
Austria	43	Greece	30	Liechtenstein	4175	
Vienna	1	Athens	1	Lithuania	370	
Azerbaidzhan	7	Guatemala	502	Vilnius	2	
Bahrain	973	Haiti	509	Luxembourg	352	
Belarus	7	Honduras	504	Malawi	265	
Belgium	32	Hong Kong	852	Malaysia	60	
Brussels	2	Hong Kong	5	Mexico	52	
Bolivia	591	Hungary	36	Mexico City	5	
Santa Cruz	33	Budapest	1	Moldova	373	
Canada	1	Iceland	354	Chisinau	2	
Montreal	514	India	91	Monaco	3393	
Ottawa	613	Bombay	22	Morocco	212	
Toronto	416	New Delhi	11	Namibia	264	
Vancouver	604	Indonesia	62	Nepal	977	
Cameroon	237	Jakarta	21	Netherlands	31	
Chile	56	Iran	98	Amsterdam	20	
Santiago	2	Teheran	21	The Hague	70	
China	86	Iraq	964	New Zealand	64	
Beijing	1	Baghdad	1	Nicaragua	505	
Columbia	57	Ireland	353	Nigeria	234	
Bogota	1	Dublin	1	Norway	47	
Costa Rica	506	Israel	972	Oslo	2	
Croatia	385	Jerusalem	2	Oman	968	
Cyprus	357	Tel Aviv	3	Pakistan	92	
Czech Republic	42	Italy	39	Islamabad	51	
Prague	2	Florence	55	Panama	507	
Denmark	45	Milan	2	Peru	51	
Copenhagen	1 or 2	Rome	6	Phillipines	63	
Ecuador	593	Venice	41	Manila	2	
Egypt	20	Ivory Coast	225	Poland	48	
El Salvador	503	Japan	81	Warsaw	22	
Estonia	372	Tokyo	3	Portugal	351	
Tallinn	2	Yokohama	45	Lisbon	1	
Ethiopia	251	Jordan	962	Qatar	974	
Finland	358	Amman	6	Romania	40	
Helsinki	0	Kazakhstan	7	Bucharest	0	
France	33	Kenya	254	Russia	7	
Paris	1	Kirgizistan	7	Moscow	095	
				St. Petersburg	812	

Saudi Arabia	966
Senegal	221
Singapore	65
Slovakia	42
South Africa	27
Spain	34
Barcelona	3
Madrid	1
Sri Lanka	94
Suriname	597
Sweden	46
Stockholm	8
Switzerland	41
Geneva	22
Zurich	1
Tadzhikistan	7
Taiwan	886
Thailand	66
Bangkok	2
Tunisia	216
Turkey	90
Istanbul	1
Turkmenistan	7
Ukraine	7
United Arab Emirates	971
UK	44
Belfast	232
Cardiff	222
Glasgow	41
London	71 (inner)
	81 (outer)
United States	1
Boston	617
Chicago	312
Dallas	214
Detroit	313
Houston	713
Los Angeles	213
Montpelier	802
New York	212
San Francisco	415
Seattle	206
Washington	202
Uruguay	598
Uzbekistan	7
Vatican City	396
Venezuela	58
Yemen Arab Republic	967
Yugoslavia	381
Belgrade	11

Metric Conversion Chart

LENGTH

I centimeter	0.394 inches
I inch	2.540 centimeters
I foot	0.35 meters
I meter	3.281 feet
I yard	0.9144 meters
I kilometer	0.6214 mile
I mile	1.6094 kilometers
I verst (Russia)	1.067 kilometers

WEIGHT

I gram	0.03527 ounce
I ounce	28.35 grams
I pound	0.4536 kilos
I kilogram	2.2046 pounds
I met. ton	0.9842 Eng. ton
I Eng. ton	1.016 metric ton

SQUARES AND AREA

I sq. centimeter	0.1550 sq. inch
I sq. inch	6.452 sq. centimeters
I sq. meter	10.764 sq. feet
I sq. foot	0.09290 sq. meters
I sq. meter	1.196 sq. yards
I sq. yard	0.8361 sq. meters
I sq. kilometer	0.386 sq. mile
I sq. mile	2.59 sq. kilometers
I hectare	2.47 acres
I acre	0.405 hectares

VOLUME

I tsp.	5 ml
I cup	0.24 liter
I liter (dry)	0.908 quart
I quart (dry)	1.101 liters
I liter (liquid)	1.0567 quarts
I quart (liquid)	0.9463 liters
I US gal. (liquid)	3.785 liters
I Imp. gal. (lqd)	4.546 liters
I liter (liquid)	0.264 US gal.
I liter (liquid)	0.220 Imp. gal.

CLOTHING SIZES

WOMEN

Suits and Dresses

American	8	10	12	14	16	18
British	10	12	14	16	18	20
Russian	36	38	40	42	44	46

Stockings

American & British	8	8½	9	9½	10	10½
Russian	0	1	2	3	4	5

Shoes

American	6	7	8	9
British	4½	5½	6½	7½
Russian	36	37	38	40

MEN

Suits/Coats

American	36	38	40	42	44	46
Russian	46	48	50	52	54	56

Shirts

American & British	15	16	17	18
Russian	38	41	43	45

Shoes

American & British	5	6	7	8	9	10	11
Russian	38	39	41	42	43	44	45

TEMPERATURE

$(°F - 32) \times 5/9 = °C$
$(°C \times 5/9) + 32 = °F$

°F	°C
100	40
90	35
80	30
	25
70	20
60	15
50	10
40	5
30	0
20	-5
10	-10
	-15
0	-20
-10	-25
-20	-30
-30	-35
-40	-40

*Russian **hat sizes** are based on the measurement, in centimeters, of the circumference of one's head, at mid-forehead level.

The Newly Independent States

The US Department of State and Department of Commerce have termed the states of the former Soviet Union the Newly Independent States, or NIS, in order to include both members and non-members of the loosely configured Commonwealth of Independent States (CIS). Founded somewhat hastily on December 8, 1991 by the heads of state of Russia, Ukraine and Belarus, the CIS' formation was the final push that led to the end of the USSR as a legal entity (which officially occurred on December 26, 1991, when the USSR Supreme Soviet voted itself, and the USSR, out of existence).

CIS MEMBER STATES

Common name	Official name	Capital
Azerbaidzhan	Azerbaidzhan Republic	Baku
Armenia	Republic of Armenia	Yerevan
Belarus	Republic of Belarus	Minsk
Georgia	Republic of Georgia	Tbilisi
Kazakhstan	Republic of Kazakhstan	Almaty
Kirgizistan	Republic of Kirgizistan	Bishkek
Moldova	Republic of Moldova	Chisinau
Russia	Russian Federation	Moscow
Tadzhikistan	Republic of Tadzhikistan	Dushanbe
Turkmenistan	Turkmenistan	Ashkhabad
Uzbekistan	Republic of Uzbekistan	Tashkent
Ukraine	Ukraine	Kiev

FORMER USSR REPUBLICS WHICH ARE NOT CIS MEMBERS

Common name	Official name	Capital
Estonia	Estonian Republic	Tallinn
Latvia	Latvian Republic	Riga
Lithuania	Lithuanian Republic	Vilnius

RUSSIAN TIME CHANGES

Russia changes to and from Summer Time on different weekends from much of the West. Between Moscow and New York, the time differences during the year are:

From the last Sunday of March to the first Sunday of April: 9 hours.
From the last Sunday of September to the last Sunday of October: 7 hours
All other times: 8 hours.

The Russian Federation

The Russian Federation is composed of 21 republics (one is *de facto*), one autonomous oblast, 10 autonomous okrugs, six krais and 49 oblasts.

REPUBLICS OF RUSSIA

Adygeya (Caucasus, near Sea of Azov); **Bashkortostan** (Central Asia, near Western Kazakhstan); **Buryatia** (Eastern Siberia, Lake Baikal); **Chechnya [Ichkeria]** (Caucasus, bordering on Eastern Georgia); **Chuvashia** (Southeast of Moscow); **Dagestan** (Caucasus, bordering on the Caspian Sea); **Gorno-Altay** (Southeastern Siberia, bordering on China); **Ingushetia** (Caucasus, bordering on Eastern Georgia); **Kabardino-Balkaria** (Caucasus, bordering on Eastern Georgia); **Kalmykia-Khalmg Tangch** (Near Northern Caspian Sea); **Karachaevo-Cherkesia** (Caucasus, bordering on Eastern Georgia); **Karelia** (Northern Russia, bordering on Finland); **Khakasia** (Southeastern Siberia, bordering Altay); **Komi** (Northwestern Siberia); **Mariy El** (Southeast of Moscow); **Mordovia [Mordvinia]** (Southeast of Moscow); **Northern Ossetia** (Caucasus, bordering on Eastern Georgia); **Sakha [Yakutia]** (Northeastern Siberia); **Tatarstan** (Southeast of Moscow); **Tuva** (Southeastern Siberia, bordering on China); **Udmurtia** (Southeast of Moscow)

AUTONOMOUS OBLAST

Jewish [Yevreyskaya] (Southern Far East, bordering on China)

AUTONOMOUS OKRUGS

Aginskiy Buryatskiy [Aga] (Southeastern Siberia, near Buryatia); **Chukotka** (Northern Far East, bordering Alaska); **Evenka** (Central Siberia, West of Sakha); **Khanty-Mansi** (Central Siberia, East of Komi); **Komi-Permyat** (Western Siberia, South of Komi); **Koryak** (Northern half Kamchatka); **Nenetsiya** (Northwestern Siberia, North of Komi); **Taymyr [Dolgano-Nenetsiya]** (Northcentral Siberia, West of Sakha); **Ust-Orda Buryat** (Southeastern Siberia, West of Buryatia); **Yamalo-Nenets** (Central Siberia, East of Komi);

FREE ECONOMIC ZONES

Free economic zones have been established in a number of cities, republics and regions of Russia, by way of singling out the region as relatively more attractive to foreign investment and trade. In concrete terms, this usually means a more beneficial tax and tariff structure (see Chapter 9).

There are presently Free Economic Zones established in or planned for: **Altay, Avachinskaya (Kamchatka), Blagoveshchensk, Chitinskaya oblast, Gorny Altay,** the **Jewish autonomous oblast, Kaliningrad (Yantar), Kurile Islands, Kuzbass, Nakhodka, Novgorod (Sadko), St. Petersburg, Sakhalin, Sheremetyevo airport, Taganrog, Vladivostok, Vyborg** and **Zelinograd.**

Russian City/Region Name Changes

Few things signify the changing of the guard in Russia more than the casting off of the names imposed on Russian cities under communism. Below is a list of Russian cities which have been returned their pre-1917 names. Lists of street name changes in Moscow and St. Petersburg are given in our books, *Where in Moscow* and *Where in St. Petersburg*, respectively.

Communist (former) name	Original (present) name
Andropov	Rybinsk
Brezhnev	Naberezhnie Chelny
Chernenko	Sharypovo
Georgiu-Dej	Liski
Gorkiy	Nizhniy Novgorod
Gorkiy oblast	Nizhegorod oblast
Gotvald	Zmiyev
Kalinin	Tver
Kalinin oblast	Tver oblast
Kaspiyskiy	Lagan
Khalturin	Orlov
Kirovabad	Giandzha
Komsomolskiy	Yugorsk
Kuybyshev (Tatar SSR)	Bolgar
Kuybyshev (Samara oblast)	Samara
Kuybyshev oblast	Samara oblast
Leningrad	St. Petersburg
Novogroznenskiy	Novovoronezh
Ordzhonokidze	Vladikavkaz
Partizanskiy	Gashun-Burgista
Petrokrepost	Shlisselburg
Rybachye	Issyk-Kyl
Ustinov	Izhevsk
Sovetskoe	Shatoy
Sovetskoe village	Kashkhatau village
Sverdlovsk	Yekaterinburg
Svetogorsk village	Shamilkala village
Teuchezhesk	Adygeysk
Voroshilovgrad	Lugansk
Zagorsk	Sergiev-Posad
Zhdanov	Mariupol

Information Resources

Interest in Russia and the Commonwealth has, in recent years, grown in direct proportion to the opening of those countries' economies and societies. Concomitant with this surge in interest has been a growth in the number and types of information resources available. The flood of potentially useful information is often overwhelming and confusing. This section strives to provide a concise and reasonably comprehensive survey of the various types of information resources (at least those relating to business and travel) available in printed, electronic and other formats.

PERIODICALS

This section is restricted to periodicals which mainly or exclusively focus on the former Soviet Union, with particular reference to business and travel issues. Thus, unless they have a particular bearing on business, travel and trade activity, they are excluded.

Publications are divided into general interest publications and special interest publications. Each listing tells the frequency of the publication, its average length, and the price for an annual subscription, unless otherwise stated. Ordering information is also provided.

For books and other information materials of use to business persons, frequent travelers or companies, refer to the next section.

General Interest Periodicals

BISNIS Bulletin and BISNIS Search for Partners, BISNIS, Room 7413, US Dept. of Commerce, 14th & Constitution Ave., NW, Washington, DC 20230, ph. 202-482-4655, fax 202-482-2293. *These two free publications of the Department of Commerce contain useful information on government programs, legal developments, calendars of upcoming events, financing information, etc. on the NIS (Newly Independent States). Search for Partners contains lists of NIS firms seeking partnership with US investors, and contains full contact and some background information on the firm. (Several times/yr.; 4-8 pp.; Free)*

Business America, Business America, International Trade Association, 14th & Constitution Ave., NW, #3414, Washington, DC 20230, ph. 202-783-3238. *General interest publication on exporting which frequently provides useful information on US trade policies as well as contact information and listings of conferences and trade shows. Frequently covers Russia. (Bi-weekly; pp.; $61)*

Business Eastern Europe, Business International Corporation, 215 Park Ave. South, New York, NY 10003, ph. 212-554-0600, fax 212-995-8837. *A pricey weekly publication which focuses on the entire region, utilizing the broad resources available to Business International and the Economist Intelligence Unit. Includes spotlights on certain industries, profiles, consideration of legal, taxation and economic issues and even some business travel. (Weekly; 12 pp.; $1,100)*

Business Update Russia, Dean & Lake Consulting, Inc., 2306 Cleburne Ridge, Marietta, GA 30064, ph. 800-308-1245, fax 800-308-1246. *A concise, top-of-the-news, single-page, twice-weekly fax letter that covers business, politics, legal developments and statistics. Exchange rates and commodity prices are also provided. A good way to keep on top of the latest developments without drowning in information. (Twice weekly; 1 pp.; $595/yr, $180/3 mos.)*

Central European, Central European, Euromoney Publications, Nestor House, Playhouse Yard, London EC4V 5EX, England, ph. 71-779-8597, fax 71-779-8689. *A monthly magazine covering business and finance (mainly the latter) in Central and Eastern Europe. A mix of brief focus articles and shorter "deals done" pieces. Also features brief announcements of new joint ventures. (ISSN 0962-2543; 10 issues/year; 40-80 pp.; $460)*

Commersant, Refco Publishing, 111 West Jackson Blvd., Chicago, IL 60604, ph. 312-930-6563. *The English version of Russia's home-grown business weekly newspaper. The Western version is a stripped-down translation of the Russian original (which is now a daily), but retains the original's distinct editorial style. (Weekly; 24-30 pp.; $265)* **Also available through Access Russia (800-639-4301, item G419)**

Countertrade Outlook, DP Publications Company, Box 7188, Fairfax Station, VA 22039, ph. 703-425-1322, fax 703-425-7911. *Provides intelligence on financing trade, projects and opportunity finance in Russia and other forex-short markets through such reciprocal trade forms as barter, counterpurchase, buyback, clearing, switch, build-operate-transfer, debt-for-equity swaps, offset, etc. (ISSN 0743-0369; 24 issues/yr.; 8 pp.; $488)*

Country Report: Russia, Business International Corporation, 215 Park Ave. South, New York, NY 10003, ph. 212-554-0600, fax 212-995-8837. *A quarterly round-up of political, foreign policy and economic developments in the Commonwealth. Astute and cogent analyses, with clear presentations of economic information. More space given to larger economic and political issues, less to business developments. Subscription also includes a country profile. Economist also publishes three other Country Reports, on the Baltics, Central Asia and Ukraine. (Quarterly; 25-40 pp.; $315)*

Current Digest of the Post-Soviet Press, Current Digest of the Post-Soviet Press, 3857 N. High St., Columbus, OH 43214, ph. 614-292-4234, fax 614-267-6310. *Translations and abstracts of articles from the Russian and Commonwealth press. Translations typically appear about 6 weeks after publication in Russia. Indexed quarterly. (ISSN 0011-3425; Weekly; 20-40 pp.; $820)*

Delovie Lyudi: Business in the Ex-USSR, Delovie Lyudi, 1560 Broadway, Ste. 511, New York, NY 10036, ph. 212-221-6700, fax 212-221-6997. *This magazine is the product of a Russo-French joint venture. The writing is done almost entirely by Russian staff (thus the English is a translation) and is oriented as much to its Russian as its Western audience. Includes monthly special reports on sectors of the economy and insightful portraits of prominent business people. It has a unique*

Opportunities feature where everything from job to trade opportunities are offered. (ISSN 1167-2137; Monthly; 100-120 pp.; $85). **Also available through Access Russia (800-639-4301, item B133)**

East Europe & the Republics: A Weekly Business Risk Alert, *Political Risk Services, 222 Teall Avenue, PO Box 6482, Syracuse, NY 13217-6482, ph. 315-472-1224, fax 315-472-1235. A weekly newsletter of expert news and analysis of late-breaking events in this fluid region. Political, economic, and ethnic events are analyzed from the perspective of business and investment risks. (ISSN 1072-1738; Weekly; 4 pp.; $895).* **Also available through Access Russia (800-639-4301, item B126)**

East European Investment Magazine, Dixon and Co., 119 Fifth Ave., 8th Floor, New York, NY 10003, ph. 212-388-1500, fax 212-254-3386. *Includes articles on finance, conversion, trade and investment. Much of the publication is given over to a listing of deals done, joint ventures signed, acquisitions and other new foreign investments in the region. Publishes much important data not available elsewhere. (ISSN 1063-4029; Quarterly; 250 pp.; $580)*

East-West Business and Trade, Welt Publishing Company, 1413 K St., N. W., Suite 1400, Washington, DC 20005, ph. 202-371-0555, fax 202-408-9369. *One of the oldest periodicals in the field, this bi-weekly has a distinctive "deals concluded" format. Concise and very eclectic in the news items it covers, a subscription to this publication includes a complimentary subscription to the monthly East/West Technology Digest. (ISSN 0731-7727; Biweekly; 4 pp.; $249)*

East-West Fortnightly Bulletin, East-West, 10 Boulevard Saint-Lazare, 1210 Brussels, Belgium, ph. 02-218-4349, fax 02-218-1985. *Mainly a listing of deals done and overviews of general business news and developments. Subscription includes monthly publication East European Statistics Service, covering output, trade, financial and consumption statistics. (Bi-weekly; 16 pp.; $1,250)*

East-West Investment and Joint Ventures News, Economic Commission for Europe, United Nations, Palais des Nations, CH 1211 Geneva 10, Switzerland, ph. 22-917-1234, fax 22-017-0036. *Monitors and analyzes legislative acts and other regulations on foreign investors' access to and activities in the countries of Central and Eastern Europe. Also contains statistical reports on foreign investment in the region, reviews of recent publications and announcements of upcoming meetings of interest to investors. (Quarterly; $80)*

East/West Business and Finance Alert, World Trade Executive, PO Box 761, Concord, MA 01742, ph. 508-287-0301, fax 508-287-0302. *Includes details of the latest business transactions, by sector, information on reliable contacts, advance information on tenders, privatization auctions and sales opportunities. (Bi-weekly; 12 pp.; $425).* **Also available through Access Russia (800-639-4301, item B111)**

East/West Executive Guide, World Trade Executive, PO Box 761, , Concord, MA 01742, ph. 508-287-0301, fax 508-287-0302. *Features longer, in-depth* analyses of current issues, with articles contributed mainly by practicing legal professionals and business people. One of the best. (Monthly; 28-32 pp.; $576) **Also available through Access Russia (800-639-4301, item B110)**

Eastern Europe Finance, DP Publications Company, Box 7188, Fairfax Station, VA 22039, ph. 703-425-1322, fax 703-425-7911. *A very good biweekly publication devoted to money and money-related issues in Eastern Europe and the FSU, with particular emphasis on currencies, trade, finance, banking and insurance. Updates on who is getting money from World Bank, EBRD, other sources public and private, and for what ends. (ISSN 1060-2518; Bi-weekly; 8-16 pp.; $437)*

Eastern Europe Reporter, Bureau of National Affairs, 1231 25th St., NW, Washington, DC 20037, ph. 202-452-4577, fax 202-452-7583. *Much in-country, often with input and reactions from government officials and private practitioners. A "deals concluded" section covers the whole region and the publication features full texts of important legislation. (ISSN 1058-7365; Bi-weekly, indexed; 40 pp.; $864)*

Eastern European Markets, Financial Times Newsletters, c/o European Business Publications, P.O. Box 891, Darien, CT 06820, ph. 203-656-2701, fax 202-655-8332. *Consists of mainly medium length articles, analyzing events and deals concluded. Focuses on the entire region. Has a nice back-page feature chronicling events of the past two weeks in the region. (Bi-weekly; 16 pp.; $827)*

FBIS Daily Reports: Central Eurasia, NTIS, Department of Commerce, 5285 Port Royal Road, Springfield, VA 22161, ph. 703-487-4630. *A daily compendium of translations from the Russian and Commonwealth press and media. (Interflo, abstracted below, reviews the contents of this for its subscribers). Also available is a publication called simply Central Eurasia, which is published twice weekly and costs $550/yr. (Daily; $625)*

Finance Eastern Europe, Financial Times Newsletters, c/o European Business Publications, P.O. Box 891, Darien, CT 06820, ph. 203-656-2701, fax 202-655-8332. *Reporting the financial side of reforms and business developments in the region. Excellent analytical reportage and current citings of deals done. (Biweekly; 16-20 pp.; $663)*

Financing Foreign Operations: Russia, Business International Corporation, 215 Park Ave. South, New York, NY 10003, ph. 212-554-0600, fax 212-995-8837. *A review of the political and economic environment plus detailed financial information and advice on foreign exchange regulations, sources of capital, short, medium and long-term financing techniques, equity financing, capital incentives, cash management, trade finance and insurance. (Twice-yearly; 25 pp.; $150)*

geoGraffity, McDonald & Woodward, PO Box 10308, Blacksburg, VA 24062, ph. 703-951-9465, fax 703-552-0210. *Billed as a meeting place of ideas and a forum for Russian scholars to address the international community, this journal focuses on the geographical concept of space, and the many ways that humans have perceived, used and represented the earth's surface. Glossy and full of photos, this is* *a thinking Russophile's National Geographic. (ISSN 1063-9837; Quarterly; 80 pp.; $30) Also available through Access Russia (800-639-4301, item G424)*

Global Forecasting Service, Economist Intelligence Unit, 40 Duke St., London, W1A 1DW, United Kingdom, ph. 71-493-6711, fax 71-499-2107. *A wide range of quality information products are published periodically EIU and its American partner, Business International. These include Global Forecasting Service, Country Risk Service, Regional Reference, and Offices and Agencies in Eastern Europe. They also publish one-off research studies of certain sectors of the Russian/USSR economy and/or analyses of investment options. On the whole, the quality of the analyses is quite high, with prices to match.*

Harriman Institute Forum, Harriman Institute, Columbia University, 420 West 118th St., Rm. 1218, New York, NY 10027, ph. 212-854-8454, fax 212-666-3481. *This publication treats contemporary issues with an analytical/academic bent. Published by a leading Russian studies institute in the United States, the Forum can be counted on to be thought provoking and of a high caliber. (ISSN 0896-114X; Monthly; 10-20 pp.; $35)*

Independent Newspaper from Russia, Independent Newspaper from Russia, Inc., Box GG, Mc Lean, VA 22101, ph. 703-827-8923. *The English-language edition of one of Moscow's most popular newspapers. A bi-weekly analysis of Russian society, politics, economics, history, and outlook straight from the source. A good supplement to Western coverage. Also available in a Russian Language Edition. (ISSN 1064-4431; Biweekly; 12 pp.; $38) Also available through Access Russia (800-639-4301, item G423)*

Interfax News Bulletin, Interfax USA, 1675 Larimer, Ste. #600, Denver, CO 80202, ph. 303-825-1510, fax 303-825-1513. *A daily fax news service covering economic and political news from around the CIS. Interfax publishes three other daily bulletins: Daily Business Report, Diplomatic Panorama and Baltnews, costing $210-240 per month. Interfax also publishes nine weekly journals: Weekly Business Report, Petroleum Report, Mining Report, Agriculture Report, Financial Report, Viewpoint, Ukraine Business Review, Statistical Report, and Business Law. Each sells for $160-250 monthly, with an extra charge for fax delivery. All are informed by the superior on-the-ground reportage of Interfax correspondents spread throughout the former USSR. Discounts for multiple and long-term subscriptions. (Daily; 40 pp.; $290)*

Interflo, Interflo: An East-West News Monitor, P.O. Box 42, Maplewood, NJ 07040, ph. (201) 763-9493. *A monthly overview of usually 250+ articles from both the Western and Commonwealth press dealing with trade and investment. Also includes excerpts or full reprints of short legal acts or US government compiled economic data of interest. One of the best periodical values. (Monthly; 30-40 pp.; $142)*

International Economic Review, US International Trade Commission, Office of Economics, Trade Reports Division, 500 E St., SW, Washington, DC 20436, ph. 202-205-3270, fax 202-205-2340. *Focuses more generally on inter-*

national economic issues and trends, but also covers events and trends in Russia and the CIS. (Monthly; 12-16 pp.; Free)

International Information Report, International Information Report, 2612 P Street, NW, Washington, DC 20007, ph. 202-333-3533. *A monthly compendium of reports, information and sources of information available in and through the US Government, foreign governments and some private sources. (Monthly; 8 pp.; $140)*

Mars, MARS, P.O. Box 53305, Washington, DC 20009. *With a specific focus on Russophiles in the Baltimore and DC area, this monthly is gossipy and light. Sometimes has job opportunities listed. Its Beets and Pieces section features useful tidbits for persons living in the DC area. (Monthly; 8 pp.; $20)*

Moscow Letter, The, Interforum Services, 565 Fulham Road, London, SW6 1ES, UK, ph. 71-386-9322, fax 71-381-8914. *A collection of short news items and directory info related to business and travel in Moscow. (ISSN 0996-4394; Monthly; 8 pp.; £220)*

New Outlook, American Committee on US-Soviet Relations, 109 11th Street, SE, Washington, DC 20003, ph. (202) 546-1700, fax (202) 543-3146. *This quarterly publication features a variety of articles on Russian life, economy and reforms. The articles' tone is varied and translations of Russian materials are often featured. (Quarterly; 100-120 pp.; members only)*

PlanEcon Business Report, PlanEcon, 1111 – 14th St., NW, Suite 801, Washington, DC 20005-5603, ph. 202-898-0471, fax 202-898-0445. *This newsletter focuses on the entire Eastern Europe and Commonwealth region with sections on privatization, legislation, the economy and foreign trade. Industry by industry reportage of developments and deals. Includes a modicum of economic data. PlanEcon also publishes two specialized quarterly publications,* **PlanEcon Energy Report** *and* **PlanEcon Chemical Report**, *which are 60-80 pages in length and sell for $800/yr, and a semiannual publication,* **PlanEcon Review and Outlook**, *which summarizes economic performance and forecasts for the future on a country by country basis, typically devoting 20-40 pages to each country and selling for $850 per country, $1000 for Russia.* **PlanEcon Report** *focuses on major macroeconomic and trade developments throughout Eastern Europe and the Commonwealth and is of most interest to academics. Typically, each 30-40 page issue will focus on particular countries or sectors and treat them in great detail both descriptively and in graphs and tables ($1600). (Bi-monthly; 20 pp.; $800)*

Post-Soviet Business International Digest, Arguments and Facts International, PO Box 35, Hastings, East Sussex, TN34 2UX, UK, ph. 424-444-142, fax 424-717-428. *A detailed monthly briefing of business and economic activity in the former USSR. Includes opinion and in-depth pieces, as well as extensive business briefs broken out by country and industry, with plenty of useful contact information. (ISSN 0957-0020; Monthly; 48-64 pp.; $600)*

Post-Soviet Business Monitor, Exchange Publications, PO Box 5757, Washington, DC 20016, ph. 800-776-1314, fax 202-296-2805. *A dense and readable bi-weekly that covers business developments, economic reform and investment opportunities around the former Soviet Union. Fine-tuned editing of Business-TASS reporting, combined with Washington-based insights provide balanced and thorough coverage of the region. (Bi-weekly; 20 pp.; $695)*

Problems of Economic Transition, M.E. Sharpe, Inc., 80 Business Park Dr., Armonk, NY 10504, ph. 914-273-1800, fax 914-273-2106. *A compilation of articles by and interviews with economists and policy-makers on the nature and direction of economic reform in Russia, translated from the Russian (ISSN 1061-1991; Monthly; 96 pp.; $599)*

RFE/RL Daily Report, RFE-RL, Inc., 1201 Connecticut Ave., NW, Suite 410, Washington, DC 20036, ph. 202-828-8784, fax 202-457-6907. *A very extensive (usually eight page) review of mainly political events and news from around the Commonwealth and Eastern Europe. Is available by mail (price below) or by fax ($1300/yr), on-line via Sovset, or free via the Internet (see On-line Information Resources section below). Also available is RFE/RL Research Report, a weekly publication which provides some detailed analysis of the week's events (price: $240, $96 for students). (Daily; 8 pp.; $450)*

Russia and the Commonwealth States, The Atlantic Council of the U.S., 1616 H Street, NW, Washington, DC 20006, ph. 202-347-9353, fax 202-737-5163. *A general overview of political and economic developments in the region. The Council also issues Occasional Papers examining issues in greater detail. (Bi-monthly; 4 pp.; Free, order individually)*

Russia Briefing, 87 Duke Road, London W4 2BW, ph. 81-995-3860, fax 81-747-8802. *Insightful political and economic analyses of the events and players shaping the Russian scene. Invaluable profiles of individuals, articles on special topics and readable synopses of recent events. (Monthly; 18 pp.; $505)*

Russia Express Executive Briefing, Russia Express, International Industrial Information, PO Box 12, Montmouth, Gwent NP5 3YL, UK, ph 600-890-274, fax 600-890-774. *This bi-weekly includes a few in-depth articles, but the majority of the publication focuses on shorter blurbs. Also a list of new opportunities and upcoming trade and exhibition events. Included is a subscription to **Russia Express Contracts**, a monthly update to a database of 4000 investment and trade opportunities available to Western companies in the former Soviet Union, grouped by 100 project classifications under eleven major headings. The company also publishes **Russia Express Geopolitical Update**, a bi-monthly overview of the region, on a country-by-country basis, as well as an overview of general key-issues. Bi-monthly, $290, reduced rate of $830 for all three publications. (ISSN 0957-0853; Bi-weekly; 28-32 pp.; $600)*

Russian and East European Finance and Trade, M.E. Sharpe, Inc., 80 Business Park Dr., Armonk, NY 10504, ph. 914-273-1800, fax 914-273-

2106. *Compendiums of academic-style articles, translated from Russian and East European journals, covering international trade, finance and reform in the former Comecon states. (ISSN 1061-2009; Quarterly; 100-120 pp.; $315)*

Russian Business Journal, 14329 Court Street, Moulton, AL 35650, ph. 205-905-0365. *Monthly coverage of political and business issues, direct from St. Petersburg. In the process of being restyled by a new US publisher, it is currently distributed free to qualified subscribers. (10 times/yr; 38 pp.; Free)*

Russian Gospel Messenger, Russian Gospel Ministries, PO Box 1188, Elkhart, IN 46515-1188, ph. 219-522-3486, fax 219-293-1932. *A free bimonthly distributed by a non-profit Evangelical Baptist group, dedicated to relating the circumstances and experiences of the Christian church in Russia and Ukraine. (Bimonthly; 4 pp.; Free).*

Russian Life Magazine, 42-32 235 Street, Douglaston, NY 11363-0158, ph. 718-279-2630, fax 718-225-8114. *For any Russophile, this handsome glossy bimonthly magazine (successor to Soviet Life) is a must. It is filled with readable, objective articles on life in Russia, with beautiful photography and composition. (ISSN 1066-999X; Quarterly; 48-64 pp.; $25)* **Also available through Access Russia (800-639-4301, item G417)**

SEER, Interforum Services, 565 Fulham Road, London, SW6 1ES, UK, ph. 71-386-9322, fax 71 381-8914. *Includes short news items and one or two longer feature articles each month. Broad-focused on political and economic events in the former USSR and Eastern Europe. (ISSN 0963-7036; Monthly; 16 pp.; £255)*

Surviving Together, ISAR, 1601 Connecticut Ave., NW, suite 301, Washington, DC 20009, ph. 202-387-3034, fax 202-667-3291. *Ostensibly oriented at exchange and educational programs, this is a good general information publication for the business person as well. (ISSN 0859-6286; Quarterly; 64 pp.; $25)*

Tracking Eastern Europe, A.M.F. International Consultants, 812 N. Wood Ave., Linden, NJ 07036, ph. 908-486-3534, fax 908-486-4084. *A collection of brief news items related to business and investment in the region, plus usually one longer piece. Heightened focus is given to Poland. Includes lists of trade events in the region, country-by-country exchange rates and investment opportunities. (ISSN 1051-7197; Biweekly; 12 pp.; $445)*

Transition, Policy Research Dept., Room N-1103, The World Bank, 1818 H Street, NW, Washington, DC 20433, ph. 202-473-6982, fax 202-676-0439. *One of the best deals going. Monthly newsletter published by the World Bank which chronicles countries of the former Eastern bloc making the transition to free market economies. Excellent analytical articles and more than just the clearinghouse of information on World Bank activities which the letter claims to be. (Monthly; 16 pp.; Free)*

We/Мы Newspaper, Izvestia/Hearst, 1350 Connecticut Ave., NW, Ste# 1020, Washington DC, 20036, ph. 202-467-6931, fax 202-467-6941. *A USA*

Today type newspaper publication published simultaneously in Russian and English for both US and Russian audiences. Features articles on business, culture, politics, sports. (Bi-weekly; 16-24 pp.; $26)

Agriculture

AgExporter, Superintendent of Documents, ATTN: AGEXPORTER, PO Box 371954, Pittsburgh, PA 15250-7954, ph. 202-783-3238, fax 202-512-2250. *Monthly agricultural trade magazine, providing information on overseas trade opportunities, reports on marketing activities, and how-tos of agricultural exporting. (ISSN 0-16-009340-6; Monthly; 50 pp.; $16)*

World Perspectives: AG Review, World Perspectives Inc., 1150 18th St., NW, Suite 275, Washington, DC 20036, ph. 202-785-3345, fax 202-659-6891. *An extensive and current analysis of US agriculture policy and international agriculture market trends. Aimed at agri-business, government and institutional readers. (Monthly; 40 pp.; $495)*

Conversion

Post-Soviet Nuclear Complex Monitor, Exchange Publications, PO Box 5757, Washington, DC 20016, ph. 800-776-1314, fax 202-296-2805. *Complete coverage of nuclear dismantlement, conversion and radioactive waste management as it is being handled in the former Soviet Union. (Biweekly; 14 pp.; $995)*

Hi-Technology/Computers

East/West Technology Digest, Welt Publishing Company, 1413 K St., NW, Suite 1400, Washington, DC 20005, ph. 202-371-0555, fax 202-408-9369. *This two-to-four page xeroxed monthly consists mainly of equipment sales offers to Western companies by Russian counterparts. (ISSN 0145-1421; Monthly; 2-4 pp.; $99)*

Eastern European & Former Soviet Telecom Report, Int'l Technology Consultants, 1724 Kalorama Rd., Suite 210, Washington, DC 20009, ph. 202-234-2138, fax 202-483-7922. *Provides a well-organized, comprehensive country-by-country reporting of political, regulatory and business developments and trends in the telecom, information processing and broadcasting sectors in the region. Each issue features an interview with a leading figure in the field, as well as company and country profiles. (ISSN 1054-6499; Monthly; 25 pp.; $679)*

JPRS Serials Reports, NTIS, Department of Commerce, 5285 Port Royal Road, Springfield, VA 22161, ph. 703-487-4630. *Translations of Russian and former USSR republics' media relating to a wide range of scientific, technology, aviation and military subjects are available on a periodical basis. Prices range from $150-850 per year, with frequency of reports ranging from less than weekly to monthly. Contact NTIS for a list of the current subject headings.*

Rel-EAST: The East-West High-Tech Business Report, EDventure Holdings Inc., 104 Fifth Avenue, 20th floor, New York, NY 10011-6987, ph. 212-924-8800, fax 212-924-0240. *A superb quarterly publication targeted at the hi-tech, computer hardware and software markets, provides insightful analyses of developments in these markets in Eastern Europe and the Commonwealth. Each issue includes invaluable contact info on companies/individuals featured. (Bimonthly; 32 pp.; $495)*

Russian and Former Soviet Republics Fiber Optics and Telecom, Information Gatekeepers, Inc., 214 Harvard Ave., Boston, MA 02134, ph. 800-323-1088, fax 617-734-8562. *A quarterly source for information on the Russian and CIS telecommunications industries. Regular profiles of CIS companies and joint venture opportunities. Monitors foreign investment activity, key contacts and upcoming conferences and events. (ISSN 1066-9612; 30 pp.; $250)*

Legal/Accounting

Business and Commercial Laws of Russia, Shepard's/McGraw-Hill, Inc., P.O. Box 35300, Colorado Springs, CO 80935-3530, ph. 719-481-7499, fax 719-481-7319. *The most current, comprehensive, and authoritatively analyzed collection of post-Soviet Russian business and commercial laws. This three volume set is arranged topically for easy research, covering everything from banking, to privatization to taxation. Accompanied by in-depth, expert analysis by both Western and Russian practitioners. Updated six times per year. Price includes one year of updates. (ISSN 0-07-172479-6; Quarterly; $840).* **Also available through Access Russia (800-639-4301, item R312)**

Business Legal Materials: Russia, Russian Information Services, City Center, 89 Main St., Suite 2, Montpelier, VT 05602, ph. 802-223-4955, fax 802-223-6105. *A monthly index of Russian legal acts relating to trade and foreign investment. Employs RIS' useful law cataloguing system to reference and organize legislation under 14 key subject headings. Full texts of all laws indexed can be ordered in translation or in Russian from RIS. (ISSN 1066-2596; Monthly; 4-10 pp.; $225).* **Also available through Access Russia (800-639-4301, item R302)**

Butterworth Central and East European Business Law Bulletin, Butterworth Legal Publishers, 90 Stiles Road, Salem, NH 03079, ph. 800-544-1013, fax 603-898-9858. *This publication looks at doing business in the region from a strictly legal point of view, with equal emphasis on theoretical examinations of legal issues and developments and the practice of doing business in light of these same issues. Includes lists of recent legislation. (Quarterly; 16-24 pp.; $385).*

Commercial Code of Russia, The, Allen, Moline & Harold, P.O. Box 1667, 10610-A Crestwood Drive, Manassas, VA 22110, ph. 800-433-2636, fax 703-361-0594. *A periodically updated "adaptive translation" of selected Russian legislation covering business, privatization, property, taxation, banking and securities. (Quarterly; $350)*

East European Business Law, Financial Times Newsletters, c/o European Business Publications, P.O. Box 891, Darien, CT 06820, ph. 203-656-2701, fax 202-655-8332. *Features extracts from recent business and trade legislation passed throughout Eastern Europe and the Commonwealth and a modicum of commentary to illuminate the texts. With a country by country treatment, commentaries of recent developments are concise and useful. (Monthly; 24-30 pp.; $708)*

Intelprop News, Interforum Services, 565 Fulham Road, London, SW6 1ES, UK, ph. 71-386-9322, fax 71-381-8914. *A monthly newsletter covering intellectual property developments and legislation in Central Europe and the former Soviet Union. Includes articles contributed by Western and Eastern specialists and practitioners as well as news briefs, joint venture announcements and texts of legislation. (ISSN 0967-3466; Monthly; 12 pp.; £260)*

Laws of Russia and the NIS: The Bottom Line, Chadbourne and Parke, 30 Rockefeller Plaza, New York, NY 10112, ph. 212-408-5310, fax 212-541-5369. *This quarterly publication is written and edited by practicing lawyers of Chadbourne and Parke and its Russian joint venture partners and can provide a useful practitioner's view. (Quarterly; 8-12 pp.; Free upon request).*

NTIS Legal Texts: Russia and Independent States, NTIS, Department of Commerce, 5285 Port Royal Road, Springfield, VA 22161, ph. 703-487-4630. *A selective translation service of major Russian and East European legislation. Subscribers place a deposit with NTIS and this deposit is debited when laws are translated and delivered. (Irregular; pp.; $150 deposit per topic).*

Russia and Commonwealth Business Law Report, Buraff Publications, 1350 Connecticut Avenue, NW, Suite 1000, Washington, DC 20036, ph. 202-862-0990, fax 202-862-0999. *Each issue includes in-depth articles on timely legal topics, English texts of key documents, round-ups of recent laws and decrees in the CIS, and analysis of legal developments that affect foreign investment and business activity. (ISSN 1064-637X; Bi-weekly; 12 pp.; $970) Also available through Access Russia (800-639-4301, item B123)*

Russia and the Republics Legal Materials, Transnational Juris Publications, Inc., One Bridge St., Irvington-on-Hudson, NY 10533, ph. 800-914-8186, fax 914-591-2688. *Translations of legislation on business, investment, taxation and trade, with digests by the editors, summarizing legal acts. (ISSN 0-929179-46-3; Updated bimonthly; Looseleaf pp.; $395, 4 volumes)*

SEEL—Survey of East European Law, Transnational Juris Publications, Inc., One Bridge St., Irvington-on-Hudson, NY 10533, ph. 800-914-8186, fax 914-591-2688. *A concise and readable monthly overview of legislative changes in the region. Includes commentaries by practicing professionals and leading academics and texts of some laws. (ISSN 1070-9185; Monthly; 16-20 pp.; $295).*

Oil/Petrochem

Hydrocarbons Brief, Commercial Dept., The Kingsgate Business Center, 12-50 Kingsgate Road, Kingston upon Thames, KT2 5AA, England, ph. 81-547-2411, fax 81-547-2157. *A thorough (stats, deals done, latest developments) overview of the month's events in the oil & gas spheres, with a few longer articles and analyses, plus brief notes. (ISSN 0967-537X; Monthly; 28 pp.; $600) Also available through Access Russia (800-639-4301, item D224)*

Oil & Gas: Russia, Central Asia and the Caucasus, Commercial Dept., The Kingsgate Business Center, 12-50 Kingsgate Road, Kingston upon Thames, KT2 5AA, England, ph. 81-547-2411, fax 81-547-2157. *With articles by both Western and Russian specialists and engineers, this magazine focuses on technical, economic and logistical issues related to oil exploration and extraction. (ISSN 0966-4505; Quarterly; 70-80 pp.; $200) Also available through Access Russia (800-639-4301, item D224)*

Russian Petroleum Investor, 14755 Ventura Blvd., #1-424, Sherman Oaks, CA 91403, ph. 818-981-7195. *An excellent, in-depth monthly covering the Russian oil & gas sectors, with independent reporting, interviews, data and analysis. Incisive tone and style. Very readable. Unfortunately, priced for the oil specialist. (Monthly; 60-80 pp.; $2,500)*

Regional Focus

Baltic Business Report, Baltic Ventures, 1075 Washington St., West Newton, MA 02165, ph. 617-527-2550, fax 617-527-2823. *A comprehensive monthly survey of business, investment, trade and economic news for the three Baltic states. Includes interviews, in-depth articles analyzing recent legislation and events, and industry briefs highlighting recent deals and decisions. (ISSN 1058-1057; Monthly; 12 pp.; $260) Also available through Access Russia (800-639-4301, item B112)*

Central Asia and the Caucasus, Arguments and Facts International, PO Box 35, Hastings, East Sussex, TN34 2UX, UK, ph. 424-444-142, fax 424-717-428. *A monthly overview of political and economic events and trends in these regions. Includes both lengthy pieces and briefs. (ISSN 0967-8689; Monthly; 16 pp.; $800)*

Russian Far East News, Alaska Center for International Business, Business Education Bldg. 203, 3211 Providence Drive, Anchorage, AK 99508, ph. 907-786-4300, fax 907-486-4319. *Focused exclusively on the Russian Far East, this concise monthly is organized by region and industry. Coverage includes politics and business as well as environmental and native issues, from a businessperson's perspective. (Monthly; 12 pp.; $100) Also available through Access Russia (800-639-4301, item B125)*

Russian Far East Update, PO Box 22126, Seattle, WA 98122, ph. 206-447-2668, fax 206-628-0979. *Exclusive focus on the Far Eastern regions of Russia. An up-to-date and comprehensive resource for persons and companies with a specific interest in this region. Short news items as well as longer reports and special features.*

(ISSN 1061-5679; Monthly; 12-16 pp.; $275, $310 int'l) **Also available through Access Russia (800-639-4301, item B124)**

Ukrainian Business Digest, Ukrainian Business Digest, 21 Bridge Square, PO Box 3127, Westport, CT 06880, ph. 203-221-7450. *A thorough information resource on business developments in Ukraine. Features good in-country reporting. Each month's issue contains 8-10 medium-length articles on current developments, tables and occasional listings of companies active in Ukraine. (ISSN 1053-4237; Monthly; 12 pp.; $245)*

Travel

CIS Russian Travel Newsletter, International Intertrade Index, Box 636 Federal Square, Newark, NJ 07101, ph. 908-686-2382, fax 201-622-1740. *A weekly publication with a target audience of travel professionals, this can also be a useful newsletter for frequent travelers to Russia and the Commonwealth. (ISSN 1059-4957; Weekly; 4 pp.; $62)*

Russian Travel Monthly, Russian Information Services, City Center, 89 Main St., Suite 2, Montpelier, VT 05602, ph. 802-223-4955, fax 802-223-6105. *From the publishers of this guide, a monthly newsletter focusing on the most significant changes in the Russian/CIS travel environment. The best way to keep up-to-date on travel issues in-between editions of* **Russia Survival Guide**. *Exchange rates, news briefs, travel journal features and more. A must for independent and business travelers. (Monthly; 8 pp.; $36)* **Also available through Access Russia (800-639-4301, item B109)**

Traveling Healthy & Comfortably, 108-48 70th Road, Forest Hills, NY 11375, ph. 718-268-7290, fax 718-261-9082. *While not focused exclusively on Russia or the NIS, it does cover important travel issues which have extreme salience for the frequent traveler and does periodically feature travel issues/problems related to this region. Covers what to eat, immunizations, pollution problems, avoiding accidents and sources of information. Ask for the back issues on Eastern Europe and the Soviet Union. (ISSN 0899-2169; Bi-monthly; 8 pp.; $29)*

BOOKS AND OTHER RESOURCES

Past editions of the Survival Guide have listed here dozens of recommended books, maps and directories. Many of them are hard-to-find and not readily available through local bookstores. With the aim of making these works more accessible, a consortium of publishers, of sorts, has been created, whereby many of these books can now be ordered through a single catalogue resource, known as *Access Russia*.

If a title below has an Access Russia order number, you may obtain the book by calling 1-800-639-4301 (1-802-223-4955 international calls, fax 1-802-223-6105).

General Interest

Atlas of Russian History, Martin Gilbert. *Over 160 maps on an extraordinary range of topics, bringing geographic clarity to the 2,000 year expanse of Russian History: from examinations of rebellion and exile to trade and military strength. (Oxford University Press; ISBN 0-19-521041-7; 160 pp.; 1993; $19.95) Access Russia order number: G432.*

Barefoot Shoemaker, The: Capitalizing on the New Russia, Vladimir Kvint. *An insightful and critical look at the Russian market – from the inside looking in. Rich with anecdotes and vivid stories of business in the Siberian outback, this unique book makes Russian business culture accessible to the Western reader. Written with primary emphasis on the Russian manager's mindset – a perspective that we have not seen effectively described anywhere else. (Arcade Publishing; ISBN 1-55970-182-X; 230 pp.; 1993; $24.95) Access Russia order number: G429.*

Bear Hunting with the Politburo, A. Craig Copetas. *A perceptive analysis of the early days (1988-89) of capitalism in the Soviet Union, with particular emphasis on the first capitalists, the* kooperativshiki. *An extremely well-written book that is required reading for anyone who wishes a realistic view of what private enterprise is up against in Russia. Don't get involved in business in Russia without reading this book. (Simon & Schuster; ISBN 0-671-79721-2; 270 pp.; 1993; $12.00) Access Russia order number: G402.*

From Nyet to Da, Yale Richmond. *An insightful look at the Russian character by a veteran foreign service officer. Includes extremely pertinent reflections on Russian national character and how understanding it can lead to more effective negotiation and social/business interaction. (Intercultural Press; ISBN 1-877864-08-0; 200 pp.; 1992; $15.95) Access Russia order number: G403.*

From Yaroslavskiy Station: Russia Perceived, Elizabeth Pond. *A description of the author's ride on the Trans-Siberian express, with interesting digressions into all the major issues and topics of Russian life. (St. Martin's Press; ISBN 0-87663-536-2; 346 pp.; 1988; $12.95) Access Russia order number: G412.*

How to Profit from the Coming Russian Boom, Richard Poe. *If you need any encouragement about the investment opportunities in Russia, this is the book for you. Full of interesting interviews with "insiders." (McGraw-Hill; ISBN 0-07-050450-4; 350 pp.; 1993; $24.95) Access Russia order number: G418.*

Directories and Reference

Buying a Business in Russia, Youry Petchenkine. *A step-by-step guide to taking part in the Great Russian Sell-off. Complete contact information for over 4,000 Russian Enterprises approved for privatization by the Russian Ministry of Finance. (D.N. Young and Associates, Inc., 203 W. Ascension, Gonzales, LA 70737, ph. 504-644-8605, fax 504-644-1663; 1991; $189)*

CIS Datafile. *Lists key contacts in selected sectors of the economy; investment related legislation and information on trade and investment facilitation services. (Central and East European Trade and Technology Assistance Center, International Division, US Chamber of Commerce, 1615 H St. NW, Washington, DC 20062, ph. 202-463-5460, fax 202-463-3114; $47.50)*

CIS Market Atlas. *Economic and statistical data on the former Soviet Union, presented graphically (through maps). (Business International, 215 Park Ave., South, New York, NY 10003, ph. 212-460-0600, fax 212-995-8837.*

Directory of U.S. Companies Doing Business in East/Central Europe and the Commonwealth of Independent States. *US addresses of over 800 companies active in Eastern Europe and the former USSR. Also includes some governmental directory and contact information. (Technology Exchange International, 5205 Leesburg Pike, Suite 1608, Falls Church, VA 22041, ph. 703-671-2053, fax 703-255-6614; 1992; 88 pp.; $39)*

Eastern European Investment Magazine Database. *A computer database cataloguing information on investors and investments in the region. Covers January 1, 1990 to the present and can be sorted and selected by country, industrial sector, investor nations and more. (Dixon & Co., 119 Fifth Ave., 8th floor, New York, NY 10003, ph. 212-388-1500; Quarterly updates; $2,000)*

Foreign Investment in Russia. Kaj Hober. *A looseleaf publication summarizing current legislation and the law as it reflects on business practices, by a noted legal authority on Russia. (Transnational Juris Publications, One Bridge Street, Irvington-on-Hudson, NY 10533, ph. 914-591-4288, fax 914-591-2688; 1992; ISBN 0-929179-99-4; $185)*

FirstBook of Demographics for the Republics of the Former Soviet Union. *Data spanning 1951-1991 on all 15 states of the FSU. Includes vital data on demographics, services and facilities, consumption and more. Available in printed format or on disk. (New World Demographics, PO Box 866, Shady Side, MD 20764, ph. 410-867-3767, fax 410-867-0549)*

To obtain items listed with **Access Russia** *order numbers:*
call 800-639-4301
(or 802-223-4955, fax 802-223-6105)

Former Soviet Union Marketing, Media & Advertising Directory. *Detailed entries for all significant media and advertising organizations, listing services and products, production data, executives, readership/audience profiles, and company activities. Also included are details for all allied trade services and suppliers, demographic data and important government contacts for all fifteen republics. (Hughes Publishing Ltd.; ISSN 1352-2485; 1994 pp.; 660; $540)* **Access Russia order number: D219.**

Gas Production Companies Directory. *Full, detailed listing of all Gazprom companies and enterprises throughout the CIS. (Arguments and Facts International; ISBN 1-873976-06-2; 1993 pp.; 205; $440)* **Access Russia order number: D221.**

Guide to EC Technical Assistance to Eastern Europe and the Former USSR. *Case studies and analysis of European aid to the region, with particular focus on PHARE and TACIS programs. (East-West Publications, Bld. St. Lazare 10, Bte 11, B1210, Brussels, Belgium, ph. 2-218-4349; 1992; $180)*

Major Ports of the Russian Far East. *A reference resource on the RFE's nine major ports, with maps, contact information, information on port specialization, infrastructure and regional trends. (Russian Far East Update, PO Box 22126, Seattle, WA 98122, ph. 206-447-2668, fax 206-628-0979; 12 pp.; $49)*

Moscow Business Connection. *Information on over 6000 enterprises in the Moscow region. Each entry includes address, phone and fax information, name of CEO, legal structure of enterprise, year started, number of employees, and types of business activity. Cross-referenced by SIC code. Also includes government and business/personal service listings. (Telebase Systems, Inc.; 1993 pp.; 340; $24)* **Access Russia order number: D218.**

New Eurasia, The: A Guide to the Republics of the Former Soviet Union, David T. Twining. *An important reference book on the diverse peoples, geography, and composition of the fifteen new republics of the Former Soviet Union. Organized by region and by country, there is basic data given for each nation. Essays examine interrelationships of culture, history, diplomacy, economics, and defense. (Greenwood Publishing Group, Inc.; ISBN 0-275-94431-X; 213 pp.; 1993; $17.95)* **Access Russia order number: G427.**

Oil and Gas Construction Companies Directory, Boris L. Krivoshein. *Detailed information about the 266 largest construction companies in the former USSR. (Arguments and Facts International; ISBN 1-873976-01-1; 1992; 175 pp.; $440)* **Access Russia order number: D222.**

Oil and Gas Russia & CIS (Upstream) Directory. *Directory information on 465 companies rated among the best potential business partners. (Arguments and Facts International; ISBN 1-873976-03-8; 1993; 340 pp.; $440)* **Access Russia order number: D223.**

Refineries and Petrochemicals Companies Directory, E. Radchenko. *Directory information on the 71 refineries and petrochemical plants in the CIS, including* *names of executive personnel, business address, telephone, fax, telex, and product and service listings. (Arguments and Facts International; ISBN 1-873976-02; 1993; 58 pp.; $370)* **Access Russia order number: D220.**

Russia: A Telecom Market Survey. *An exhaustive and thorough study of the burgeoning Russian telecom market, from the regulatory environment to equipment to market assessments (ITC, 1724 Kalorama Road, Suite 210, Washington, DC 20009, ph. 202-234-2138, fax 202-483-7922; 1993; 145 pp.; $2,250)*

Russian and CIS Telecom 1993. *A concise compilation of over 300 abstracts from the Russian and CIS press covering telecom issues during 1993. Fully indexed. (Russian Information Services; 1994; 73 pp.; $125)* **Access Russia order number: R313.**

Russian Commercial Banks: An In-Depth Directory. *Detailed and current information on 53 banks listing officers, scope of services/activities and correspondent Western banks. (Bridge Productions, Inc.; 1993; $232.50)* **Access Russia order number: D217.**

Russian Defense Business Directory. *A publication providing current information on the conversion process in Russia, with a list of over 200 converting enterprises, discussion of export controls and relevant laws and agreements. Be sure to get all three installments. [NTIS, 5285 Port Royal Road, Springfield, VA 22161, ph. 703-487-4650. Order numbers PB93-101509 ($19.50), PB93-183366 ($25) and PB94-100211 ($27)]*

Russian Employee Compensation Report. *Based on detailed interviews with 50 Western firms employing over 1000 Russians, this concise report answers all the important questions related to hiring and retaining Russian personnel. (The Richmark Group; 72 pp.; $820 per issue)* **Access Russia order number: R304.**

Russian Government Today. *An incomparable directory of 8,500 Russian officials, indexed by government function, geography and name. From top central government officials, to provincial leaders. Includes informative organizational charts that make it easier to understand the complex Russian bureaucracy. To be revised and updated every six months. Price includes an update volume to be published by mid-1994. (Carroll Publishing Company; Nov. 1993; 770 pp.; $195)* **Access Russia order number: D209.**

Russian News Abstracts: 1993. *A compilation of English-language abstracts of over 2000 of the most important Russian and CIS news articles of 1993. Catalogues over 50 important newspapers not elsewhere indexed, particularly the newer business and economic journals. Indexed by subject, geography and company name. 1992 volume also available. (Russian Information Services; 1993; 132 pp.; $48)* **Access Russia order number: R303.**

Russian Yellow Pages. *Printed in Russian, this unique book is the definitive how-to guide to life in the United States for newly-immigrating Russian speakers. Covering everything from how to return defective goods, to how to find work, make up a resume,* *rent an apartment, pay taxes and use the post office (and much more). A great gift for frequent visitors or newly-arriving friends. (Liberty Publishing House; 1992 pp.; 544 pp.; $16.95)* **Access Russia order number: D215.**

Transportation Handbook for Russia and the FSU, The. *Includes profiles of 70 transportation centers, detailed information on sea ports, railway facilities, airports, highways and customs posts. (ASET Consultants; ISBN 0-9638667-3-7; 1993; 136 pp.; $477)* **Access Russia order number: R308.**

WA-2 Directory. *A three volume directory of 28,000 large industrial enterprises of the former USSR, with address and contact information, plus sphere of activity or goods produced. Indexed by name and goods and services provided. (Interlink Consulting Group, Inc.; $280)* **Access Russia order number: D211.**

Where in Moscow and **Where in St. Petersburg.** *For information on these qualitative yellow and white page directories of the two Russian capitals, see the Travel and Travel Essay section below.*

Who is Who in Russia. *A unique software package, updated quarterly, that provides contact information for 52,000 local and federal officials, plus other information by industry classification, product and region, at the push of a button. Toggles between English and Russian. (D.N. Young and Associates, Inc., 203 W. Ascension, Gonzales, LA 70737, ph. 504-644-8605, fax 504-644-1663; 1991; $499, $69 for yearly updates)*

World Aviation Directory Regional Report – Russia/NIS. *Directory and guide to doing business in the Russian aviation industry. Over 400 listings of Russian companies and agencies active in the sector. (WAD Marketing Services, 1200 G Street, NW, 9th floor, Washington, DC 20005, ph. 800-551-2015, fax 202-383-2439)*

Yellow Pages Moscow. Lists over 35,000 Russian and foreign businesses and government offices located in Moscow with up-to-date address, phone and fax numbers. (Marvol USA; ISBN 3-928614-03-7; 1993; 550 pp.; $46.50) **Access Russia order number: D225.**

Language & Dictionaries

Business Dictionary for Russian. *A new English-Russian, Russian-English dictionary of 3,600 entries for over 18,000 terms and phrases for business people. (Wiley (in Russia); ISBN 5-88182-004-5; 615 pp.; 1993; $28.50)* **Access Russia order number: L537.**

Business Russian, Svetlana Aleksandroff. *A practical guide to learning the Russian you need for doing business in the new Russia. From the publishers of this*

To obtain items listed with **Access Russia** *order numbers:*
call 800-639-4301
(or 802-223-4955, fax 802-223-6105)

---

guide. (Russian Information Services; ISBN 1-880100-14-2; 200 pp.; 1993; $16)
Access Russia order number: L501.

Colloquial Russian. *The best value in a Russian short-course for the beginner or those who want to consolidate their basic knowledge. (Routledge; ISBN 0-415-05784-1; 280 pp.; 1993; $35)* **Access Russia order number: L535.**

Modern Russian I and II. *The most in-depth and comprehensive, audio-based course for learning Russian (to intermediate level). Used by hundreds of American universities. (Jeffrey Norton Publishers, Inc.; $235 per unit)* **Access Russia order number: L506 and L507.**

Oxford Russian Dictionary. *A brand-new, single-volume issue of the best Russia/ English, English/Russian dictionary in the field. Contains over 180,000 words (over 5,000 recent additions) and phrases and 290,000 translations in over 1300 crisply typeset pages. (Oxford University Press; ISBN 0-19-864122-2; 1300 pp.; 1993; $45)* **Access Russia order number: L511.**

Pocket Oxford Dictionary. *The pocket version of the previous entry. Over 60,000 terms; comes in a vinyl cover to withstand years of use. (Oxford University Press; ISBN 0-198641-22-2; $12.95)* **Access Russia order number: L504.**

RELEX PC-based Russian Dictionary. *A truly usable and well-conceived Russian-English and English-Russian dictionary that operates seamlessly with DOS-based word processors. Over 30,000 entries. Add-on modules are also available: Petrolex features 25,000 terms and definitions specific to the oil & gas industry. The science/ computer/business/legal module contains 40,000 vital terms and definitions. (Karoma Publishers; $175)* **Access Russia order number: L513.**

The Russian Desk: A Listening and Conversation Course, Martin, Robin. *An innovative course focusing on developing listening comprehension and oral proficiency, using authentic audio and text materials from contemporary Russian TV, radio, and press. For the intermediate to advanced student. Includes book and cassette. (Slavica Publishers, Inc.; ISBN 0-89357-218-7; 136 pp.; 1991; $18.95)* **Access Russia order number: L529.**

Maps

Atlas of Russia and the Post Soviet Republics. *A large-format (24 x 33 cm) atlas of the former USSR. Scaled at 1:3,000,000 and with names printed in English, this is a valuable resource. (A&F International, PO Box 35, Hastings, East Sussex, TN34 2UX, UK; 48 pp.; £40 or $90)*

New Moscow City Map and Guide, The (2nd ed.). *A totally revised second edition of what is arguably the definitive city street map of Moscow. Includes feature and street indexes and measures 2' x 3' when unfolded. Laminated wall version also available. (Russian Information Services; ISBN 1-880100-23-1; 1994; $6.95)* **Access Russia order number: M600.**

New St. Petersburg City Map and Guide, The. *The most current and usable map of the Imperial City. As with Moscow map, includes full city map, an expanded city center map, a walking map of Nevskiy prospekt, a metro and regional map. Fully indexed. Laminated wall version also available. (Russian Information Services; ISBN 1-880100-17-7; 1993; $6.95)* **Access Russia order number: M602**.

Oil and Gas Map of the Former Soviet Union (Laminated). *A full-color, physical map of the former USSR providing the most comprehensive overview available of the oil and gas industries in that area. (Pennwell Books; 1994; $165)* **Access Russia order number: M621**

Road Atlas of the Former Soviet Union. *A hard-bound book with over seventy 12" x 10" maps of the FSU, showing major roads, cities, railroads, waterways and regions. Fully indexed. In Russian (1993; $29.95)* **Access Russia order number: M605**.

Russia and Post-Soviet Republics Wall Map (Laminated). *An up-to-date color map of Russia and the new states, encased in 3 mil plastic. Shows all new republics within Russia. In English (Kartographia; 1993; $32)* **Access Russia order number: M621**

Russian Far East: Territorial Maps by District. *Computer-generated maps of the seven regions of the Russian Far East (Russian Far East Update, PO Box 22126, Seattle, WA 98122, ph. 206-447-2668, fax 206-628-0979; 1994; 12 pp.; $45)*

See also the section following on US Government (CIA) maps.

Travel and Travel Essay

Blue Guide: Moscow & Leningrad, Evan and Margaret Mawdsley. *Never mind the part about Leningrad in the title, there is no more detailed yet compact guide to the tourist sites of Moscow and St. Petersburg. Organized in a 'walks through the cities with narration' format. (W.W. Norton; ISBN 0-393-30773-5; 400 pp.; 1991; $22.50)* **Access Russia order number: B104**.

Central Asia: The Practical Handbook, Giles Whittell. *Jam-packed with highly-practical details, this beautifully designed book is indispensable for the traveler to this region. Useful regional and city walking maps, colorful descriptions of locales and insider knowledge of the region. (The Globe Pequot Press; ISBN 1-56440-227-4; 330 pp.; 1993; $15.95)* **Access Russia order number: B114**.

International Travel Health Guide: 1994, Stuart R. Rose, M.D. *A current and comprehensive guide to planning a safe and healthy trip abroad. Covers every conceivable affliction and eventuality. (Travel Medicine, Inc.; ISBN 0-923947-44-2; 400 pp.; 1994; $16.95)* **Access Russia order number: B120**.

Journey for Our Time: The Russian Journals of the Marquis de Custine. *Required reading for any serious student of Russia. An extremely insightful and realistic, albeit hardly positive, description of 18th century Russia, much of which,* the reader soon realizes, still applies some 150 years later. *(Regnery Gateway; ISBN 0-68-970672-3; 246 pp.; 1987; $8.95) Access **Russia** order number: G410.*

Trans-Siberian Rail Guide, Robert Strauss. *Completely updated in a new third edition, this book is full of facts and information on traveling the several lines of the Trans-Siberian. Contains easy-to-follow strip maps of railway routes. (Hunter Publishing, Inc.; ISBN 0-9520900-0-7; 275 pp.; 1993; $16.95) Access **Russia** order number: B113.*

Where in Moscow (4th ed.), Paul E. Richardson, ed. *Offers concise and invaluable yellow and white pages directory information to the essential goods and services that business people, students and independent travelers need when traveling to Moscow. Many entries are cross-referenced to a 30-page indexed color city street map, located in the back of the book (see maps section above) (Russian Information Services; ISBN 1-880100-19-3; 230 pp.; 1994; $13.50) Access **Russia** order number: B105.*

Where in St. Petersburg (2nd ed.), Paul E. Richardson, ed. *The first ever yellow pages guide to St. Petersburg. Includes yellow and white page directories and a colorful city street map – with all three elements cross-referenced. (Russian Information Services; ISBN 1-880100-13-4; 218 pp.; 1994; $13.50) Access **Russia** order number: B106.*

Where Nights are Longest, Colin Thubron. *Perhaps the best-written, most insightful travel essay written about the crumbling Soviet Union. Based on the renowned travel author's driving tour of Western Russia, Ukraine and the Baltics. (Atlantic Monthly; ISBN 0-87113-167-6; 210 pp.; 1984; $9.95) Access **Russia** order number: G413.*

ON-LINE INFORMATION RESOURCES

Currently, very good resources are available from a variety of electronic channels which provide information on developments in Russia and the CIS. And because of the ever-expanding reach of electronic information resource networks like Compuserve, Telenet and the Internet, in most cases you can simply call a local phone number and pay $15-20 an hour for usage, or about the cost of a long distance phone call.

There are some services which are dedicated to the Russian and Slavic areas. Other, mass-user networks provide additional, useful resources. Electronic mail services for communicating with partners in Russia, which most of the networks below also feature, are treated in some detail in Chapter 6.

Dedicated On-Line Services

• *AFS International Group*, 300 Spring Building, Suite 900, Little Rock, AR 72203, ph. 501-376-9997, fax 501-374-2770. $5 per minute.

While not an on-line service, this company does provide indirect access to a huge database of over 25,000 FSU firms, searchable by industry, SIC code, region, etc. The company also offers a database accessing full-text English language translations of the

Customs and Tarriffs laws of all CIS and Baltic states. You call in with your information request and AFS staffers perform the searching and data output.

• **EVPNet**, East View Publications, 3020 Harbor Lane North, Minneapolis, MN 55447, ph. 612-550-0961, fax 612-559-2931.

On-line access to full-texts of Russian newspapers (Kuranty, Nezavisimaya Gazeta and others), as well as East View's substantial catalogue of Russian-published books, periodicals and maps.

• **Sovam Teleport**, 3278 Sacramento Street, San Francisco, CA 94115, ph. 800-257-5107, fax 415-931-2885 (access via Telenet). Cost $15 per hour.

This San Francisco-based company, using its joint venture in Moscow (with nodes in other cities – see the City Guide, Chapter 6) has established what is arguably the best, most cost-effective Email system between the US and Russia (see Chapter 7). Recently, the service added user-friendly **Internet Access***, with menus to help users access Russia/ CIS-focused NewsGroups. The company also offers subscribers a number of database and information services, including:*

Radio Liberty Daily Reports: *Daily political and economic news from around the former USSR.*

BISNIS: *Text of BISNIS (See Government Information below) reports and newsletters.*

Newsbytes, Teleputing Hotline *and* **NASA Headline News:** *A comprehensive reporting of developments in the Russian and Commonwealth computer, telecom and space industries, respectively.*

• **Sovset**, Comtex, 2900 Seminary Road, Suite 800, Alexandria, VA 22311, ph. 703-820-2000, fax 703-820-2005. Academic rate: $27/mo. Corporate rate: $40/mo. Access via the Internet is free. $9/hr for access via Telenet.

Founded mainly for Slavic studies academics (by CSIS in Washington), this is a sleeper resource, not used to its maximum potential by the business community. In addition to Email capabilities accessible from Russia, Sovset provides several unique information services. Management of the service was recently (Dec. 1993) taken over by Comtex, and new services are expected to be added in coming months. Some of the better resources currently on-line include:

Radio Liberty Daily Report: *Also available in a weekly version, this is an easily-accessible and comprehensive daily news source on the Commonwealth and Baltics.*

Federal News Service: *Texts of Kremlin news conferences, speeches of executive and legislative body leaders and related documents.*

Express Chronicle: *An independent weekly newspaper published and edited in Moscow since August 1987. Some of the best political coverage available from reporters around the Commonwealth.*

Interlegal: *A monthly newsletter produced jointly by the Interlegal Research Center in Moscow and Postfactum News Agency. Covers ecclesiastical, environmental, human rights and aid issues.*

ITAR-TASS, *news feed from the top daily news agency in Russia.*

• *Russica*, 210 E. State Street, Batavia, IL, 60510, ph. 708-406-6411, fax 708-879-8807. $145 per year, plus $39 per hour of connect time. [also accessible through Communicate! (800-777-9243), DataTimes (800-642-2525), Lexis-Nexis, (800-544-7390, 71-488-9187 in UK), Datastar (800-221-7754, 71-930-5503 in UK, and GBI in Germany (89-957-0064)]

A new privately-owned service connected with the huge Dialog concern in Russia, this company is now providing some of the best on-line information on Russia currently available, including:

Russian Press Digest: *15-20 new articles per day (over 24,000 stories going back to 1990) of most potential interest to international subscribers. Gleaned from over 100 newspapers. Allows searching by date of publication or keyword within the text.*

BizEkon Daily Reports: *A parallel service to RPD, this dates back to 1991.*

BizEkon Business Directory: *Addresses and company information from over 10,000 Russian firms which have done business with foreign firms. Checked quarterly for accuracy.*

Who is Who Directory: *Data on some 1500 of Russia's leading individuals.*

Moscow News OnLine: *Full text services of Russia's leading weekly.*

Russian Public Association Directory: *Information on over 3000 religious, social, ecological, labor human rights and other organizations.*

Russian Far East Report: *News reports from an independent news agency in Vladivostok, covering news of the Eastern and Siberian regions.*

RusLegisLine: *Database of full-text translations of Russian legal acts related to foreign trade and investment. Over 500 laws in late 1993. It is the primary source for* Business and Commercial Laws of Russia *(see Periodicals Section above).*

Postfactum: *Updated twice-daily with information generated by the 55 regional news bureaus of PostFactum throughout the FSU.*

Non-Dedicated On-Line Systems

• *Compuserve*, Customer Services, P.O. Box 20212, Columbus, OH 43220, ph. 800-848-8990.

This popular information service instituted, in the wake of the August 1991 coup, a forum for monitoring events in the former Soviet Union. You get there by typing GO USSR (when logged on to Compuserve). The forum gives access to the following services:

Soviet Crisis Newsclips: *A special clipping service continually updated with reports from the Washington Post and major international wire services, including Reuters, UPI, and ITAR. (access directly by entering GO USSRCLIPS)*

Any user who signs up for Executive Option service on Compuserve can create a similar type of clipping file oriented to their particular interests (i.e. using keywords such as "Russia" and "oil").

U.S. Department of State Travel Advisories: *Accesses travel advisories on any country, including the former Soviet Union (still listed under Soviet Union at the time of printing). Type GO STATE to get directly to this service.*

International Entrepreneurs' Forum: *Useful files on doing business in Russia. Often companies post business opportunities through this forum. (GO PROFORUM)*

• **Dialog**, 3460 Hillview, Palo Alto, CA 94303, ph. 800-334-2564

This mega-information provider can provide searchable access to the full text of over 1600 periodical, newspaper and newsletter publications. This, plus company reports on North American and European companies, business and news wires, and more. Of course, this comes at a price, of anywhere from $15 to over $100 per hour, plus telecom charges. Several periodicals reviewed in the Periodicals section above are included, too many to list here ($45 sign-up fee w/ $50 usage credit; annual service fee of $35).

• **MCI Mail**, 1150 17th Street, NW, Suite 800, Washington, DC 20036, ph. 800-444-6245.

*This Email provider (see Chapter 6 below) can also provide access to the Dow Jones News Service (//NEWS), which has daily news and which can conduct customized searches for users (//QUEST). A clipping file can also be created (//CLIP). News of the former USSR is also available on the Dow Jones service (.R/UR). In all cases, the services are a bit pricey ($2-3 per minute during prime time and $0.50 to $2 for non-prime time), but user-friendly and mainly efficient. For users of **Prodigy** and **PC Telemail** or **SprintNet**, these services offer similarly-configured access to news and clipping services.*

• **NewsNet**, 945 Haverford Road, Bryn Mawr, PA 19010, ph. 800-345-1301 or 215-527-8030.

Access to a number of useful news and information services, for a premium price. In addition to International Information Report, Russia Express and Russia Express Contracts (profiled in the Periodicals section above), it also allows access to the Federal News Service (see above under Sovset). The cost is $15 per month, plus $1.50 per minute for usage time. A special starter kit is available for $79.95.

FAX RETRIEVAL SERVICES

This new technology allows the user to dial from his/her fax machine, enter a document code, and receive a document immediately by fax. You pay only the cost of the phone call. Four services are currently available.

Flashfax BISNIS Bank: *Maintained by the Business Information Service for the Newly Independent States (BISNIS) at the US Department of Commerce, this service includes trade opportunities, calendars of trade events, market information and aid/investment support opportunities. To access the service, dial* **202-482-3145** *from any touch tone phone and follow the instructions.*

The Export Hotline: *Maintained by International Strategies, Inc. and underwritten by AT&T, KPMG Peat Marwick, Business Week, Delta Airlines and others. Call from the phone on your fax machine to* **617-248-9393** *and follow instructions.*

US Centers for Disease Control: *Runs a fax retreival service on issues of concern to travelers, including regional health alerts and immunization recommendations. Call* **404-332-4559** *from any touch-tone telephone and follow the instructions.*

US Department of State Travel Advisories: *You can receive copies of the most current advisories by fax by dialing* **202-647-3000** *and following the directions.*

UNITED STATES: INFORMATION AND RESOURCES

For the sake of brevity, the addresses of government organizations which provide various kinds of information are listed immediately below, with any specific phone numbers or offices noted within references:

[BISNIS] Business Information Service of the Newly Independent States, US Department of Commerce, Room H-7413, Washington, DC 20230, ph. 202-482-4655; fax 202-482-2293

[DoS] Department of State, 2201 C St. NW, Washington, DC 20520, ph. 202-647-4000

[DoC] Department of Commerce, 14th St. and Constitution Ave., NW, Washington, DC 20230, ph. (202)482-2000

[E/IB] Export/Import Bank, 811 Vermont Avenue, NW, Washington, DC 20571, ph. 202-566-4490; fax 202-566-7524; or 11000 Wilshire Blvd., Los Angeles, CA 90024, ph. 310-322-1152; fax 310-322-2041

[ITC] International Trade Commission, 701 E St. NW, Washington, DC 20436, ph. 202-205-2000

[OPIC] Overseas Private Investment Corporation, 1100 New York Ave., NW, Washington, DC 20527, ph. 202-336-8799; fax 202-408-9859

Adoption

Current law allows adoptions in Russia and Ukraine, although most US citizens attempting the procedure have faced a steep uphill battle, particularly in Russia. If you seek the most current information on adopting a child from any of the countries of the former USSR, contact the DoS' Office of Consular Services at 202-647-3444.

Export Licensing

ELECTRONIC APPLICATION FILING

• Electronic communication is speeding export control processes. The Department of Commerce's ELAIN system allows for electronic filing of license applications. Within the ELAIN system there is also a system known as EXPERT, which helps exporters determine if a given technology is export controlled.

For more information on Electronic Filing of Export License Applications, contact IBEK Corporation, 202-463-0904 or OCR International, 301-208-0700. Both are officially licensed with DoC.

EXPORT ADMINISTRATION REGULATIONS

• The regulations are a publication of the Department of Commerce, and may be ordered from the Superintendent of Documents, U.S. Government Printing Office, Washington, DC 20402, ph. 202-783-3238, fax 202-512-2233. The price is $87 per year (stock # 903-017-00000-7).

OTHER USEFUL NUMBERS
- **Bureau of Export Administration**, DoC, 714-660-0144
- **Export License Voice Info System**: 202-482-4811
- **Tracking Export License Applications**: 202-482-4811

Export Financing and Insurance

PUBLICATIONS
- The publication of BISNIS, *Sources of Finance for Trade and Investment in the Newly Independent States*, is the most informative and detailed resource available on this subject. Free publication. Call 202-482-4655.

HOTLINE
- The **E/IB** operates an Export Financing Hotline at 202-566-4423, 800-424-5201 outside DC.
- The **International Trade Administration** operates a US Export/Import Bank Automated Information System at 800-424-5201.

FINANCE
- The **E/IB** offers: medium and long term loan guarantees with repayment protection against both political and commercial risks for private sector loans; medium and long term direct loans to foreign buyers of US exports and intermediate loans to responsible parties that extend loans to foreign buyers – at up to 85% of the export value. In the case of the latter financing options, the buyer must approach a Russian bank designated by E/IB as a sovereign borrower (i.e. VneshTorgBank and Vnesheconombank or a private bank which E/IB has established a guarantee arrangement with, i.e. Tokobank and International Moscow Bank).
- **OPIC** offers: direct loans of $500,000 to $6 mn to small and medium-sized companies for up to 50% of the cost of a new venture and 75% of the cost of an expansion; investment finance (loan guarantees) of $200 mn for investors with significant equity and management stake in a Russian venture.
- The **Small Business Administration** offers: loan guarantees to small businesses for fixed assets and working capital; a guaranteed, one-year rolling line of credit to support financing of labor and materials for manufacturing or wholesaling for export, for developing foreign markets, for financing foreign accounts receivable, and, in come cases, for funding foreign business travel and trade show participation; loan guarantees for the purchase or upgrading of facilities or equipment within the US, for production of export oriented goods and services. To locate the SBA office nearest you, call 800-U-ASK-SBA, or fax 202-205-7064.
- The **International Finance Corporation** (IFC) provides loans for up to 25% of the cost of large ($25-400 mn) ventures oriented to private investment. Call IFC Corporate Relations Unit at 202-473-9331.
- The **European Bank for Reconstruction and Development** (EBRD), of which the US Government is a founder, offers equity investment and debt guarantees to "foster the transition toward open market-oriented economies

and to promote private and entrepreneurial initiative." Target industries (with emphasis on privatization) are telecom, energy, infrastructure, goods and services distribution, banking and financial services. Contact EBRD via the International Trade Administration DoC, ph. 202-482-1246, fax 202-482-5179.

INSURANCE

• **OPIC** now offers investment insurance to protect US firms against currency inconvertibility, expropriation and political violence. The government corporation has specialized programs for financial institutions, leasing, oil and gas, natural resources and for contractors and exporters. They also have a small business insurance package which offers streamlined application procedures.

• **E/IB** offers short and medium-term export credit insurance, through loans or reimbursement, protecting investors against losses should a foreign buyer default. It also offers working capital guarantees, to encourage local lenders to make loans to US businesses for various export activities.

• **Multilateral Investment Guarantee Agency** (MIGA) offers guarantees to investors against losses caused by non-commercial risks, ph. 202-473-0179.

INSURANCE AND FINANCE INFORMATION

• **Finance and Countertrade Div.**, DoC, Rm 1104, ph. 202-482-4434.

• **USDA** has established an alternative export arrangement division to help stimulate non-conventional agricultural trade. Call 202-720-6211.

• **American Association of Importers and Exporters**, 11 W. 42nd Street, New York, NY 10036, ph. 212-944-2230, fax 212-382-2606.

• The **E/IB** holds periodic seminars on ways to start exporting to the CIS. Call 202-566-4490 for more information.

Geographical Information

• Declassified **CIA maps** on the former USSR can be ordered through the NTIS order desk at 703-487-4650. But first get a copy of the free catalogue by calling the Public Affairs office at 703-351-2053.

• Defense Mapping Agency **nautical maps** and **aeronautical maps** of the former Soviet Union can be had for a song. Reap the peace dividend and call and ask for a catalogue to be sent to you: 301-436-6990.

• For current city maps of Moscow and St. Petersburg, and commercial maps of Russia and the FSU, call RIS at 802-223-4955.

Information, General

• **BISNIS, DoC:** 202-482-4655, fax 202-482-2293. Ask for a current and complete package of information on accessing the Russian/CIS market. Also ask to be put on the mailing list for their free newsletter.

• **Commerce Business Daily**, published by the DoC, it includes Requests for Proposals, and Requests for Applications relating to export contracts. To subscribe, call the Superintendent of Documents at 202-783-3238, fax 202-512-2233 (cost is $324 per year, or $275 for second class delivery).

• **DoC Russia and Independent States Desk:** 202-482-2354, fax 202-377-8042.

• **DoS Russia and Independent States Desk:** 202-647-9370; Commercial Visas/Exchange Department: 202-647-8956

• **Eastern European Business Information Center:** 202-482-2645

• **Export Hotline** (Fax Retrieval Service), fax 617-248-9393

• **Flashfax BISNIS Bank,** fax 202-482-3145

• **OPIC** offers advisory services, investment missions, and an Opportunity Bank (buyer-seller database), as well as an Investor Information Service.

• Information on **World Bank** and **EBRD** aid activities and tender possibilities are included in the Flashfax BISNIS Bank (see above). Detailed information in this area is also available by subscribing to *East European Finance* (see Periodicals section above) or by calling the DoC liaison at the World Bank 202-458-0118.

• For information on the activity of non-governmental organizations in Russia and the NIS, contact **Citizens Democracy Corps** at 800-394-1945.

CIA PUBLICATIONS

To subscribe to all CIA declassified publications, the annual subscription fee is just $375. To order, call 202-707-9527 or write to DOCEX, Exchange and Gifts Division, Library of Congress, Washington, DC 20540-4230. Among these are directories of leaders, maps, economic data resource and reference publications.

Market Studies, Contacts and General Reports

• **Country Market Studies:** A market study of Russia ("Industry Sector Analysis") or any of the other Commonwealth states, based on research by the International Trade Administration, is available through DoC district offices. Call 800-872-8723 for the closest district office.

• **Finding Russian contacts:** The DoC's Agent/Distributor Service (ADS) is now available for Russia via DoC district offices. First, contact your local district office (call 800-872-8723 to get the coordinates of the closest one), where they will review your product literature. This will be forwarded on to DoC officials in Moscow, who will locate and contact potential agents and distributors. Within 60-90 days, you will receive a list of up to six of the best qualified and most interested contacts, along with relevant contact and background information. The cost of the service for Russia is $250. You can also call BISNIS for more information.

• **OPIC** has a Project Development Program for funding up to $150,000 (50-75%) of the cost of feasibility studies of proposed investments in the region. This program is administered by Ernst & Young, 1225 Connecticut Ave., NW, Washington, DC 20036, ph. 202-327-6439, fax 202-327-6399.

• **US Trade and Development Program**, SA-16, Room 309, Washington DC, 20523-1602, ph. 703-875-4357; fax 703-875-4009. Funds feasibility studies, training programs, etc. which have priority status in the CIS and relate to US Export potential and have untied financing. Feasibility studies to be funded are typically listed in *Commerce Business Daily*. Prior to conduct of feasibility studies, TDA contracts with private consultants to do Definitional Missions (DM) or desk studies of the project, to see if it meets TDA criteria. For current DM tenders, call the DM liine at 703-875-7447.

• *See also Technical Assistance below.*

Statistics

EAST-WEST TRADE

• **DoC** can provide some statistics on trade and investment for a fee. Contact DoC at 202-482-5291 to get connected with your district office Trade Specialist. BISNIS can also provide general info.

Technical Assistance

CONVERSION

• **BISNIS** issues a publication *Russian Defense Business Directory*, which lists key converting enterprises and summarizes important legislation and activity in this area. See the Books, Directories and Reference section above.

• **DoC** has established, together with the Russian government, an Intergovernmental US-Russian Business Development Committee, which has a subcommittee on Defense Conversion. Contact ph.: 202-482-3701.

• The **Geonomics Institute**, while not a governmental organization, has begun a project under its Breadloaf Charter to encourage and assist US and Russian conversion processes. Contact: Geonomics Institute, 14 Hillcrest Ave., Middlebury, VT 05753, ph. 802-388-9619, fax 802-388-9627

• The **US Department of Defense** has allocated some $800 million in funding for conversion assistance. Contracts which may be bid on are published in *Commerce Business Daily* (see General Information above).

COUNTERTRADE

• The **Financial Services and Countertrade Division** (FSCD) of DoC provides assistance to companies seeking to get started in barter and other countertrade operations. Call 202-482-4471, fax 202-482-5702.

• Two **publications** prepared by FSCD are available from the Superintendent of Documents, ph. 202-783-3238, fax 202-512-2233: *International Countertrade: A Guide for Managers and Executives* (#003-009-00613-9), and *Individual Country Practices in International Countertrade* (#003-009-00614-7).

• See *Countertrade Outlook* in periodicals section above.

ENVIRONMENT

• **ISAR**, a private, not-for-profit organization, has established an **International Clearinghouse on the Environment**, to facilitate and enhance communication on environmental issues. The project involves setting up centers for such transnational communication in Russia and the US. For more information, contact ISAR at 1601 Connecticut Ave., NW, Suite 301, Washington, DC 20009, ph. 202-387-3034.

EXPORT ASSISTANCE

• The **CABNIS** program begun by DoC (Consortia of American Businesses in the Newly Independent States) seeks to encourage companies in an industry area to establish consortia that will provide economies of scale for businesses seeking to do business in and export to the NIS. A consortia, established with the help of a CABNIS grant, will provide members with export information, marketing and promotion services, and establish an on-the-ground presence in the NIS.

• The DoC has extended its **Office Away from Home** service to Moscow. This service allows US companies, for a very modest fee, access to office space and support services while traveling in Moscow, including an answering service, international phone and fax, and meeting rooms. Contact them in advance by dialing direct to Moscow at 011-7-502-224-1105, fax 011-7-502-224-1106. From Moscow, their number is 255-4848, fax 230-2101.

• The DoC also has extended its **Gold Key Service** to Russia. This service uses DoC specialists to help American companies develop a market strategy for Russia, and to set up appropriate meetings with the government, firms and individuals prior to your arrival in Moscow. Six key contacts are identified for $300. For each day's meetings there is a $100 charge. Three week advance notice is required to use this service. Contact BISNIS or the US Commercial office in Moscow (see previous note-for more information.

FOREIGN AID/INVESTMENT FUNDS

• **USAID** has set up several programs, in areas from health care to private sector development to environmental protection to energy efficiency to encouraging democratic pluralism, all under its Bureau for Europe and the NIS, Center for Trade and Investment Services, ph. 202-663-2667, fax 202-663-2670. Proposal and Application Requests are published regularly in *Commerce Business Daily* (see General Information above).

• The **Russian-American Enterprise Fund** was created in 1993 by USAID (with $300 mn for the next 4-5 years) with the aim of providing loans and/ or investments in small- and medium-sized businesses in the Russian Federation, including in US-Russian joint ventures. See the Fund's address below.

• The **Eurasia Foundation**, a new privately-managed organization financed by USAID, supports, through grants (generally $50-75,000), activities designed to develop the private sector, reform the public sector, or develop and support media and communications. Contact the Eurasia Foundation at 1527 New Hampshire Ave., NW, Washington, DC 20036, ph. 202-234-7370.

• The **Russian Country Fund** is a $100 mn investment fund to provide equity investment in larger newly-formed or privatized enterprises in Russia. It will focus on joint ventures with ties to the US economy or that will generate hard currency income through exports (primarily in mining, oil and gas). It is administered by Paine Webber, ph. 212-713-3214, fax 212-713-1087.

TRAINING

- The **International Executive Service Corps** (a non-governmental organization) sends retired US business persons to Russia to aid and consult with privatizing and reforming enterprises. IESC, Stanford Harbor Park, 333 Ludlow St., Stanford, CT 06902, ph. 203-967-6000, fax 203-324-2531.
- **SABIT**, the Special American Business Internship Training program run by the DoC, provides 3-6 month subsistence grants for Russian internees in American businesses. Priority sectors are energy, pharmaceuticals, agribusiness, telecom, financial services, housing, medical equipment, conversion, and the environment. Phone 202-482-0073, fax 202-482-2443.
- **Citizen Democracy Corps** (a private organization) offers volunteer opportunities in Russia and the former USSR. Call 800-394-1945.
- **USIA** saw its budget for NIS-related exchange and educational projects double in the last year. Programs include support for NIS graduate, undergraduate and non-degree students to study in the US, exchange programs, visiting professorships and professionals in residence in the NIS. Contact USIA at ph. 202-619-4355, fax 202-619-6988.
- The **Peace Corps** has started sending volunteers to work in the NIS. To find out how to serve, talk to the Peace Corps' Russia desk at 202-606-3973.

Travel Information

PASSPORT INFORMATION

- For information on getting a passport, call 202-647-0518.

TRAVEL ADVISORY INFORMATION

- For the latest **travel advisories**, call 202-647-5225, or write to Overseas Citizens Services, Bureau of Consular Affairs, DoS, Room 4800. This is also valid for emergency information, such as the death of a US relative while that person is abroad. Advisories are also accessible on Compuserve (GO STATE) and via a fax back service (call 202-647-3000).
- The **Bureau of Diplomatic Security** at DoS operates an electronic bulletin board, updated daily, providing useful information about security risks and emergencies involving Americans abroad. As well, it gives current information on entry requirements for visiting other countries and information about foreigners visiting the US. Dial, by modem, 202-647-9225.
- *See periodicals section above, especially* **Russian Travel Monthly**.

Important Associations and Organizations

- **American-Ukraine Business Council**, 321 North Clark Street, Suite 550, Chicago, IL 60610, ph. 312-853-5980.
- **Amtorg Trade Inc.**, 15 West 56th St., 6th Floor, New York, NY 10018, ph. 212-956-3010, fax 212-956-2995. Liaisons between Russian trade organizations and large enterprises and US companies. Among its new mandates is establishment of **US-NIS Chamber of Commerce and Industry**, reachable at the same address.

- **Citizen Democracy Corps**, 2021 K Street, NW, Suite 215, Washington, DC 20006, ph. 202-872-0933 or 800-394-1945, fax 202-872-0923. Information on aid and service organizations active in the CIS.
- **Eurasia Foundation**, 1527 New Hampshire Ave., NW, Washington, DC 20036, ph. 202-234-7370.
- **Moscow Chamber of Commerce**, ul. Chekhova 13, Moscow 103050, Russia, 095-299-7612.
- **New England East-West Trade Council**, PO Box 60, Boston, MA 02130, ph. 617-524-5454, fax 617-524-0013.
- **Russian Agency for International Cooperation and Development**, ul. Vozdvizhenka 18, Moscow, Russia ph. 095-290-0903, fax 095-975-2253.
- **Russian-American Chamber**, 731 8th Street, SE, Washington, DC 20003, ph. 202-546-3275, fax 202-546-4784.
- **Russian-American Enterprise Fund,** c/o Federal Reserve Bank of New York, 33 Liberty Street, Room 1101, New York, NY 10045.
- **Russian-American Trade Association,** 8344 E. RL Thornton Fwy., #108, Dallas, TX 75228-7186, ph. 800-393-4833, fax 214-324-4792.
- **Russian Chamber of Commerce and Industry**, ul. Kuybysheva 6, Moscow K-5 103684, Russia, ph. 095-921-0811, telex 411126.
- **Russian Trade and Cultural Center**, 35th floor, West, One World Trade Center, New York, NY 10048, ph. 212-432-2989, fax 212-682-1961.
- **St. Petersburg Chamber of Commerce**, nab. Krasnovo Flota 10, St. Petersburg 190000, Russia, ph. 812-314-9953.
- **Trade Representation of the Russian Federation**, 2001 Connecticut Ave., NW, Washington DC 20008, ph. 202-232-5988; fax 202-232-2917.
- **UNIDO Investment Promotion Services**, 1020 17th St., NW, Suite 800, Washington, DC 20036, ph. 202-659-5165, fax 202-659-7674.
- **US-Russian Business Council**, 1701 Pennsylvania Ave., NW, Suite 650, Washington, DC 20006, ph. 202-956-7670, fax 202-956-7674.
- **US Information Agency**, Washington, DC 20547, ph. 202-619-5055, fax 202-619-6988.

BRITISH GOVERNMENT/PRIVATE OFFICES & SERVICES

Government offices

- **Department of Trade and Industry**, Ashdowne House, 123 Victoria Street, London SW1E 6RB, ph. 71-215-5000, fax 71-828-3258, telex 8813148 DIHQ G.
- **Foreign and Commonwealth Office**, King Charles Street, London SW1A 2AH, ph. 71-270-3832, fax 71-270-3282.

Private Associations and Organizations

- **Britain-Russia Chamber of Commerce (BSCC)**, 42 Southwark St., London SE1 1UN, ph. 71-403-1706, fax 71-403-1245. *Provides in-depth assistance for members. They maintain a Moscow office which supports members in their* *visits to Russia, and organize seminars and group visits to Russia. Members receive a monthly internal newsletter and the BSCC Journal. Members are also entitled to discounts on individual accommodations while in Moscow.*

- **The Britain-Russia Centre**, 14 Grosvenor Pl., London SW1X 7HW, ph. 71-235-2116, fax 71-259-6254. *The British East-West Centre is a subsidiary of the above. Based from the same location, they deal with non-Russian republic concerns.*

Other Resources

- **European Bank for Reconstruction and Development**, One Exchange Square, London EC2A 2EH, ph. 71-338-6000, fax 71-338-6100

CANADIAN GOVERNMENT/PRIVATE OFFICES & SERVICES

Government

- **Department of Foreign Affairs and International Trade**, Central & East European Trade Development Division, 125 Sussex Drive, Ottawa, K1A OG2, ph. 613-996-6835, fax 613-995-8783.

Private Associations and Organizations

- **CUBC**, 2 First Canadian Place, Suite 2125, P.O. Box 11, Toronto, M5X 1A9, ph. 416-862-2821, fax 416-862-2820. *Provides full trade and consulting support to members, both in Canada and Russia, with substantial capability in Ukraine as well. Publishes bi-monthly newsletter. Office in Moscow.*

EUROPEAN AND JAPANESE CHAMBERS OF COMMERCE

All of the following are very active agents for their members, liaisoning with both Russian and home governments. Most all have offices in Moscow.

Finland

Finnish-Soviet Chamber of Commerce, Annankatu 32A, 00100 Helsinki, ph. 90-693-1066, fax 90-693-1442, telex 121589 FISOP.

France

French-Russian Chamber of Commerce, 22 Avenue Franklin Roosevelt, 75008 Paris, ph. 1-42-25-9710, fax 1-43-59-7473, telex 615909

Germany

Association of German Chambers of Industry and Commerce, Adenauer Allee 88, 53113 Bonn, Germany, ph. 228-104-188, fax 228-104-179

Ost-Ausschuss der Deutschen Wirtshaft, Gustav Heinemann Ufer 84, 50968 Koeln, ph. 221-3708-417, fax 221-3708-540

Bundesstelle fuer Ausenhandles Information, Agrippa Strasser 7893, 50676 Koeln 1, ph. 221-20571, fax 221-2057-212

Italy

Italian-Soviet Chamber of Commerce, via San Tomaso 5, 20121 Milano, ph. 720-04-008, fax 805-2009, telex 333821.

Japan

Japan-Russia Trade Association, Sanko Building 6-4-3, Kojimachi Chiyodaku, Tokyo, ph. 03-3262-8401, fax 03-3262-8403, telex J 27213

Netherlands

Nederlands-Russische Kamer van Koophandel, Lange Voorhout 86, Apt. #5, 2514 EA Den Haag, Netherlands, ph. 70-345-1600, fax 70-362-5231

Russian Embassies in Foreign Countries

AUSTRALIA

Embassy: 78 Canberra Avenue, Griffith A.C.T. 2603, Canberra, ph. 6-295-9033, fax 295-1847; (Consular Dept.) 295-9474, telex 61365 SOVPOSOL AA, (Consular Dept.) 62602 SOVPOSOL AA.

Consulate: 7-9 Fullerton Street, Wolluhra, Sydney, N.S.W. 2025, ph. 612-326-1188, 326-1866, 326-1702, fax 327-5065; telex 73606 SOVCON AA.

AUSTRIA

Embassy: Reisnerstrasse 45-47, 1030 Wien, ph. 222-713-12-15, 712-12-29, (Consular Dept.) 712-32-33, telex 47136278.

Consulate: Burgelsteinstrasse 2, 5020 Salzburg, ph. 6212-241-84, telex 47632655.

BELGIUM

Embassy: 66 Avenue De Fre, 1180 Bruxelles, ph. 2-374-68-86, 374-34-06, telex (Consular Dept.) 4665272.

Consulate: Della Faililaan 20, 2020 Antwerpen, ph. 3-829-16-11, telex 4435779.

CANADA

Embassy: 285 Charlotte Street, Ottawa, Ontario, K1N 8L5, ph. 613-235-4341, 236-1413, telex 26(21)0533332, (21)0533514.

Consulate: 3655 Avenue de Musee, Montreal, P.Q., H1W 1S1, ph. 514-843-5901, 288-0932, telex 26(21)05560071, 26(21)05560469.

DENMARK

Embassy: Kristianiagade 5, 2100 Kobenhaven, ph. 31-42-55-85, 42-55-86, (Consular Dept.) 38-23-70, telex 5516943.

FINLAND

Embassy: SNTL: Suurlahetysto, Tehtaankatu 1 B, 00140 Helsinki, ph. 0-66-18-76, 66-18-77, 60-70-50, fax 66-10-06 (Consular) 66-14-49, telex 57125577.

FRANCE

Embassy: 40-50 Boulevard Lannes, 75016 Paris, ph. 1-45-04-05-50, (Consular Dept.) 45-04-05-01, telex: 45044409, (Consular Dept.) 42642830.

Consulate: 3 avenue Ambroise-Pare, 13008 Marseille, ph. 91-77-15-25, telex 42440272.

GERMANY

Embassy: Waldstrasse 42, 53177 Bonn, ph. 49-228-31-20-85, 31-20-87, 31-20-74, (Consular Dept.) 31-20-89, telex (Consular Dept.) 41885615 VISAD.

Consulate: Unter-den-Linden 63-65, Berlin 1080, ph. 30-229-1129, telex 69114024 BERLIN DD.

GREAT BRITAIN

Embassy: 13 Kensington Palace Garden, London W8 4QX, ph. 71-229-3628, 229-3620, 229-6412, (Consular Dept.) 229-8027, fax 229-3215, telex (Consular Dept.) 51261420.

GREECE

Embassy: Palais Psychico, 28 Nikiforou Litra, Athens, ph. 1-672-5235, 672-6130, (Consular Dept.) 647-1395, 647-2949, telex 601223553.

ICELAND

Embassy: 33 Gardastraeti, Reykjavik, ph. 1-1-51-56, 62-04-55, fax 62-06-33 telex (Consular Dept.) 5012200.

INDIA

Embassy: Shantipath, Chanakyapuri, New-Delhi 110021, ph. 11-60-60-26, 60-61-37, 60-58-75, telex: 3182016 USSR IN.

Consulate: 42 Jamogandas Marg (Old Nepean Sea Road), Bombay: 40006, ph. 22-363–3627, 363-3628, telex: 811175939 SOVK IN.

Consulate: 31 Shakespeare Sarani, Calcutta 700017, ph. 33-44-20-06, 44-49-82, telex 81217774 SUSG IN.

Consulate: 14 Santhome High Road, Madras 600004, ph. 44-83-23-20, telex 81417515 SOCV IN.

IRELAND

Embassy: 186 Orwell Road, Rathgar, Dublin 14, ph. 1-92-35-25, 92-20-48, telex (Consular Dept.) 50033622.

ITALY

Embassy: via Gaeta 5, 00185 Roma, ph. 6-494-1681, 494-1683, 494-1680, 494-1649, telex (Consular Dept.) 43622310.

Consulate: via Sant'Aquilino, 20148, Milano, ph. 2-404-6741, 404-6742, telex 43326571.

Consulate: via Ghirardelli Perscetto 16, Genova, ph. 10-31-54-10, telex: 43222899.

JAPAN

Embassy: 1-1 Azabudai, 2-chome, Minato-ku, Tokyo, 106, ph. 3-583-4224, 583-5982, 583-4297, fax 505-0593 (Consular Dept.) 583-4445, telex (Consular Dept.) 7224231 SOVPOSOL J.

Consulate: Osaka-fu Toyonakashi Nishi Midorigaoka 1-2-2, ph. 6-848-3452, telex 7265908.

Consulate: 826 Nishi 12-chome, Minami 14-jo, Chuo-ku, Sapporo, 064, ph. 11-561-3171, telex: 720932305.

MEXICO

Embassy: Jose Vasconselos 204 (Condesa), Delegacion Cuanthema, 06140, ph. 5-273-1305, 273-1305, telex (Consular Dept.) 221772516 URSS ME.

Consulate: Avenida Vicitimas, 5 y 6 de Julia N 1045, Veracruz.

NETHERLANDS

Embassy: Andries Bickerweg 2, 2517 JP Den Haag, Holland, ph. 70-345-1300, (Consular Dept.) 364-6473, telex 07034585.

NEW ZEALAND

Embassy: 57 Messines Road, Karori, Wellington, ph. 4-476-61-13, (Consular Dept.) 476-67-42, fax 476-3843, telex (Consular Dept.) 7431727 SOVPOSOL NZ.

NORWAY

Embassy: 0271 Oslo 2, Drammensveien 74, ph. 2-255-3278, 255-3279, (Consular Dept.) 260-3035, telex 22550070.

SPAIN

Embassy: Madrid-6, c/Maestro Ripoll, 14, ph. 1-411-0807, 564-2049, 411-2524, (Consular Dept.) 411-2957, telex 5245632 URSS E, (Consular Dept.) 5247677 KOSU E.

SWEDEN

Embassy: Gjorwellsgatan 31, 11260 Stockholm, ph. 8-13-04-40, 13-04-41, 13-04-44, (Consular Dept.) 619-0470, telex (Consular Dept.) 5414830.

Consulate: St. Sigfridsgatan 1, Box 5093, 40222 Goteborg, ph. 31-40-80-84, 40-84-00, 20-60-93, telex 6182703.

SWITZERLAND

Embassy: Brunnadernrain 37, 3006 Berne, ph. 31-352-0566, (Consular Dept.) 352-6460, telex (Consular Dept.) 3526460.

Consulate: Rue Schaub 24, 1202 Geneve, ph. 22-734-7955.

UNITED STATES

Embassy: 1125 16th Street, N.W., Washington, D.C. 20036, ph. 202-628-7551, 628-7554, fax 347-5028, telex 232248400, (consular) 232248708.

Consulate: 1825 Phelps Place, Washington, DC 20008, ph. 202-939-8907, 8913, 8918; Information dept.: 202-232-6020

Consulate: 2790 Green Street, San Francisco, CA 94123, ph. 415-202-9800, fax 415-929-0306, telex 184945.

Consulate: 9 East 91st St., New York, NY 10128, ph. 212-348-0926, fax 831-9162.

Consulate: 2323 Westin Building, 2001 Sixth Ave., Seattle, WA 98121, ph. 206-728-1910, fax 206-728-1871.

Newly Independent States' Embassies in the US

Due to space limitations, only embassies in the United States can be listed here. The Russian embassy in any other country can give you addresses of the embassies of other former Soviet republics. You may also, of course, inquire via the republic's embassy in the US, at the address below.

ARMENIA: Embassy of the Republic of Armenia, 1660 L St., NW, Suite 210, Washington, DC 20036, ph. 202-628-5766, fax 202-628-5769

AZERBAIDZHAN: Turkish Mission to the United Nations, 821 United Nations Plaza, 10th Floor, New York, NY 10017, ph. 212-949-0150, fax 212-949-0086

BELARUS: Embassy of Belarus, 1619 New Hampshire Ave., NW, Washington, DC 20009, ph. 202-986-1606, fax 202-986-1805

ESTONIA: Embassy of Estonia, 630 Fifth Ave., Suite 2415, New York, NY 10111, ph. 212-247-1450, 212-247-7634, fax 212-262-0893

GEORGIA: Direct inquiries c/o Russian Embassy

KAZAKHSTAN: Embassy of Kazakhstan, 3421 Massachusetts Ave., NW, Washington, DC 20007, ph. 202-333-4504, fax 202-333-4509

KIRGIZISTAN: Embassy of Kirgizistan, 1511 K Street, NW, Suite 705, Washington, DC 20005, ph. 202-347-3732, fax 202-347-3718

LATVIA: Embassy of Latvia, 4325 17th St. NW, Washington, DC 20011, ph. 202-726-8213, fax 202-726-6785

LITHUANIA: Embassy of Lithuania, 2622 16th Street NW, Washington, DC 20009, ph. 202-234-2639, fax 202-328-0466; Consulates: 41 W. 82nd St., Apt. 5B, New York, NY 10024, ph. 212-877-4552; 3959 Franklin Ave., Los Angeles, CA 90027, ph. 805-496-5324

MOLDOVA: Moldovan Mission to the US, 573-577 Third Avenue, New York, NY 10016, ph. 212-682-3523, fax 212-682-6274

TADZHIKISTAN: c/o International Commodity Traders, Inc., 1825 I Street, NW, Suite 400, Washington, DC 20006, ph. 202-429-2026, fax 202-429-9574

TURKMENISTAN: Turkmenistan Mission to the US, c/o Russian Mission to the UN, 136 East 67th Ave., New York, NY 10021, ph. 212-472-5921, fax 212-772-2589

UKRAINE: Embassy of Ukraine, 3350 M St., NW, Washington, DC 20007, ph. 202-333-7507, fax 202-333-7510

UZBEKISTAN: Uzbekistan Mission to the United Nations, 866 UN Plaza, Suite 326, New York, NY 10017, ph. 212-486-7570, fax 212-486-7998

US Diplomatic Representations

Listed below are the US embassies and consulates in Russia and the Newly Independent States of the former USSR, plus, for the latter and where available, each state's chamber of commerce for the encouragement of foreign trade. See Chapter 2 for a list of these states' embassies in Moscow.

RUSSIA

MOSCOW

Embassy: Novinskiy bulvar 19-23, Moscow, ph. 095-252-2450, fax 095-255-9965, telex 413160 [after hours ph. 095-252-1898] *Commercial Office:* Novinskiy bulvar 15, *International:* ph. 502-224-1105, fax 502-224-1106, telex 413205; *from Moscow:* 095-255-4848, fax 095-230-2101.

ST. PETERSBURG

Consulate: Furshtadtskaya ul. 15, St. Petersburg, ph. 812-274-8235, telex 64121527. *Commercial Office,* Hotelship Peterhof, Nab. Makarova, V.O., ph. 812-119-6045, fax 812-213-6962, telex 005831401452.

VLADIVOSTOK

Consulate and Commercial Office: ul. Mordovtseva 12, Vladivostok, ph. 4232-258-458 or 509-851-1011, fax 4232-268-445, telex 213206.

OTHER NEWLY INDEPENDENT STATES

ARMENIA

US Embassy, Gen Bagramian 18, Yerevan, ph. 885-215-1144, fax 885-215-1122; **Armenian Chamber of Commerce,** Kutuzov st. 24, Yerevan, ph. 885-277-390.

AZERBAIDZHAN
US Embassy, Hotel Intourist, Baku, ph. 8922-926-306.

BELARUS
US Embassy, Starovilenskaya 46, Minsk, ph. 0172-347-642, fax 0172-347-853; Belarus Chamber of Commerce, Ya Kolasa 65, Minsk, ph. 0172-660-460.

ESTONIA
US Embassy, Kentmanni 20, Tallinn, ph. 2-455-313, international via Finland (358): 49-303-182, fax 49-308-17; Estonian Chamber of Commerce, Toom-Koolo 17, Tallinn, ph. 2-444-929, fax 2-443-656, telex 173254.

GEORGIA
US Embassy, Antonelli 25, Tbilisi, ph. 8832-989-967, fax 8832-742-052; Chamber of Commerce, Chavachavadze pr. 1, Tbilisi, ph. 8832-222-554.

KAZAKHSTAN
US Embassy, Seyfullina 551, Almaty, ph. 3272-631-375, fax 3272-633-883; Commercial Office, ul. Furmanova 99, ph. 3272-631-770, fax 3272-633-883, telex 251375.

KIRGIZISTAN
US Embassy, Erkindick 66, Bishkek, ph. 3312-222-270, fax 3312-223-551; Kirgiz Chamber of Commerce, Frunze st. 435, Bishkek, ph. 3312-264-942.

LATVIA
US Embassy, Raina bulvaris 7, ph. 2-210-005, fax 2-220-502, telex 161211, international via Finland (358): ph. 49-311-348, fax 49-314-665; Latvian Chamber of Commerce, Brivibas bulvaris 21, ph. 2-332-205, fax 2-332-276.

LITHUANIA
US Embassy, Akmenu 6, Vilnius, ph. 2-628-049, fax 2-222-779; Chamber of Commerce, Algirdas 31, ph. 2-661-550, fax 2-661-542.

MOLDOVA
US Embassy, Strada Alexei Mateevich 103, Chisinau, ph. 2-233-494, fax 2-233-494.

TADZHIKISTAN
US Embassy, Hotel Independence, Ainii st. 39, Dushanbe, ph. 3772-248-233; Tadzhik Chamber of Commerce, Sh. Rustaveli st. 31, ph. 3772-226-968.

TURKMENISTAN
US Embassy, Yubileynaya Hotel, Ashgabat, ph. 3632-244-925.

UKRAINE

US Embassy, Vul. Yuriy Kotsubinskoho 10, Kiev, ph. 044-244-7349, fax 044-244-7350, telex 131142; **Commercial Office,** Kudryavskiy Uzviz 7, 2nd floor, ph. 044-417-2669, fax 044-417-1419; **Ukranian Chamber of Commerce,** Bol. Zhitomirskaya st. 133, Kiev, ph. 044-222-911.

UZBEKISTAN

US Embassy, Chilanzarskaya 82, Tashkent, ph. 3712-776-986; **Consulate,** Chilanzarskaya 55, ph. 3712-771-407, fax 3712-776-953; **Uzbekistan Chamber of Commerce,** Pr. Lenina 16a, Tashkent, ph. 3712-336-282.

Travel Agents/Visa Services

While any travel agent can arrange travel to Russia, some companies have built a specialty on, or have specific experience with, travel to Russia. Many also can provide visa expediting services. Those with more experience and good contacts in Russia can also set up ground transportation and qualified translators.

AUSTRALIA

Intourist, Underwood House, 34-49 Pitt Street, Sydney NSW 2000, ph. 02-277-652, telex INTAUS AA 176604

Red Bear Tours, 320B Glenferrie Rd., Melbourne, Victoria 3144, ph. 3-824-7183, fax 3-822-3956, telex AA38615 Kewtel

Gateway Travel, PO Box 451, Strathfield N.S.W. 2135, ph. 2-745-3333, fax 2-745-3237

AUSTRIA

Intourist, Schwedenplatz 3-4, 1010 Wien, ph. 63-95-47; telex 114524

CANADA

Canadian Gateway, 7000 Bathurst, Unit C-8, Toronto, Ontario L4J 7L1, ph. 800-668-8401; fax 416-660-7004; telex 06-964737 (visa expediting and both group and individual travel arrangements)

Intours, 1013 Bloor St. West, Toronto, Ontario M6H 1M1, ph. 416-537-2165; fax 416-537-1627; telex 06-218557

P. Lawson, 4 King St. West, Suite 805, Toronto, Ontario, M5H 1B6, ph. 416-862-8020; fax 416-862-2390.

ENGLAND

Alpha-Omega, Amadeus House, 6 Lidgett Lane, Garforth, Leeds, LS25 1EQ, ph. 532-862-121, fax 532-864-964.

East-West Travel Limited, 15 Kensington High St., London W8 5NP

Goodwill Holidays, Manor Chambers, The Green, School Ln., Wellyn, Hargeshire AL6 9EB, UK, ph. 438-716-421, fax 438-840-228

Intourist, Intourist House, 219 Marsh Wall, Isle of Dogs, London E14 9FJ, ph. 71-538-3202, fax 71-538-5967, telex 27232 INTMOS

Intravel Ltd., World Trade Centre, International House, 1 St. Catherine's Way, London E1 9UN

Overseas Business Travel, Ltd., 117-119 Leman St., London E1 8EX

Russia House, Ltd., 37 Kingley Ct., Kingley St., London W1R 5LE, UK, ph. 71-439-1271, fax 71-434-0813

Visa Shop, The, 44 Chandos Place, London, WC2N 4HS, ph. 71-379-0419

FRANCE

Intourist, 7 Boulevard des Capucines, 75002 Paris, ph. 47-42-47-40; telex 680180 INTOUR.

FINLAND

Area, Pohjoisesplanadi 2, Helsinki, ph. 90-7661-491

Intourist, Etela Esplanaadi, 14, 00130 Helsinki 13, ph. 90-631, telex 124654 INTOUR.

GERMANY

Intourist, Friedrichstrasse 153A, 1080 Berlin, ph. 229-1948, 228-1492, telex 115173 INTOUR • 1000 Berlin, Kurfurstendamm 63, ph. 030-88-00-70, telex 185392 INTOUR • Stephanstrasse 1, 6000 Frankfurt am Main 1, ph. 069-28-57-76, telex 414232 INTOUR.

ITALY

Intourist, Piazza Buenos Aires 6/7, 00198 Roma, ph. 86-38-92; telex 626367 INURSS.

JAPAN

Intourist, Roppongi Heights, 1-16, 4-chome Roppongi, Minato-ku, Tokyo, ph. 03-584-6617, 03-584-6618, telex 27645.

SWITZERLAND

Intourist, Usteristrasse, 9 Lowenplatz, 8001 Zurich; ph. 01-211-3335; telex 813005 TOSU CH.

UNITED STATES

AmeriRuss Cruises, 1873 S. 45 West, Orem, UT 84059, ph. 800-279-4454, fax 801-226-1881. (Russian river cruises)

Barry Martin Travel, 19 West Street, Suite 3401, New York, NY 10004, ph. 212-422-0091, fax 212)344-1997.

Bolshoi Cruises, 379 N. University Ave., Suite 301, Provo, UT 84601, ph. 800-769-8687, fax 801-377-8800. (Volga river and Karelia cruises)

Cruise Marketing International, 1601 Industrial Way, Ste. A, Belmont, CA 94002, ph. 800-578-7742. (Cruises and ship-hotel in Moscow)

Cultural Access Network, PO Box 4410, Laguna Beach, CA 92652, ph. 714-497-6809, fax 714-497-6809.

East-West Discovery, PO Box 69, Volcano, HI 96785, ph. 808-985-8552.

East-West Tours & Travel Consulting, 10 E. 39th St., Suite 1124, New York, NY 10016, ph. 212-545-0737, fax 212-889-2009

East West Ventures, Inc., P.O. Box 14391, Tucson, AZ 85732, ph. 602-795-5414.

Express Visa Service, Inc., 2150 Wisconsin Ave., Suite 20, Washington, DC 20007, ph. 202-337-2442, fax 202-337-2253. (visa expediting).

IBV Bed and Breakfast Systems & Capital Visa, 13113 Ideal Drive, Silver Spring, MD 20906, ph. 301-942-3770, fax 301-933-0024.

Intourist, 630 Fifth Ave. #868, New York, NY 10111, ph. 212-757-3884, 757-3885, fax 212-459-0031, telex REP INTUR 62614 UW.

ITS Tours and Travel, 1055 Texas Ave., Suite 104, College Station, TX 77840, ph. 800-533-8688, fax 409-693-9673.

Mountain Travel/Sobek, 6420 Fairmount Ave., El Cerrito, CA 94530, ph. 800-227-2384, fax 510-525-7710. (Adventure travel)

New Solutions, 912 S. Juanita Ave., Redondo Beach, CA 90277, ph. 800-768-9535, fax 310-543-9839.

Pioneer East/West Initiatives, 88 Brooks Ave., Arlington, MA 02174, ph. 617-648-2020, fax 617-648-7304.

Rahim Travel, 12 South Dixie Highway, Lake Worth FL 33460, ph. 800-556-5305, fax 407-582-1353, telex 362788.

REI Adventures, PO Box 1938, Sumner, WA 98390, ph. 800-622-2236 (Adventure travel: from trekking in the Altai to biking Baikal).

Russia and Beyond, 1201 Third Ave., Suite 1800, Seattle, WA 98101, ph. 800-841-1811 or 206-461-2348, fax 206-554-7211.

Russia Travel Bureau, 225 East 44th Street, New York, NY 10017, ph. 212-986-1500, fax 212-490-1650.

Tour Designs, Inc., 616 G Street, SW, Washington, DC 20024, ph. 202-554-5820, fax 202-479-0472, telex 904266.

Visa Advisors, 1930 18th St., NW, Washington, DC 20009, 202-797-7976 (visa expediting).

Your Own World, 796 Crestmoor Dr., San Jose, CA 95129, ph. 800-473-6165 or 408-253-0264, fax 408-253-0266.

Other Services

Access to certain types of professional services and opportunities may be faciliated by the following lists of firms *active in Russia and the CIS.* Due to space limitations, mainly US addresses are listed.

ACCOUNTING FIRMS

Arthur Andersen, 1345 Avenue of the Americas, New York, NY 10105, ph. 212-708-4125.

Coopers & Lybrand, 1251 Avenue of the Americas, New York, NY 10020, ph. 212-536-2000, fax 212-536-3038.

Deloitte & Touche, 1001 Pennsylvania Ave., NW, Washington, DC 20004-2505, ph. 202-879-5600, fax 202-879-5607.

Ernst & Young, International Business Services, 787 Seventh Ave., New York, NY 10019, ph. 212-773-3000; **In Moscow:** Korovy val 7, office 10, ph. 095-237-1250, fax 095-230-2202.

Price Waterhouse, 1801 K St., NW, Washington, DC 20006, ph. 202-296-0800, fax 202-466-3918.

EXECUTIVE SEARCH SERVICES

Ernst & Young, International Business Services, 787 Seventh Ave., New York, NY 10019, ph. 212-773-3000.

Gilbert & Van Campen, 420 Lexington Ave., New York, NY 10170, ph. 212-661-2122, fax 212-599-0839.

Preng & Associates, 211 Picadilly, London W1V 9LD, ph. 71-548-9860, fax 71-895-1361.

EXHIBITION SERVICES

Arche International F.R.L., via Valassina 24, Milan, Italy, 20159, ph. 2-6680-4640, fax 2-6680-4710.

Comtek International, 43 Danbury Road, Wilton, CT 06897, ph. 203-834-1122, fax 203-762-0773.

Glahe International, 1700 K Street, NW, Suite 403, Washington, DC 20006, ph. 202-659-4557, fax 202-457-0776.

International Trade and Exhibitions, Ltd., Byron House, 112A Shirland Road, London W9 2EQ, ph. 71-286-9720, fax 71-286-0177.

Messe und Ausstellungs Gesellschaft, Heinickestrasse 2, D2000 Hamburg 20, Germany, ph. 40-460-3001, fax 40-460-4276.

Nowea International, PO Box 320203, Stockumer Kirchstrasse 61, D4000, Dusseldorf 30, Germany, ph. 211-456-002, fax 211-456-0740.

East-West Exhibition, 20 Summer St., Stamford, CT 06901, ph. 203-323-8922.

LAW FIRMS

While Western thousands of lawyers are active in Russia, for the sake of brevity, the list below (as with the lists of accountants and executive search firms) lists US addresses of firms that have been consistently involved over the past several years. Most have offices in Russia (see our *Where in Moscow* or *Where in St. Petersburg* for addresses of these offices).

Akin, Gump, Strauss, Hauer & Feld, 1333 New Hampshire Ave., NW, Suite 400, Washington, DC 20036, ph. 202-887-4000, fax 202-887-4288.

Arnold & Porter, 1200 New Hampshire Ave., NW, Washington, DC 20036, ph. 202-872-6929, fax 202-872-6720.

Baker & McKenzie, 2 Embarcadero Center #2400, San Francisco, CA 94111, ph. 415-576-3000, 415-576-3099.

Chadbourne & Parke, 30 Rockefeller Plaza, New York, NY 10112, ph. 212-408-5100, fax 212-541-5406.

Cole, Corette & Arbutyn, 805 15th St., Suite 900, NW, Washington, DC 20005, ph. 202-872-1414, fax 202-296-8238.

Coudert Brothers, 200 Park Avenue, New York, NY 10166, ph. 212-880-4400, fax 212-557-8137.

Davis, Graham and Stubbs, 370 17th Street, Ste. 4700, Denver, CO 80202, ph. 303-892-9400, fax 303-893-1379.

Debevoise & Plimpton, 875 Third Ave., New York, NY 10022, ph. 212-909-6000, fax 212-909-6836.

Hale & Dorr, 60 State Street, Boston, MA 02109, ph. 617-526-6000, fax 617-526-5000.

Heller, Ehrman, White & McAuliffe, 333 Bush St., San Francisco, CA 94104, ph. 415-772-6000, fax 415-772-6268.

Hughes Thorsness, Gantz, Powell and Brundin, 509 West Third Ave., Anchorage, AK 99501, ph. 907-274-7522, fax 907-263-8320.

Latham & Watkins, 520 South Grand Ave., Suite 200, Los Angeles, Ca 90071, ph. 813-891-1200, fax 813-891-7123.

Leboeuf, Lamb, Leiby & Macrae, 125 West 55th St., New York, NY 10019, ph. 212-424-8000, fax 212-424-8500.

Lord, Day & Lord, Barret Smith, 1675 Broadway, New York, NY 10019, ph. 212-969-6453, fax 212-969-6100.

Milbank, Tweed, Hadley & McCloy, One Chase Manhattan Plaza, New York, NY 10005-1413, ph. 212-530-5000, fax 212-530-5219.

Pepper, Hamilton & Scheetz, 1300 19th St. NW, Washington, DC 20036, ph. 202-828-1200, fax 202-828-1665.

Salans, Hertzfeld and Heilbron, 750 Lexington Ave., 14th floor, New York, NY 10022, ph. 212-644-0800.

Steptoe & Johnson, 1330 Connecticut Ave., NW, Washington, DC 20036, ph. 202-429-3000, fax 202-429-9205.

Stroock & Stroock & Lavan, 1150 Seventeeth St., NW, Suite 600, Washington, DC 20036, ph. 202-452-9250, fax 202-293-2293.

Tuttle & Taylor, 1025 Thomas Jefferson St., NW, Washington, DC 20007, ph. 202-342-1300, fax 202-342-5880.

Vinson and Elkins, 1455 Pennsylvania Ave., NW Suite 700, Washington, DC 20004, ph. 202-639-6500, fax 202-639-6604.

Vorys, Sater, Seymour and Pease, Suite 1111, 1828 L Street, NW, Washington, DC 20036, ph. 202-467-8800, fax 202-467-8900.

White & Case, 1155 Avenue of the Americas, New York, NY 10036, ph. 212-819-8200, fax 212-354-8113.

RUSSIAN BUSINESS CARDS

As mentioned several times in this book, it is a real plus, if you are traveling to Russia on business, to have business cards printed in both Russian and English. The following firms have some experience in typesetting and printing such cards.

Exclusively Russian!, 87 Windwhisper Ln., Annapolis, MD 21403, ph. 800-473-9517, fax 410-263-2878

Hermitage, PO Box 410, Tenafly, NJ 07670, ph. 201-894-8247.

Russian Language Specialties, 1801 E. 27th Ave., Anchorage, AK 99508, ph. 907-272-0327, fax 907-274-6999.

Tangent Graphics, 9609 49th Ave., College Park, MD 20740, ph. 301-441-1880.

• If you want to try typesetting cards yourself and all you need are Russian fonts, the best set is the *Cassady & Greene Glasnost Cyrillic Font Library* (five different font families for PC/Windows or Mac), which can be ordered through the *Access Russia* catalogue, ph. 800-639-4301, ask for item number L517 (PC) or L518 (Mac). Price is $156.50 plus $3 s&h.

RUSSIAN LANGUAGE STUDY PROGRAMS

Learning Russian can be the best investment a business person makes in their Russia-based ventures. Listed below are programs for Russian language study offered by or associated with universities, either for study in Russia or the United States.

American Council of Teachers of Russian, 1776 Massachusetts Avenue, NW, Suite 300, Washington, DC 20036, ph. 202-328-2287 (both summer and year-long programs in Russia)

Council for Scholarship in Russia, 1456 Corcoran Ave., NW, Washington, DC 20009, ph. 202-387-0471. (summer program in St. Petersburg)

Department of Russian and Slavic Languagues, 340 Modern Languages, University of Arizona, Tucson, AZ 85721, ph. 602-621-7341. (course in Moscow and St. Petersburg)

Intensive Summer Language Program. Department of Russian, 235 Jessup Hall, Univ. of Iowa, Iowa City, IA 52242. (intensive summer language program at Moscow State University)

Middlebury College, American Collegiate Consortium, 14 Hillcrest Ave., Middlebury, VT 05753. (summer and year-long programs)

Mir Language Programs, 85 South Washington Street, #210, Seattle, WA 98104, ph. 206-624-7289. (summer program in St. Petersburg)

Moscow Internship Program, Boston University, Div. of International Programs, 232 Bay State Road, Boston, MA 02215, ph. 617-353-9888. (summer program with business internships in Moscow and St. Petersburg)

Norwich University, The Russian School, Box 793, Northfield, VT 05663, ph. 802-485-2165. (summer program in Vermont)

People To People International, 501 E. Armour Blvd., Kansas City, MO 64109-2246, ph. 816-531-4701(summer language and business courses)

Perelingua Sprachreisen, Varziner Str. 5, D12159 Berlin, ph. 30-851-8001, fax 30-851-6983. (in Moscow, St. Petersburg and other cities)

Pushkin House, Stouffer Pl. 12-10, Lawrence KS 66044, ph. 913-864-3313. (summer and semester courses at the Russian Academy of Sciences of Russian Literature in St. Petersburg)

Red Bear Tours, 320B Glenferrie Rd., Malvern, Victoria, 3144 Australia, ph. 3-824-7183. (four week intensive courses in Moscow, year-round)

Rostov-on-Don Summer Program, UNC-CH Study Abroad Office, 12 Caldwell Hall, CB 3130, Chapel Hill, NC 27599-3130, ph. 919-962-7001. (summer study program in Rostov-on-Don)

Russian Language Institute, Bryn Mawr College, 101 North Merion Ave., Bryn Mawr, PA 19010-2899, ph. 215-526-5187. (eight week, two semester program in Bryn Mawr)

Russian School, The, Middlebury College, Middlebury, VT 05753, ph. 802-388-3711. (summer programs in Vermont)

Russian Summer Language Institute, Department of Slavic Languages and Literatures, University of Pittsburgh, 1417 CL, Pittsburgh, PA 15260, ph. 412-624-5906. (summer program, through third year, in Pittsburgh)

Summer in St. Petersburg Program, Center for Slavic, Eurasian & East European Studies, Box 90260, Duke University, Durham, NC 27708, ph. 919-684-2765. (summer language study in St. Petersburg)

Summer Intensive Russian Program, Slavic Languages and Literature, University of Washington, DP-32, Seattle, WA 98195, ph. 206-543-6848. (summer program, through 4th year, in Seattle)

Summer Intensive Russian Program, Monterey Institute of International Studies, 425 Van Buren St., Monterey, CA 93940, ph. 408-647-4115. (summer program in Monterey)

Summer Intensive Russian Program, Office of International Education, HAB, SUNY New Paltz, New Paltz, NY 12561, ph. 914-257-3125. (summer program in Moscow and St. Petersburg)

SWEEL, Dept. of Slavic Languages & Literature, Ballantine Hall 502, Bloomington, IN 47405, ph. 812-855-1648. (10 week intensive summer workshop in Russian and other Slavic Languages, in Bloomington)

SALES AGENTS & REPRESENTATIVES

One of the best ways to access the Russian market, if you have something you feel would sell there, but don't know where to start, is to use the services of agents who can represent your product in Russia and the CIS and provide you with office space while you are there. Moscow addresses are given for some of the longer-established firms of this type. The law and accounting firms listed above will also be able to make some suggestions, and can perform important tasks like due diligence on prospective clients.

Argus Trading Ltd., ul. Skakovaya 9, floor 4, ph. 945-2777, fax 945-2765, telex 612171 *(general trading)*

Axel Johnson AB, Kutuzovskiy pr. 13, kv. 131-132, ph. 243-5025, fax 230-6348, telex 413154 *(representation)*

Camco, Krasnopresnenskaya nab. 12, office 1340, ph. 253-1575, fax 253-1340, telex 413523 *(oilfield equipment)*

FMC Corporation, Gruzinskiy per. 3, kv. 201-202, ph. 254-4119, fax 200-2291

Ipatco, ul. Petrovka 15, office 19-20, ph. 924-5893, fax 200-1228, telex 413310 *(representation)*

Overseas Marketing Corporation Limited (OMC), Krasnopresnenskaya nab. 12, office 1405, ph. 253-1701, fax 253-9487, telex 413672 *(trading)*

RCMI, Inc. (Research Consultation Management Intl.), ul. Chekhova 15, ph. 209-9814, fax 209-1398 *(representation, market research)*

Satra Corporation, Tryokhprudny per. 11/13, ph. 299-9169, fax 200-0250, telex 413360 *(aerospace, automotive)*

Scott-European Corporation, Krasnopresnenskaya nab. 12, office 502, ph. 253-1048, fax 253-9382, telex 411813 *(hospital/medical equipment, pharmaceuticals, construction, mining and oilfield equipment)*.

ZigZag Venture Group, Plotnikov per. 12, ph. 241-3593, fax 244-7235, telex 411636 *(consulting, trading)*

2

Preparations & Visas

What to Do Before You Leave

BUSINESS TRIPS

The most important thing to do is to gather information. The previous section of this book details the sources and types of information available. Since the direct costs and opportunity costs of a business trip to Russia are quite great, you should do everything you can to make your trip as worthwhile as possible. You cannot over prepare. To summarize the advised preparation:

• Talk to people who have made the same type of trip – find out what went right and what went wrong, and why. Travel essay books can also provide useful insights. See Chapter 1.

• Study up on the state of development of the area of the economy you are interested in. This is relatively easy to do if you have access to a major university or city library. Review the types and sources of business information surveyed in Chapter 1 to select those of most use to you.

• Also check if your local city chamber of commerce has resources it can provide (for a list of international chambers of commerce, see Chapter 1). State commercial and development offices can also often be of assistance.

There are also some other advised preparatory measures to take:

• Apply early for a visa (see section below, *Visas and Visa Support*).

• Be certain your contacts will be in Moscow when you are there. July to September is vacation time in Moscow. Late December to early January is also slow, as is the first week of May (see the table below on Russian holidays).

• Use government agencies (where applicable and possible – see the previous section), and private Russian companies (see the Yellow Pages in our *Where in Moscow* or *Where in St. Petersburg*), to help arrange meetings with Russians in advance. Western law and consulting firms with offices in Moscow or St. Petersburg can also be of assistance in this regard (see the list in Chapter 1, plus the afore-mentioned Yellow Pages). It is best to arrange at least a few meetings before you leave.

• Similarly, arrange for transport support and translation services before you leave, if either is something you will need. Accommodation must likewise be reserved ahead of time, often long in advance (see Chapter 3, Accommodation and Travel, for information on hotels and other accommodation and travel alternatives. See also the list of Travel Agents in Chapter 1).

• If you plan to work toward a joint venture agreement or contract of some type, prepare a draft agreement (both on paper and on computer disc) before you leave, and have it translated into Russian.

THINGS TO TAKE ALONG

If you have not left already, you should consider including some or all of the following items to make your trip more pleasurable, successful, comfortable, etc.:

• One bottle of Pepto-Bismol and a few rolls of antacids;
• One bottle of aspirin;
• Some disposable syringes in case of emergencies;
• Proof of health insurance coverage, and a claim form if you are staying for a long time;
• Small tube of laundry soap if you are staying in an apartment;
• Spare roll of toilet paper;
• Pocket-pack tissues and wet-wipe type towelettes;
• An umbrella if you are going between March and October;
• Galoshes or shoes you do not mind soiling (city sidewalks are grimy in summer, icy, salty and slushy in winter);
• *Very* warm clothes if traveling October-April (including a hat and overcoat); a warm trench coat for May and September;
• Business cards, preferably with Russian on one side (see Chapter 1);
• Small, business-type gifts, i.e. pocket calculator, pens, pocket flashlight, lighter or other gadgets, preferably with your firm name on them;
• 10 blank business letterheads for typing an unexpected letter to a Ministry or an invitation to visit your home country;
• A personal and/or business checkbook (see Chapter 5);
• A couple of spare one-dollar bills for a luggage cart at the airport;
• Pocket dictionary of Russian-English (or relevant first language);
• Power converter for hair dryer, shaver, etc. **Russia is on 220 volts, 50 Hz**, the plug is a two-pin, European plug;
• Telephone plug adaptor if you plan to bring a laptop with modem and send faxes or Email (available at 1-802-223-4955, ask for item A710);
• Battery-operated alarm clock;
• Universal flat bathtub stopper if you expect to do laundry in your sink (a golf ball also works);
• Extra pair of glasses or contact lenses;
• Two copies of all relevant phone numbers;
• A list of credit cards and their numbers carried in a separate place;
• Photocopy of your passport and visa, kept separately from the originals in case of loss or theft;
• Prescription medication – if you suffer from dry skin, bring some lotion in winter, indoors it will be very warm and dry;
• If you are in the US, call Magellan's (800-962-4943) and get their travel catalogue. It will provide other ideas (money belts, water filters, etc.);
• *Russia Survival Guide; Where in Moscow; Where in St. Petersburg*

Visas and Visa Support

All foreigners must have a visa to enter and exit Russia. Your visa, along with your passport, will be carefully inspected each time you enter and leave the country.

A visa is a sheet of paper which lists information about you, including your name, year of birth, passport number, etc., and indicates the dates during which you may be in Russia, which cities you may visit, the purpose of your visit, and which organization has sponsored your visa. **Four different types of visas exist for non-diplomats: tourist visas, private individual visas, transit visas and business visas.** Each type can be valid for various lengths of time. Existing USSR visas are still honored in Russia (and some of the Commonwealth), if their term has not expired.

TOURIST AND PRIVATE VISAS

A **tourist visa** is arranged through a tourist agency when booking travel to Russia. You will fill out a visa application form like that printed in this chapter, and your travel agent will submit this on your behalf. Many travel agencies now offer not only packaged group tours, but also individualized travel packages (see list of travel agents in Chapter 1). In both cases, the agent should arrange for your visa as part of their services.

A **private individual visa** is based on an invitation issued on your behalf by a Russian citizen, through their local UVIR (visa registration) office. This is a *comparatively long and tortuous process* and not recommended as a first option. Most Russians have contacts with a local business that will agree to sponsor your visa (see below), and it is advised to go that route first.

If, however, you seek a private individual visa, you will need to obtain three applications from the Russian embassy. Attach a passport photo to each completed application and send two of them to your Russian friend. They will take these to UVIR or their local militia for approval and for issuance of official permission (извещение – *izveshcheniye*). Once this has been issued, send the application you retained to the Russian consulate or embassy, along with two more passport photos and a photocopy of the identification pages of your passport.

Both tourist and private visas are typically single-entry visas good for a specified period of time.

Russian National Holidays

January 1-2	New Year's
January 7	Russian Orthodox Christmas
March 8	International Women's Day
May 1-2	Holiday of Spring Labor
May 9	Victory Day (WWII)
June 12	Independence Day
November 7	Anniversary of the October Revolution

TRANSIT VISAS

If you are only planning on passing through Russia on your way to another destination (including to another republic of the former USSR), you can obtain a transit visa relatively easily.

You must submit to the Russian embassy/consulate a visa application form, as printed opposite, a copy of your passport identification page, a xerox copy of the visa for the country which is your destination (if such is required), and a copy of your airline tickets showing your booking to your final destination. A transit visa will allow you to spend 24 hours in the transit city, usually Moscow. See below on *Airport Visas* for extending a transit visa.

BUSINESS VISAS

Persons visiting Russia on business are granted **business visas** by the Ministry of Foreign Affairs. In order to obtain a business visa, you must be sponsored by a Russian organization that can "support" your visa, i.e. demonstrate to the Ministry of Foreign Affairs that it is necessary for you to visit Russia and that it is in a position to be responsible for helping to facilitate your stay in the country. Only ministries, state organizations, joint ventures and/or enterprises which are officially registered in the city soviet (city council) can support visas.

Single-Entry Business Visa

This is the predominant, recommended and simplest type of visa to obtain. And until you have an established reason for a long term business relationship (be it a joint venture or other activity requiring multiple-entries), this is the type of visa you will receive. What follows is a description of the process you and your Russian contacts must go through each time you need a single-entry business visa.

Inform your business contacts or partners that you wish to visit Russia. It is best to give at least one month's notice of your desire to visit, if this is possible. The major difficulty in getting a visa is that the process can be slow the first time. When you and your Russian contacts have agreed on a date for your visit, add a couple of days onto each end of the time period to allow for slow arrival of the visa and possible extensions of your visit.

Send your contacts/partners:

❶ *Your passport data: number, date of birth, date and location of passport issuance and expiry. Your passport must be valid at least three months beyond the date of your planned departure from Russia.*

❷ *The dates of your visit and a list of the cities you will need to visit.*

❸ *The name of the city from which you will be departing immediately before entering Russia. If, for example, you are flying to Moscow via Helsinki, you will list Helsinki as the departure city, even if your travels originated somewhere else. Your departure city is the last stop before landing in Russia.*

After your sponsoring organization has received all the required information from you, it should send you a written invitation via telex, fax or letter, inviting you for a business visit for the time period specified (and specifying

Sample Visa Application Form

КОНСУЛЬСТВО (консульский отдел посольства) СССР в _____

страна

Форма № 95

QUESTIONNAIRE

ATTENTION! Please type, or print using ballpoint pen. Incorrect information may cause denial of visa, denial of permission to cross the USSR border, or annulment of visa on the USSR territory.

В И З О В А Я   А Н К Е Т А

ВНИМАНИЕ! Писать четко, обязательно шариковой ручкой или на машинке. Неправильные данные могут повлечь за собой отказ в визе, в пересечении границы СССР или аннулирование визы на территории СССР.

Place for photograph

1	Nationality	Национальность
2	Present citizenship (if you had USSR citizenship when and why you lost it)	Гражданство (если Вы имели гражданство СССР, то когда и в связи с чем его утратили)
3	Surname (in capital letters)	Фамилия
4	First name, patronymic (names)	Имя, отчество (имена)
5	(if changed, your surname, name (names) and patronymic before the change)	(Если изменяли, то Ваша фамилия, имя и отчество (имена) до изменения)
6	Day, month, year of birth 7. Sex	Дата рождения Пол
8	Object of journey to the USSR	Цель поездки в СССР
9	USSR department, organizations proposed to be visited	В какое учреждение
10	Route of journey (points of destination)	Маршрут следования (в пункты)
11	Date of entry 12. Date of departure	Дата начала действия визы Дата окончания действия визы
13	Passport N° 14. Категория, вид и кратность визы	
15	Index and name of the tourist group Индекс, наименование туристской группы	
16	Place of work or study, position its address, telephone number Место работы или учебы, должность, адрес, номер телефона	
17	Permanent address, telephone number Адрес постоянного местожительства, номер телефона	
18	Place of birth (if born in the USSR, when and where-to emigrated) Место рождения (если Вы родились в СССР, то куда и когда эмигрировали)	
19	Number of previous trips to the USSR Сколько раз были в СССР	Date of the latest trip Дата Вашей последней поездки

	Surname Фамилия	First name, patronymic Имя, отчество (имена)	Date of birth Дата рождения	Permanent address Адрес местожительства
20. Children under 16 years travelling with you Дети до 16 лет, следующие с вами				
21. Relatives in the USSR Ваши родственники в СССР				

I declare that the data given in the Questionnaire are correct
Я заявляю, что все данные, указанные в анкете, являются правильными

1639

Date _____
Дата
Personal signature _____
Личная подпись

the information listed above). *If you are being invited by a private company, be sure to have your contacts also send a copy of their company's registration certificate.*

When you receive your invitation, you must send the following items to the nearest Russian embassy or consulate (see addresses in Chapter 1):

❶ *A completed visa application form;*

❷ *A copy of your invitation and the inviting company's registration certificate;*

❸ *A xerox copy of the identification page(s) of your passport, trimmed to the size of the original and stapled to the upper left hand corner of the application form;*

❹ *Three passport-size photos. One of these should be stapled to the marked box in the upper-right corner of the application form, the other two stapled to the copy of your passport identification page. Photos can be black and white or color, preferably on matte paper. Write your name on the backsides of the photos; A cover letter from you or your company, explaining who is going, where, when and with what purpose;*

❺ *A processing fee of $20 (money order or company check); £10 in the UK;*

❻ *A self-addressed, stamped return envelope. In the US, if you include a prepaid airbill (i.e. for Fedex), your visa will be express mailed back to you. Otherwise it will be sent by certified mail.*

You now wait until this embassy or consulate issues your visa. This may end up being the most time consuming part of the process. The turn-around time of visa applications has become much shorter and more predictable in the last couple of years. Processing typically should take about 10 working days.

You can speed the visa issuing process by enclosing a rush fee, instead of the $20 fee noted above. The cost is $30 (£40) for four day service, $60 (£60) for next day, and $100 for same day service.

It does happen that permission for a visa is denied. This can be because the invitation was issued by a non-registered Russian organization or company (registration must be with the local city soviet, i.e. it must be a legally functioning enterprise or organization). But it can also be because the Russian government has identified a problem of some sort in your record.

While it is rare that an explanation accompanies a specific visa refusal, in the past, illegal currency exchange and/or other types of interaction with the black market during previous visits to Russia were grounds for refusal. Other possible reasons for refusal are previous violation of visa rules, violations of customs regulations and/or criminal behavior. Refusals on political grounds have, to the best of our knowledge, ceased.

If something happens to disrupt your travel plans and you, for some reason need to extend the duration of your visa before you depart, you will need a new invitation from your host organization. Send this and your visa with a $10 fee to the consulate or embassy and your visa will be extended.

Dual-Entry Visa

The breakup of the Soviet Union has led to widespread use of this type of visa. If your itinerary requires you to exit and reenter Russia (i.e. Moscow – Riga-St. Petersburg), you can apply for a dual-entry visa instead of having to get an exit and reentry visa when you are in Moscow (see below for procedures). You simply must specify your itinerary as such in your cover letter and application. See below for information on visa requirements of the other republics of the former USSR.

Multiple-Entry Business Visa

If you foresee traveling frequently to Russia over the next several months, you may wish to seek a multiple-entry (многократная—*mnogokratnaya*) visa. These visas are now issued for a one-year or two-year period and allow the bearer to enter and exit at will, without getting a new visa for each visit.

This visa, however, is a bit more difficult and time consuming to obtain. Your contact in Russia, instead of sending you the invitation letter directly, must apply at the Ministry of Foreign Relations, and the latter must send a telex to the embassy in your home country for that embassy to clear a multiple-entry visa request.

If your passport is lost or stolen in Russia

For a passport: immediately apply for a replacement at your embassy or consulate.

For a visa: you must have a valid passport. If your passport is a replacement of a lost one, you need a new visa; if you only lost your visa, you simply need a new visa. For either operation, you must go to UVIR, in Moscow it is located at ul. Pokrovka 42.

If permission from the Ministry of Foreign Relations is granted, your contact/sponsoring organization should send you a copy of the visa support letter, which you then forward with your application to the Russian embassy (follow the application procedures listed in the section on Single-Entry Visas; note that **the cost for processing a multi-entry visa is $120).**

If you are just beginning to develop a business relationship with people in Russia, you will find it much easier to simply get a single-entry business visa, as described above, for each trip to the country. If you find later that a multiple entry visa is necessary, it is suggested that you seek to have one issued while you are in Moscow for a business trip (see below for procedures). With a bit of pushing and savvy on the part of your Russian partner, this is a much easier task to manage while you are in-country.

Employees of joint ventures and members of their families, as well as persons who are working on contract with state organizations or ministries, will want to obtain (and have an easier time obtaining) multiple entry visas. While more difficult to get at the outset, having one means fewer hassles.

Airport Visas

If you are in a hurry, you can get a visa at Moscow's Sheremetevo airport, upon arrival for $72 (good for 24 hours), $90 (good for 48 hours) or $110 (good for 72 hours). At St. Petersburg's Pulkovo airport the cost is $100 for a 24 hour visa. In both instances, you could obtain such a short term visa and then get this visa extended at the local UVIR office with your contact organization's assistance. The one drawback is that you may be required to book overpriced, low-quality accommodation. The safeguard against this is to make direct reservations with a JV or other hotel (see Chapter 3) and have them fax you confirmation of accommodations, which you can show upon your arrival at the airport. Also check with your airline to make sure they do not have a policy barring passengers from boarding without a valid visa.

Important note: While Moscow and St. Petersburg authorities have announced the availability of Airport Visas, **this means of getting a visa is largely untested and, as such, is at present a highly uncertain means of getting a visa.** If you seek to enter Russia on an Airport Visa, be warned that you may run the risk of being refused entry.

Registration Upon Arrival

You are required to register with UVIR within 72 hours of your arrival in Russia. If you are staying in a hotel, the hotel will hold your passport for 1-2 days and take care of the registration for you. If you are not staying in a hotel, make sure that someone in your sponsoring organization takes your passport to UVIR and registers you. You can also go to the UVIR office yourself, although, of late, UVIR officials have expressed a marked preference for foreign citizens to send their Russian sponsor/contact to handle the registration process for them. In Moscow, UVIR is located at ul. Pokrovka 42, in St. Petersburg it is at ul. Saltykova-Shchedrina 4.

Foreigners are no longer required by law to register with the militia, but it is still a recommended procedure if you are staying in an apartment and are going to be in Russia long-term (more than a few weeks). To do this, simply go to the local militia (the пасспортный контрол – *passportny kontrol* office). The militia officer responsible will examine your passport and note down where you are staying and for how long.

If you are planning a stay longer than a week, and particularly if you plan on traveling outside the capitals, it is advisable to register with your embassy. It usually takes just a few moments (in the case of US citizens) and, at the very least, can often make things go a bit smoother if you lose your passport during your trip.

Avoiding Visa Headaches

There are two things you can do to avoid the headache and worry over a late issue of a visa.

❶ As suggested above, request that your visa be valid from a few days prior to your scheduled departure date.

❷ After receiving your visa support letter from your Russian contacts, send all your materials to a company that specializes in expediting visas. These companies deliver your documents to the correct offices, make follow-up calls to check on the status of your visa, and will express mail it to you the day it is issued. See Chapter 1 under *Travel and Visa Agencies* for a short list of such organizations.

Alternatively, by enclosing an additional fee (see above under *Single Entry Business Visa*), you can receive "rush service" from the Russian embassy itself. In most cases, the piece of mind is worth the extra charge.

Length of Visa

It is unwise to stay in Russia past the expiration date on your visa. It is simple enough to have your partners extend your visa dates (see the following section). If your visa does expire before you leave the country and you have not extended it, you may be required to pay a fine and open yourself to harassment, bribery and potential detainment. Further, the next time you try to get a visa to enter the country, you could face difficulties and long delays. It could also place your sponsoring organization in a difficult position.

CHANGING YOUR VISA STATUS

Once you are in Russia, you may wish to change your visa status. This section focuses on how to extend a visa, how to change a visa sponsor, and how to obtain a multiple entry visa if you already have a single-entry visa. The information (prices in particular) was valid at the time of publication.

Extending a Visa

To extend your current visa, you will need to have the organization that invited you (your current visa sponsor) write a letter asking for your visa to be extended to a particular date. The letter *must include all your current passport and visa information and exactly correspond to the format and wording requested by UVIR* – if you have any questions on this latter score, there are sample letters on the wall at UVIR. UVIR will not process a request accompanied by a non-standard support letter. You (actually much better if you take a Russian friend or have a Russian go for you) then go to UVIR, taking along your passport and current visa. At UVIR, they will give you a form to fill out on the spot which asks for the basic information found on your visa and passport. You then hand this in with your passport, visa and letter. *No payment is necessary for this procedure*. Your visa should be ready to be picked up the next working day. Don't be surprised, however, if you have to go back to UVIR a few times. UVIR officials can be somewhat strict in specifying the exact wording of visa support letters.

Changing a Visa Sponsor

If you are seeking to change your visa sponsor, you use essentially the same procedure as outlined above for extending your visa. The only difference is in the letter. Instead of having a letter from your current visa sponsor, *you must have a letter from your new sponsor* asking that your visa be extended to a particular date. This letter *must include all your current passport and visa information*. You should make sure that your new sponsor is a *registered enterprise* – a joint venture, a Russian enterprise or a individually owned

GENERAL VISA REGISTRATION INFORMATION

UVIR (the Office of Visa Registration for Foreigners), is located at ul. Pokrovka 42 in Moscow, and ul. Saltykova-Shchedrina 4 in St. Petersburg. The office is open on Mondays, Tuesdays and Thursdays from 10-18:00 and on Friday from 10-17:00 with lunch each day from 13-15:00.

You can go to UVIR by yourself, but it is *highly recommended* that you take along your Russian visa sponsor or a Russian friend.

Sberbank: For some operations related to extending your visa or changing your visa status, you will be required to make payment to UVIR's Sberbank (Savings Bank) account. You can make payment at any Sberbank (in Moscow, there is a Sberbank branch directly accross the street from UVIR) to UVIR's account, which is: Kommercheskiy Narodny Bank account number **101-308-02**. To make payment you fill in a *kvitantsiya* (квитанция) or receipt form. This receipt is your proof of payment for services anticipated and will accompany your letter/application for different operations.

business. This means your new sponsor must be registered at Russian Consular Services and have one of the familiar officially registered round stamps. You then go to UVIR with your letter, passport and present visa. At UVIR, they will give you a form to fill out on the spot which asks for the basic information found on your visa and passport. You then hand this in with your passport, visa and letter. *No payment is necessary for this procedure.* Your visa should be ready to be picked up the next working day.

Note that UVIR will just extend your current visa as is, so that your old sponsor will still appear on your visa. This is only a problem if you are trying to get a multiple-entry/exit (многократная—*mnogokratnaya*) visa (see below).

Obtaining a Multiple-Entry Visa

First and most importantly, to get a multiple-entry visa, *the organization/ sponsor on your current visa must be the sponsor for your multiple-entry visa*. It is virtually impossible to get a multi-entry visa if you are switching visa sponsors at the same time.

Have the organization which sponsored your original, single-entry visa, and which will also sponsor your multiple-entry visa write a letter containing all current visa and passport information. In the letter, be sure to *note your local address of residence and include in which region and militia district your address is located. You must also include a general phrase that states "personal and property security is guaranteed."* Have your organization stamp the letter with their registered round stamp.

At this point, you go to any Sberbank (see General Visa Registration Information), and fill out a *kvitantsia* or receipt form. You must *pay a nominal ruble fee to UVIR's account* (check at UVIR first to get the current fee). The teller will give you a receipt.

Take this receipt from the bank teller, along with your passport, current visa, two passport photos, and the stamped letter to UVIR. At UVIR, they will give you a form to fill out on the spot which asks for the basic information found on your visa and passport. You then hand this in with your passport, visa, photos and letter. Technically speaking, your visa should be ready within 3-4 working days.

Again, UVIR will not give you a multiple-entry visa if the sponsoring organization in your letter is different from your original visa sponsor (the one printed on your current visa). In this case, they will only extend your visa, but not change it to a multiple-entry. The only proven way to change sponsors and get a multiple-entry visa is to leave the country and reenter on a new single-entry visa from your new sponsor. You can then change it over to a multiple-entry visa when in Russia.

TRAVELING TO OTHER CITIES IN RUSSIA

It used to be that, by law, foreigners could only travel to those cities which were indicated on their visa. This is ending. Visas are not required for any cities, and foreigners can travel to any city which is not "closed" (for security reasons). There is also no longer a restriction on foreigners forbidding travel outside a 40 kilometer limit from the city which they are visiting. For detailed travel contact information on over 75 Russian cities, see Chapter 4.

VISAS TO STATES OF THE FORMER USSR

Whereas in Soviet times, one visa served all 15 republics of the Soviet Union, now each republic/country is setting its own requirements. Your best bet (except perhaps for travel to the Baltics) is to get a Russian visa while in the West and deal with a visa to the other CIS country, if need be, once in Moscow. Fees will be lower and waits shorter. If you do seek to get a visa directly from the country's embassy in the US, contact them at the number listed in Chapter 1 and get the low-down on what you need to submit.

Here is the latest republic-by-republic wrap-up of what you need for a visa to the republics and how to get it once in Moscow (most consular sections accept visa applications during morning hours, and don't forget to bring a passport size photo with you). Some consular sections require also a xerox-copy of your passport and a Russian visa. Information is based on inquiries made to the separate Moscow and US embassies and is subject to change.

ARMENIA: Citizens of the US and most European countries may still use their Russian visas.

AZERBAIDZHAN: To enter the country, US and European citizens need an Azeri entry visa. The visa can be obtained at the Azeri embassy in Washington or at the airport in Baku if you have a Russian visa. The embassy in Moscow does not issue entry visas, but they may renew an Azeri entry visa. There is a price difference between business and tourist visas. The cost of a visa can be queried via the consular department in Baku (8-8922-93-6034) or from the information department of Azeri Ministry of Foreign Affairs (8-8922-93-2377).

BELARUS: A Russian visa is not valid for travel to Belarus. An invitation is required. You can apply for your visa at the Belarus embassy in the US, in Moscow, or at the airport if you fly direct to Minsk. A single-entry business visa costs $60, a single-entry tourist visa costs $20 and a multiple-entry visa costs $300.

ESTONIA: Effective June 1, 1993, US citizens no longer need a visa to enter Estonia. Just a valid passport is required. You still need visas for travel to the two other Baltic states, however. Citizens of other countries must have an invitation and a 1" x 1.5" photo to obtain an entry visa. A single-entry visa costs $3 and can be obtained at the Estonian embassy in Moscow in seven days.

GEORGIA: You cannot use your Russian visa for travel to Georgia. A Georgian visa can be obtained at the Georgian Embassy in Moscow in 1 day for $30, or at the Tbilisi airport if you fly direct from the US. You should have a valid passport, business cards and 2 1" x 1.5" (3 cm x 4 cm) photos.

KAZAKHSTAN: A Russian visa is not valid for travel to Kazakhstan. A Kazakh visa cannot be obtained at the Kazakh embassy in Moscow. You can obtain an entry visa at Almaty international airport without an invitation. The cost is $150 for a three-day visa. If you need to renew/extend this visa, you must apply to UVIR. To visit the country as a tourist, you may simply purchase a tourist voucher from Russian Intourist ($30 for 7 days, $50 for 14 days, $70 for a month and $200 for a year). There is difference between tourist and business visas. If you are on business trip, you need to have an official pro-forma invitation from your Kazakh partner to get a business visa. A single-entry visa costs $108, a multiple entry costs $200 (for a year).

Embassy Addresses in Moscow
(bolded number is consular department)

Armenia: Armyanskiy per. 2, ph. 924-1269.
Azerbaidzhan: ul. Stanislavskovo 16, ph. 202-4730; **202-7407**
Belarus: ul. Maroseika 17/6, ph. 924-7031; **924-7095**
Estonia: Kalashny per. 8, ph. 290-5013; **290-3178**
Georgia: ul. Nozhovy 6, ph. 290-6902; **241-9633; 241-9645**
Kazakhstan: Chistoprudny bulvar 3a, ph. 208-9852; **208-3775**
Kirgizistan: ul. Bolshaya Ordynka 64, ph. 237-4882; **237-4481**
Latvia: ul. Chaplygina, ph. 925-2707; **921-1422**
Lithuania: Borisoglebskiy per. 10, ph. 291-2643; **291-7586**
Moldova: Kuznetskiy Most 18, ph. 928-5405; **924-5546**
Tadzhikistan: Skatertny per. 19, ph. 290-6102
Turkmenistan: Per. Aksakova 22, ph. 291-6636; **296-6591**
Ukraine: ul. Stanislavskovo 18, ph. 229-6475; 229-3251
Uzbekistan: Pogorelskiy per. 12, ph. 230-0076; **230-1301**

KIRGIZISTAN: A Russian visa is sufficient for entry into Kirgizistan, but to stay, you will need a local visa. Single-entry visas cost: $30 for seven-days and $40 for a month. Multiple-entry visas cost $150 for six-months, $200 for a year and $400 two years. You apply for your visa at the Consular Department of the Kirgiz Foreign Ministry, upon arrival in Bishkek.

LATVIA: You can get a visa within 3-10 days in Moscow by calling the Embassy. They do not distinguish between business and tourist visas and Latvia does not charge a visa fee for many countries with which they have a reciprocal agreement. For citizens of other countries, they charge $10 for a single-entry visa, $30 for a multiple visa, $7 for a dual-entry transit visa and $40 for a multiple-transit visa. Overnight visa-processing is available by paying twice the normal fee for the visa.

LITHUANIA: You can get a visa within two days by applying to the Lithuanian Embassy in the US or Moscow. You may also bet a visa at the Vilnius airport. If your trip is to last longer than three weeks, you will need an official business or tourist invitation. A single-entry visa is valid for three weeks and there is no difference between business and tourist visas. Fees vary for citizens of different European countries, but there is no fee for US citizens. You pay a fee only if you need your visa issued urgently ($10 for 24 hour processing). British citizens are not required to have visas.

MOLDOVA: A Russian visa is not valid for Moldova. You can apply at the Moscow or US embassy for a visa. The Moldovan embassy in Washington reports that you may obtain a visa at the border (if you arrive with an invitation, passport and three photos). Your partner should notify UVIR or the Ministry of Foreign Affairs (if your partner is a company) of your arrival when an invitation is issued. There is a difference between tourist and business visas. A single-entry tourist visa is $25-30, a single-entry business visa is $30, a transit visa is $25. A multiple-entry visa for one year costs $160-180.

TADZHIKISTAN: A Russian visa suffices, although Dushanbe should be listed as a destination city on your visa, which requires an invitation from the Tadzhik Ministry of Foreign Affairs (MFA) or from a state organization. You can also get a visa via the Russian Embassy with such an invitation. After your arrival in Dushanbe you have to register with UVIR or MFA within 3 days.

TURKMENISTAN: A Russian visa is not sufficient. The Turkmen Embassy in Moscow does not issue entry visas. Visas are issued in the US via the Russian embassy. An entry visa can also be obtained at the Ashgabat airport, but better yet, send a fax to Ashgabat Consular Service of the Turkmen Ministry of Foreign Affairs, at (3632) 25-3583 (phone/fax) or (3632) 25-1463; 25-6320 with your passport information beforehand. The cost varies from $10 to $170, depending on the length of stay. A visa support letter from a partner company is desirable, but not obligatory.

UKRAINE: A Ukrainian visa is required. You can apply at the embassy in Moscow or the US, if you have an invitation from your Ukrainian partner. A single-entry visa costs $30, a multiple-entry $120.

UZBEKISTAN: A Russian visa is not valid. To obtain an Uzbek visa, a business person or individual needs to have a letter of support from an Uzbek company (a copy of the letter should be submitted to a consular section of the Uzbek Ministry of Foreign Affairs, which will send Moscow confirmation of permission) or a voucher from Uzbek Intourist (phone in Moscow is 238-5632). You can apply for your visa at the Uzbek Embassy in Moscow (the Uzbek embassy in the US does not have a Consular Department yet), or at the Tashkent airport if you fly direct, but the host Uzbek company needs to apply to the Uzbek Ministry of Foreign Affairs beforehand (as indicated above), so that the consular bureau at the airport is notified. The cost for a visa good for 1 week is $40, for 2 weeks, $50, for a month, $60.

THE RE-ENTRY VISA

If you need to leave Russia for a period of time and then reenter, the organization sponsoring your visa must write a letter which includes all your present passport and visa details. The letter *must cover where you are going, the date you are leaving and the date you are coming back to Russia.* You then go to any Sberbank (see previous section), and fill out a *kvitantsia* or receipt form. There you must *pay a nominal ruble fee to UVIR's account* (check at UVIR first for the current fee) and the teller will then give you a receipt.

You take this receipt, two passport photos, your passport, current visa and the letter to UVIR (see previous section). At UVIR, they will give you a form to fill out on the spot which asks for the basic information found on your visa and passport. You then hand this in with your passport, visa, photos and letter. Usually, they will have your green exit-entry visa ready within three to four working days. You will get back your original visa, so for a time you will have both. When you leave the country, the border passport control officer will take half the new green visa. They will take the other half when you return. While you do not need your current (original) visa, it is best to keep it with you, should any questions arise.

Reportedly there is no need for a reentry visa if you are visiting a former USSR republic that accepts the Russian visa, but it is best in these changing times not to take risks and go through this procedure in any case.

Russians Traveling Abroad

If you decide that it is necessary to meet with your Russian partners or contacts in your home country, they will have to get international passports before they can leave Russia. The new law on emigration and foreign travel no longer requires Russian citizens to have an exit visa (as expected, actual implementation of this law is going slowly – it was originally to have been in force on January 1, 1993). Russians now approach the embassy of their destination country directly, but, for that, they must have an international passport.

Every country has different procedures regulating visitor or business visas. Here we cover only the US requirements.

First you must invite your associates by means of an official "Letter of Invitation" on your company letterhead. This letter must include the following information in your own language (Russian is optional):

- ❶ The full name, address and passport number of the person being invited;
- ❷ The full name of your company;
- ❸ The full address and phone numbers of your company inside the country your guests will visit, plus a short description of the nature of your business (your company address cannot be in Canada if your guests will be going to the United States);
- ❹ An outline of planned meetings or conferences, with as exact an itinerary as possible and an exact statement of the purpose of the trip;
- ❺ Dates of the trip.

The letter must be notarized. This is very important. The easiest way to do this in Moscow is at your embassy or consulate. Go letter in hand (call ahead to find out when you can get such a letter notarized) and have it notarized on the spot.

The US Commercial Office (USCO) has introduced a special service enabling easier processing of entry visas for Russians invited on business to the US by American companies. Your contact must take the invitation letter, his or her passport, two photographs, and a typed, completed visa application (also available from USCO) to the USCO office (Novinskiy bulvar 15, in Moscow) between 4:30 and 5:30 Monday, Wednesday or Friday. For more information, contact the USCO office in Moscow at 252-4848.

Customs Regulations

ARRIVING BY PLANE

You will know you are in Russia when you begin the process of passport control, baggage collection, and customs. The process is slow (but improving), has long lines, and can be arbitrary and chaotic, particularly at Sheremetevo Airport in Moscow.

At passport control, your visa and passport will be scrutinized by young border guards. If your visa is in order and you have not arrived outside the effective dates of your visa, you should have no problems and be through in about 15-30 minutes, depending upon lines.

The arrival of your bags on the conveyer belts can take anywhere from 10 minutes to an hour. While you are waiting for your bags to come, you can track down a customs declaration form if you were not given one on the plane, and fill it in. You may not be able to locate one in your native language. For this reason, and to let you know what to look for, a sample form is printed in this chapter. You will be asked to declare all money, jewelry, videotapes, electronic items, and other objects of value. *Write down everything* of this sort. The obvious implication of this declaration procedure is that, upon leaving,

---

US Dept. of State Travel Advisories, ph. (202) 647-5225
Fax-back service (dial from a fax phone): (202) 647-3000

Sample Customs Declaration

FOR OFFICIAL USE

A. Cleared on entry to (exit from) the Russia

No.	Description of objects	Quantity (in words)

Keep for the duration of your stay in the Russia or abroad. Not renewable in case of loss.

Persons giving false information in the Customs Declaration or to Customs officers shall render themselves liable under laws of the Russia.

broad

CUSTOMS DECLARATION

Full name

Citizenship

Arriving from

Country of destination

Purpose of visit(business, tourism, private, etc.)

My luggage (including hand luggage) submitted for Customs inspection consists of _____ pieces.

With me and in my luggage I have:

e of Bank

I. Weapons of all descriptions and ammunition

II. Narcotics and appliances for the use thereof

III. Antiques and objects of art (painting, drawings, icons, sculptures, etc.)

IV. Russian rubles, Russian State Loan bonds, Russian lottery tickets

V. Currency other than Russian rubles (bank notes, exchequer bills, coins), payment vouchers (cheques, bills, letters of credit, etc.), securities (shares, bonds, etc.) in foreign currencies , precious metals (gold, silver, platinum, metals of platinum group) in any form or condition, crude and processed natural precious stones (diamonds, brilliants, rubies, emeralds, sapphires and pearls), jewerly and other articles made of precious metals and precious stones, andscrap thereof, as well as property papers:

Description	Amount/quantity		For official use
	in figures	in words	

VI. Russian rubles, other currency, payment vouchers, valuables and any objects belonging to other persons

I am aware that, in addition to the objects listed in the Customs Declaration, I must submit for inspection: printed matter, manuscripts, films, sound recordings, postage stamps, graphics, etc. plants, fruits,seeds, live animals and birds, as well as raw foodstuffs of animal origin and slaughtered fowl.

I also declare that my luggage sent separately consists of _____ pieces.

Date   Owner of luggage (signed)

you should not be taking anything out with you that you cannot prove to have brought in with you or purchased in a hard currency shop (save your receipt), nor should you have more currency than you came in with.

If your luggage is lost *en route*, report immediately to the lost luggage office off to the side of the baggage claim area. This is a frequent enough occurrence anywhere in the world, much less Moscow, to suggest that the traveler have in a carry-on what is needed to survive for two days. In fact, recently problems with baggage theft and "pillaging" have been on the rise. Valuables should therefore be in a carry-on, and *a hard sided suitcase that can be locked is recommended* for check-through.

Upon collecting your baggage you proceed to customs. There are now green (nothing to declare) and red (something to declare) channels. The lines for the red channel are always long. If you want to be able to progress through the green channel you should not have more than $50 worth of hard currency (including cash and travelers' checks) with you. There is no limit to the amount of money a foreigner can bring into the country (for Russians there is a $500 limit without bank documentation), and there are no longer any limits on "luxury items" such as cigarettes, perfume or alcohol (although there are limits on taking them out).

In reality, passing through the green channel means you will not be able to take *out* more than $50. If you plan to spend all the cash you have brought with you, pass through the green channel. Be certain, however, that any personal possessions of value (personal computer, diamond rings, Rolex watch) are indicated on the second side of your customs declaration form and duly noted by the customs officer (they will circle the items noted in such a manner that additional items cannot be written in later).

There is a duty free shop before you go through customs at Sheremetevo (Moscow) or Pulkovo (St. Petersburg) and you can buy some luxury items there if you want to bring them in as gifts or for personal consumption.

If you are traveling on a business visa, you are probably less likely to have your baggage searched, particularly if you travel light. Those who look suspicious (unfortunately this is often judged by skin color) or who travel heavy seem to have their bags checked more closely (Russian citizens are also subjected to greater scrutiny than are foreigners). On the way out of Russia, the same general rules apply, but with recent customs crackdowns it is more often that an outgoing passenger's bags are checked, at least cursorily.

The customs officer will verify your customs declaration (if you go through the red channel) and make some marks on it. Your customs declaration will then be given back to you. *Your customs declaration is a very important document. Do not lose it.* Keep your declaration slip with you and/or your passport at all times. You will have to fill in another declaration upon leaving the country.

If you lose your incoming declaration you, theoretically, will not be allowed to take out any of the money or goods on your export declaration, because you will be unable to prove you came in with them. In reality, however, you will probably be treated as if you came in through the green channel – you will not be allowed to take out more than $50 cash. It is probably not likely that your personal valuables will be scrutinized, if they are not somehow "suspicious" (i.e. if you have lots of gold rings). Still, all of this is heavily subject to the mood and demeanor of the customs official you will be dealing with. As in all things of this nature in Russia, it is best to be forthright, apologetic and humble. Avoid any behavior that might suggest you are trying to "get away with something."

You can request that your embassy write a letter to Central Customs, Komsomolskaya ploshchad 1a, Moscow, requesting issuance of a duplicate declaration, but most often replacement declarations are not granted.

It does happen that customs officials ask to see the wallets of travelers in order to verify the amount of money being brought in or out. In other words, lying about this figure is not in your interest. It will only cost you grief and probably bring you little gain.

For departure from Russia, *allow 60-90 minutes for customs before check-in time at your airline.* Thus, it is good practice to arrive at the airport about two hours before your flight time. If you are flying Aeroflot, it is advisable to arrive closer to three hours in advance of the flight time.

ARRIVING BY TRAIN

If you come into Russia from Helsinki or elsewhere by train, you will want to be very mindful of the customs regulations just mentioned and those discussed below. Whether arriving in or departing from Russia by train, it is logical and true that the customs officers will have more time and opportunity for customs inspection. Expect more customs difficulties when traveling by train. Expect to have your papers and belongings subjected to much closer scrutiny.

CUSTOMS RESTRICTIONS AND LIMITATIONS

Recent legal acts have drastically limited the number of items subject to import duties. Still, there are certain items subject to different types of restrictions and limitations. These are summarized below.

Art, icons and precious metals: Objects of art, gold, precious stones, icons, and the like are all being monitored tightly at exit customs control. Be sure that anything like this which you buy can be taken out of Russia duty free.

Anything which may be deemed of historical or cultural value is forbidden from export. Items of historical or cultural value are (for example): sculpture, graphics and paintings by outstanding artists of any period or country, icons and other religious items, Russian and foreign manuscripts, books dating before 1977, porcelain and crystal, rugs and tapestries, coins and jewelry, restored furniture. If you are in doubt about a specific purchase, Russian customs authorities can be consulted at Komsomolskaya ploshchad 1a, ph. 975-4460.

Objects of art can be exported if you go through the proper procedures. This requires registration of the object with the Ministry of Culture to obtain a *spravka* (справка), which can take up to a month (as any item must be examined by an expert committee responsible for that sort of item). If the Ministry of Culture determines that the object may be exported, a letter is prepared for customs with the tax to be charged (100 percent of the value of the item). To have the object evaluated and obtain a *spravka* (or to get more information), take the object to the Ministry of Culture at ul. M. Dmitrovka 29 (open Tuesdays 10-14) in Moscow (on Thursdays, go to ul. Neglinnaya 8 between 11-14), ph. 921-3258. The Ministry of Culture requires three photographs of the object. Get them done ahead of time.

Do not worry about declaring souvenirs (but be sure they are souvenirs and not valuable works of art) you have picked up on the Arbat, Izmailovo Park or other open-air markets. But do not try taking out a suitcase-full of Palekh lacquered boxes. Items purchased for hard currency can be taken out without limit, so long as you retain the receipt (see *Gifts* below).

Caviar and Consumer goods: Russian customs regulations state that the export of sturgeon and salmon caviar by foreign citizens is permitted without limitation on condition of presentation of a receipt that the caviar was purchased for hard currency "according to established procedures." Caviar obtained through other channels (i.e. for rubles) is not permitted for export.

Regulations also limit the export of other consumer items. The value of consumer goods (and presumably gifts, but this is not so strictly enforced) purchased for rubles which may be taken out of the country may not exceed 300,000 rubles. In effect, this makes export of foodstuffs, medicines, etc. completely forbidden (unless purchased for hard currency).

No more than 1.5 liters of vodka, 100 cigarettes and 2 liters of wine may be taken out (this can be overridden by considerations of what you may have brought in and stated on your declaration, or by goods you can prove to have purchased at hard currency stores).

Computers and electronics: There is some confusion as to whether personal computers and other consumer electronics can be brought in duty free. As with many things, the law is inconsistently applied. There is a law which requires you to pay a deposit upon entry with such items, and the deposit is refunded if you leave with the items.

In reality, this deposit requirement is not being applied. You should resist its application in the case of a personal laptop computer or shortwave radio, etc. (see Personal Use Doctrine below) If, however, you are bringing in consumer electronics to sell (which is legal) you should be prepared to pay the duty. If you can prove you are bringing in electronics as gifts, you will have a $2,000 duty-free allowance.

Even though Russia is now a member of CoCom, there are still come CoCom restrictions on exporting computers into Russia from member countries. For the most part, any off-the-shelf type computer may be exported under General License. Only larger, mainframe-type or super-mini type computers require special licensing procedures.

By way of guidelines, you may export Pentium (and slower processor) machines with up to 32 megabytes of RAM, with a processing speed of up to

66 mhz. An internal hard disk of up to 2 gigabytes is allowed (with up to 5 additional hard disks and a total storage space of 10.3 gigabytes) and LAN support but no wide area networking is allowed. Finally, the system cannot exceed a data signalling rate of 20 mn bits and cannot have an internetwork gateway. If any of these limits are exceeded, a Validated License is necessary.

You may wish to contact your Department of Commerce or Foreign Trade (or relevant chamber of commerce – see Chapter 1) for the most up-to-date information. In the United States call the Office of Technology and Policy Analysis at (202) 377-0899.

Private individuals cannot bring into the country radio-telephones and certain other high-frequency devices.

Currency and monetary instruments: Import and export of rubles is no longer forbidden. Yet, you cannot take more hard currency or rubles out of Russia than you brought in (and you may only bring in R500,000). Technically you are required to write down on your customs declarations (in and out) all travelers' checks and any monetary instruments made payable to you, but many people do not.

Gifts: The law states that foreign citizens can bring in up to $2,000 worth of goods in gifts without duty. Expect this law, as with many Russian laws, to be applied erratically and arbitrarily.

Meanwhile, the law also says you may only export 300,000 rubles ($200 at the time of publication) worth of goods along with your personal property that was reported upon entry. Gifts in excess of this amount are to be dutied at 600%. Again, expect this law to be applied erratically. The safest course is to buy high-value souvenirs for hard currency and get a receipt.

Narcotics and firearms: Narcotics and firearms may not be imported into or exported from Russia.

Prescription Drugs: Many Western over-the-counter drugs theoretically require permission from the Ministry of Health to be brought into the country, but allowance for personal use is given.

Printed and recorded material: Pornography and defamatory material may not be brought into (or out of) Russia. Russian standards of pornographic material are still much stricter than in the West. Sexually explicit photographs constitute pornography.

Written material must, theoretically, be declared, but do not sweat this one. In theory "sensitive" items can be confiscated and have been in the past. Just use common sense. Don't bring in original manuscripts or documents without leaving a copy at home. If you are carrying into or out of the country internal (Russian) government documents which might be deemed of a sensitive nature, you should have a letter from the appropriate ministry or department which gave you the documents, vouchsafing the fact that you have proper authority to be carrying these papers on your person.

Video tapes are the focus of current crackdowns. Current regulations allow five cassettes for personal use. Leave these sealed if you can for entry, so there will be no chance they will be seen as recorded material. Customs regulations forbid import into Russia of recorded video cassettes (meaning commercial movies, not personal recordings).

Trade samples: You can take trade samples both into and out of Russia without much problem, provided you have the proper documentation and provided the samples do not infringe any of the restrictions mentioned above. To exit with trade samples, have the company which has given you the samples prepare a letter in Russian, with the appropriate stamps, attesting to the fact that these are   samples and should not be subject to export restrictions. If you feel the need, you can prepare a similar letter for samples which you are importing.

A final consideration: A guiding principle for what you should or can bring in with you without any difficulty or duty could be called the **Personal Use Doctrine**. If you can reasonably claim that the items you are bringing in with you are for your personal use, whether they be cosmetics, film, a laptop computer, or books, then you should have no problem. If you are bringing in 10 pairs of new jeans or 40 blank video cassettes (keep blank video cassettes wrapped when entering), it will be very difficult to claim these are for personal use (unless perhaps you are staying for an extended period).

Confiscation: In the event you have something confiscated upon entry, you will normally be issued a receipt for the item. This receipt, or *kvitantsiya* allows you to reclaim the item on your way out (in theory). Undeclared currency or undeclared valuable property may be subject to permanent confiscation. If the items confiscated are considered "contraband", a protocol detailing the reasons for the seizure will also be made out. Contraband and items confiscated upon exit will not likely be returned to you.

3

Travel & Accommodations

Getting to Russia

There are any number of options and travel combinations for getting to Russia. And new ways are constantly opening up. The most common path of entry, of course, is by air.

There are direct flights to Moscow and St. Petersburg from the US, Canada, and most European countries. In the US, only Delta and Aeroflot have direct flights into Russia. In Europe, national airlines, i.e. British Airways, Lufthansa, SAS, Finnair, have direct scheduled flights, as does Aeroflot. As well, these European carriers (and others) have connecting flights out of New York, Washington, D.C., Miami (Finnair and Air France), Chicago, and other major US and Canadian cities. Alaska Airlines now also has direct flights from Seattle and Anchorage to Magadan, Vladivostok and Khabarovsk in the Russian Far East.

The obvious advice, of course, is to seek the learned input of your travel agent or one of those listed in Chapter 1 of this book. They should know how to get you the best fares. And unless you are traveling at the last moment, there is no reason you should pay full fare to get to Russia. There are so many empty seats on flights to Russia now that it is rightly a buyer's market.

One alternative, whether you are going for business or pleasure, is to travel with a group. Often the package group fares (airfare, accommodations and food included), can be less than a standard airfare. Certainly if you factor in hotel room costs that you would pay traveling alone, this can be a good way to travel. Of course, you will want to be very careful about the hotel(s) the group is staying in (make sure it is centrally located), and will want to gain the assent of the group leader for your departure from the planned itinerary – something totally acceptable now, but unthinkable in Soviet times. Again, see the list of travel agents in Chapter 1.

If you are traveling from North America, compare the option of a European stopover to that of a direct flight. European airlines have run special deals that include a free overnight in Frankfurt, Prague or London. Likewise, taking Finnair to Helsinki and riding the train to St. Petersburg (six hours) or Moscow (13 hours) can be both cost-effective and enjoyable. The train from Berlin is a bit longer ride. There are also ways to take ferries and boats into St. Petersburg from Helsinki and Stockholm, depending on the time of year.

You can now purchase a Eurail-type railpass for Russia, called the Russian Flexipass. This railpass allows unlimited travel along selected routes in Russia for four days within a 15-day period, for about what you might pay for a single round trip train ride from Helsinki to Moscow. For more information, call the US agent at (914) 682-2999.

Accommodations

The situation with travel accommodations in Russia is improving. First, the growth of private enterprise has led to a flourishing of private tour agencies and bed and breakfast operations. Second, the activity of joint ventures and Western investment has led to renovation of a handful of landmark Moscow and St. Petersburg hotels. While space is often still hard to come by, if you know where and how to look, you will find that, as opposed to even a year or two ago, accommodation choices have become better and more numerous.

If you or your host have not already arranged for accommodation, it is suggested you begin settling this issue well in advance of any travel to Russia. And even if you have traveled to Russia frequently, you will want to survey some of the newer alternatives now open to you. Whereas in years past all bookings for independent travel had to go through Intourist, now booking a room can be as easy as sending a fax or telex to a hotel, or contacting a Western representative of a Russian hotel or bed and breakfast service. Of course, you can still arrange for a room through a local travel agent or Intourist (see Chapter 1 for addresses).

At present there are basically two accommodation choices for the individual traveler: hotels, of which there are joint venture hotels and Russian state-owned hotels, and accommodation in private homes.

HOTELS

Joint venture hotels are former state-owned hotels that have been renovated and/or are being managed by a Western-Russian joint venture. The level of service tends to be very high, as do the prices. Wholly Russian-owned hotels, if only because they have not had the benefit of outside investment, usually offer a much lower quality of service. Over time, prices for an overnight in such hotels have been declining, which means you can, increasingly, stay in a passable hotel for a reasonable price.

Despite the inroads being made by large Western hotel chains, such as Radisson, Novotel and Intercontinental, there remains a certain characteristic Russian (some would say Soviet) quality to major hotels in Moscow and St. Petersburg. This said, it is noteworthy that service personnel in some of the new joint venture hotels are better paid and thus more motivated, and are more responsive to the usual expectations of the Western traveler. This is gradually leading to a "warming" of the atmosphere at such landmark hotels, and away from the unaccommodating service and poor facilities characteristic of hotels in the Soviet period.

In wholly Russian-owned hotels (many of which are still state-owned), Soviet habits unfortunately still cling to deep roots. The staff remains underpaid and under-motivated and thus generally unhelpful. The front desk is more often a place of dread and red tape rather than for problem-solving and services. Room service is difficult to come by and staff can be intrusive (expect maids to come into your room without knocking). Support and business services, as well as hotel sundries stores are on the rise, but generally still not adequate. Finally, of late some of the seedier former state-owned hotels have become havens for both local and out-of-town black marketeers and less-desirable elements.

In the warped ruble/dollar economy which now exists in Russia, you can expect that hotels where foreigners stay will continue to attract people hawking souvenirs and trinkets. These merchants used to be known as "black marketeers" but can now operate freely and openly (assuming they have paid off the right people). While it is no longer "illegal" to deal with these merchants, it still pays to be very cautious and wary. Shams, scams and cons are on the rise. Gypsy beggars, secret rendezvous' and cab rides without known destination are to be avoided at all costs (see *Crime* in Chapter 5). The fact is that there is little available through this sort of trading that cannot now be obtained through commercial shops or at places like Izmailovo Park and the Arbat in Moscow or Klenovy (Maple) alley in St. Petersburg.

Most major tourist hotels, especially the non-joint venture hotels, still retain some variation of the hall lady (дежурная—dezhurnaya) system, whereby a woman monitors your hotel floor around the clock. In the European fashion, you exchange your key for your hotel entrance pass (пропуск—propusk) with her (or with someone at a more centralized location) when you are leaving the hotel, and do the reverse when you return. She is the first person to turn to when you need a shirt ironed, when you want bottled water, a taxi, room service, when something does not work in your room, etc. A tasteful gift to one of these ladies upon arrival may help to make most any ensuing accommodation problems melt away.

Along with the generally better level of business and support services which the newly refurbished joint venture hotels offer, quite often they also offer an easier access to money changing (with more plentiful supplies of rubles). The day when all major tourist hotels had exchange points is past and these newer hotels often maintain exchange point services exclusively for their clientele.

The table on the following pages summarizes the relative quality, size and prices of major Moscow and St. Petersburg hotels. Booking numbers or fax numbers for these hotels are also given. Some of these numbers are in the West (especially in the case of chains) some (those preceded by the country code 7) are the hotel's number in Moscow or St. Petersburg. For addresses and locations, see our *Where in Moscow* or *Where in St. Petersburg*. If you don't find a hotel listed in the table, it is because foreigners very rarely stay there, because the hotel opened after this edition of *Russia Survival Guide* was printed, or because the hotel does not register on the rating scale. *If you book a room independently, always get a confirmation or reservation number.*

	Class	No. Rooms	Cost Single	Cost Double	For reservations (* = fax)
Moscow Hotels					
Aerostar	★★★★	200	$265	$314	1-800-843-3311
					7-502-222-1104*
Arbat (Oktyabrskaya II)	★★	107	$120	$150	7-095-244-0093
Baltschug-Kempinskiy	★★★★★	234	$300	$330	1-800-426-3135
					7-501-230-9503*
Belgrade	★	450	$80	$90	7-095-230-2129*
Danilovskiy	★★	100	$180	$220	7-095-954-0750*
Inflotel (Aleksandr Blok)	★★	71	$140	$170	7-095-253-9578*
Intourist	★★	437	$110	$130	7-095-956-8450*
Kosmos	★★	1767	—	$120	7-095-215-8880*
Leningradskaya	★	516	$50	$82	7-095-975-3032
Marco Polo Presnya	★★★★	68	$228	$240	43-1-715-553-0430
					7-095-230-2704*
Metropol	★★★★★	377	$330	$370	1-800-462-6686
					7-501-927-6010*
Mezhdunarodnaya I	★★★	250	$219	$264	7-095-253-2051*
Mezhdunarodaya II	★★★	250	$219	$229	7-095-253-2378
Minsk	★	240	$50	$60	7-095-299-1213
Moskva	★★	700	$60	$80	7-095-292-2008

NOTE:

The information in this table was gathered just prior to publication. Room rates include VAT and are subject to change without notice. Always inquire if prices already include the VAT (23%) or not. The ratings for hotels are based on a polling of travel agents and business people who travel frequently to Russia and use the following parameters:

★★★★★   **Highest class hotel.** The finest restaurants in the city; unsurpassed support services; modern amenities.

★★★★   **High class hotel.** Would be a first-class hotel in any world capital. Fine restaurants, customer service and business services.

★★★   **Very good to excellent hotel.** Good restaurants. Good to excellent customer service and business services. Comfortable, but either a bit inconveniently located or a bit "soviet" in its style of service.

★★   **Average to good hotel.** Restaurants OK but not consistent. Customer service standards low; few or no business services.

★   **Passable hotel.** Restaurants not suggested. Customer service is poor to non-existent. No business services.

	Class	No. Rooms	Cost Single	Cost Double	For reservations (* = fax)
Novotel	★★★★	488	$191	$216	1-800-221-4542
					7-502-220-6604*
Olympic Penta	★★★★★	498	$360	$448	1-800-225-3456
					7-502-224-1119*
Palace Hotel	★★★★★	221	$275	$335	43-1-715-553-0430
					7-503-956-3151*
Pekin	★★	80	$82	$113	7-095-209-2442
President	★★★	220	$200	$240	7-501-239-2318*
Pullman-Iris	★★★★	211	$220	$250	1-800-221-4542
					7-502-220-8888*
Rossia	★	3091	$40	$60	7-095-298-5541*
Savoy	★★★★	86	$265	$380	7-095-230-2186*
Slavyanskaya-Radisson	★★★★	431	$275	$300	1-800-333-3333
					7-502-224-1225
Ukraine	★	1622	$75	$100	7-095-956-2078*
Zolotoe Koltso	★	450	$53	$73	7-095-248-7395*

St. Petersburg Hotels

	Class	No. Rooms	Cost Single	Cost Double	For reservations (* = fax)
Astoria	★★★★	220	$170	$220	7-812-315-9668*
Commodore	★★★	344	$110	$120	468-666-3406*
Grand Hotel Europe	★★★★★	301	$295	$345	1-800-843-3311
					7-812-329-6001*
Helen (in Sovietskaya)	★★	120	$94	$135	7-812-113-0860*
Sankt Peterburg	★★	720	$75	$95	7-812-248-8002*
Moskva	★★	777	$67	$82	7-812-273-2130*
Nevskiy Palace	★★★★★	301	$265	$315	43-1-715-553-0430
					7-812-275-2001*
Okhtinskaya	★★	300	$70	$80	7-812-227-2618*
Olympia	★★★★	146	$150	$175	1-800-843-3311
					7-812-119-6805*
Peterhof	★★★	109	$55	$140	41-55-272-755
					7-812-850-1406*
Pribaltiyskaya	★★	1200	—	$80	7-812-356-0094*
Pulkovskaya	★★★	1600	$120	$140	7-812-264-6396*

ACCOMMODATION IN APARTMENTS

Accommodation in private homes (apartments) has the advantage over hotels in being somewhat more flexible and inexpensive. The educational aspect also should not be overlooked. This option runs the gamut from bed and breakfast arrangements to staying with friends and acquaintances, which up until a few years ago was not legal.

When staying with friends, you will be responsible for dealing with visa registration yourself; read up on this in Chapter 2 under *Visa Support*.

The new bed and breakfast alternative offers an entirely different experience from accommodation in hotels, and can be particularly desirable for longer stays. A number of Western companies have solid Russian counterparts they work with to arrange this type of accommodation. As well, Moscow or St. Petersburg-based travel companies or apartment leasing companies (see the Yellow Pages in our *Where in Moscow* or *Where in St. Petersburg*) can offer such services. The terms, prices and procedures of each varies. Generally, it is recommended to work through a Western partner of a bed and breakfast venture. Often they can also arrange for your visa support, thus taking care of two problems at once (in fact it only makes sense to work through a company that can handle visa support as well). To that end, some such companies are listed below. Where possible, available cities and pricing information have also been included.

American International Homestays, Route 1, Box 68, Iowa City, IA 52240, ph. 319-626-2125, fax 319-626-2129. [Moscow, St. Petersburg, Irkutsk and major capitals].

Cultural Access Network, Box 4410, Laguna Beach, CA 92652, ph. 714-497-6773, fax 714-497-6809. [Moscow, St. Petersburg, ph. $75 per night].

East-West Ventures, Inc., P.O. Box 14391, Tucson, AZ 85732, ph. 800-833-4398. [Moscow, St. Petersburg, Kiev, Sochi, ph. $42-64 per night; also offer visa support, driver and translator services]

I.B.V. Bed and Breakfast Systems, 13113 Ideal Drive, Silver Spring, MD 20906, ph. 301-942-3770, fax 301-933-0024.

International Bed and Breakfast, P.O. Box 823, Huntington Valley, PA 19006, ph. 800-422-5283, fax 215-663-8580.

New Solutions, 912-S. Juanita Ave., Redondo Beach, CA 90277, ph. 800-768-9535, fax 310-543-9839

Pioneer East/West Initiatives, 88 Brooks Ave., Arlington, MA 02174, ph. 617-648-2020, fax 617-648-7304.

Progressive Tours, 12 Porchester Pl., Marble Arch, London W2 2B5, England, ph. 71-262-1676.

Red Bear Tours, 320B Glenferrie Road, Melbourne, Victoria 3144, Australia, ph. 3-824-7183, fax 3-822-3956, telex AA38615 Kewtel [Moscow and St. Petersburg, $25 a night with meals; also visa support, translators].

The Two Capitals

One of the first problems to be faced when arriving in Moscow or St. Petersburg (or any Russian city) is arrangement of transport. If this is not something a host organization is looking after, then you should bone up on the range of options open to you. But first, you should get the lay of the land.

GETTING ORIENTED IN MOSCOW

It always helps to get an understanding of the geography of a city before trying to get around it. It also makes the place seem a bit less foreign.

Moscow is a city founded on a river. Actually, it is founded on three rivers, but two have been put largely underground. The Moscow (Москва) river is the most important geographical feature in the city, but it can also provide the greatest source of confusion in navigation. This is because it does not flow in a straight line through the city, but snakes its way north and south, forming something of a tongue and groove feature in the city center (where the Kremlin lies in the center of the tongue).

Your best bet is not to use the river as a source of orientation, except in the city center. You are better off orienting to the fact that the major city roadways are a series of concentric rings with major arteries intersecting them and stretching outward. The two major rings are the Boulevard Ring and the Garden Ring. Navigating with respect to these two rings (and sometimes the outer Ring Road) and a major cross road will help you remember which end is up. It is helpful to remember that the metro system is similarly organized around a main ring line. For a detailed, current map of Moscow, see *The New Moscow City Map and Guide*, which is also printed in page format in our *Where in Moscow* (see the ordering information in the back of the book).

Sightseeing

Should your trip allow sightseeing time, your best bet is to have a native (either one of your hosts or even a taxi driver) give you a drive through the center of Moscow. There are more than enough attractions to see in and around Red Square and the Kremlin. For further points of interest, check your more conventional tourist guide books (see the notes on *Books* in Chapter 1) or ask the service bureau at your hotel for some help (be prepared in the latter case to pay hard currency).

A further interesting way of sightseeing can be via trams. More frequently than buses they allow you to sit down and see out (except in winter when the windows are usually fogged up). Their routes can take you through some of the more interesting, older neighborhoods of Moscow (as this was the first form of public transport in Moscow), and they offer you the advantage of being able to get off at virtually any stop, cross the tracks and take the same numbered tram back to where you started.

Boat rides on the Moscow river in summer are also a relaxing way to see the city and the outlying areas. Boats stop at many landings along the river and run fairly frequently during daytime hours. For a good half-day trip, start at the Kievskiy Train Station stop and ride around the peninsula to get off at Gorkiy Park and go for a stroll there.

The view from Sparrow Hills (formerly Lenin Hills) on a clear day is also not to be missed. For a quiet afternoon in a park atmosphere, try a stroll around Novodevichy or Danilovskiy monastery, Kolomenskoye, Sokolniki, the Botanical Gardens, Tsaritsyno or Izmailovo Park.

If you are interested in hitting the pavement and stopping in shops, we recommend Pyatnitskaya, Tverskaya and Petrovka Streets, and the Arbat, for their high shop-density and uniqueness. The old section of town known as Kitay Gorod (Chinese City), where foreigners lived under the Czars, was a major commercial center and may pose some interest for that reason. Likewise, the section near and around Novokuznetskiy metro station has much charm.

The Pushkin and Tretyakov Museums are considered to be the best the city has to offer. But there are also many specialized museums and newer, private galleries. See our *Where in Moscow* for the most current listings.

For serious shopping for souvenirs, there are two popular places to go: the Arbat and the Vernisage at Izmailova (weekends only, go to Izmailovo Park metro station). Over time, the wares for sale have gotten progressively "*kitschier,*" but there are still always deals to be had.

If you are looking for a day trip outside the city, there are a number of places in close driving range to visit. Most notable are Sergeyev Posad (formerly Zagorsk), Arkhangelskoye, Abramtsevo, and Gorkiy Leninskiye. A bit farther off are Klin and Borodino.

GETTING ORIENTED IN ST. PETERSBURG

St. Petersburg, for over 200 years Russia's capital, is a city founded on a river delta with the specific purpose of being a maritime city. The river Neva is therefore the most important geographic feature of this "Venice of the North."

The plethora of bridges and canals between the city's 44 islands in the Neva's delta are enough to create significant confusion for the first time visitor.

Your best bet is to focus on the "half-circle" of the city center which is bordered by the river Fontanki on its round edges and the river Neva along its "straight" edge. This half-circle can then be seen as divided into wedges by the three major avenues, Nevskiy Prospekt, ul. Dzerzhinskovo, and Prospekt Mayorovo. Nevskiy Prospekt is the most important area of commercial activity in the city.

There are then two major islands which form the other half of the circle, on the other side of the Neva. These are Vasilevskiy island, where the University is located, and Petrogradskiy island, to which Peter-Paul Fortress is attached. Both are mainly residential, and most industrial activity is in the southern regions of the city near the airport, or on the "Vyborg side," also across the river from the main commercial center.

Two key points for orientation in St. Petersburg are the spires of Peter-Paul Fortress and the Admiralty, which can both be seen from most places near the center. The Admiralty spire, golden with a silhouette of a sailing ship at its peak, is the true center of the city and is the apex of the three main avenues in the "half-circle." The taller spire of Peter-Paul Fortress is topped with a cross.

The metro is not as central a part of public transport in St. Petersburg as is the case in Moscow, particularly in navigating the city center. Many points are easily accessible by trolley buses. If you have a lot of ground to cover, rent a car or stick to cabs. For maps and the most up-to-date directory information on St. Petersburg, pick up a copy of our *Where in St. Petersburg*, which includes, in page format, the most current and useful city street map of St. Petersburg, *The New St. Petersburg City Map and Guide* (see the ordering information in the back of the book).

Sightseeing

St. Petersburg is more compact than Moscow and easier to navigate on foot. Aside from that, you cannot get the flavor of the canals or the beautifully decorated facades from driving around in cars or trams, so sightseeing on foot is a necessity.

Be sure to see St. Isaac's Cathedral, Peter-Paul Fortress and Palace Square (дворцовая площадь—*dvortsovaya ploshchad*). If you have a spare day in the city, spend it at the Hermitage and/or the Russian Museum, with a side trip to the restored Menshikov Palace across the river from the Winter Palace. But these are just some highlights; St. Petersburg is filled with points of artistic, architectural and historical interest, all of which are detailed in conventional tourist guides (see the notes on *Books* in Chapter 1).

Boat rides on the canals (except in winter) are an inexpensive and interesting way to see the city. Boats depart every 15 minutes from Anichkov bridge (where Nevskiy Prospekt meets Fontanka embankment) or opposite the entrance to the Hermitage.

If you are interested in shopping, a walk up and down Nevskiy Prospekt is the recommended itinerary. Start at Palace Square and walk up one side at least to Gostiny Dvor, then cross and walk back. You'll get your fill. Klenovy (Maple) alley is the newest venue for street souvenir sales.

For a quiet afternoon in a park, try Kirov Park on Yelagin island. It has walking paths, boating, a bathing beach as well as an exhibition hall and theaters. Boating is also possible at Park Pobedy (Victory Park). Lenin Park and the Botanical Gardens, on opposite sides of Petrogradskiy ostrov (island), are also nice.

If you want to get outside the city, visit the former Imperial palaces in Petrodvorets, Pushkin or Pavlovsk, all in close range. Boats and trains service these palaces, or you can rent a car and drive.

PUBLIC TRANSPORT

In general, given the loads it must carry, public transport in both Moscow and St. Petersburg is good. And because it is ridiculously inexpensive, it is crowded and not always your best bet for getting places in a hurry. As well, bus and tram routes are not easily understandable to the non-Russian speaker or non-resident. The metro, however, can be a good way to get around on your own if you can read some Cyrillic (or simply count stops).

The metro system dates from the 1930s in Moscow and from the 1950s in St. Petersburg. Trains run, during daytime hours, about every 2-3 minutes (usually more frequently). The metro is to be avoided at all costs during rush hours, between 7-10 a.m. and 4-7 p.m., unless you have a deep yearning to "get close" to Russia.

One pays for the metro ride by depositing a metro token (which you can buy at a change window, sometimes a few at a time when supplies are short) in automated entry gates inside metro stations. Buses and trams require you to purchase *talony* (талоны) or tickets at metro stations, kiosks, or on the buses and trams themselves, and to validate them by stamping them in punches hanging on the inside of the cabin. Prices for public transport have risen incredibly (over 500%) in the past year, and this trend will continue (at press time, the metro cost 50R and trams 40R). Still, in real dollar terms, the fare will likely stay under 25 cents per ride for the foreseeable future.

You can also buy a **monthly pass** good for unlimited travel on all public transport (again prices are constantly changing, but are usually pegged at around 100 times the price of a single ride). If you plan on riding public transport often, have your Russian contact buy this *yediny bilet* (единый билет) for you before your arrival as they are only on sale at selected metro stations beginning the middle of a month for the coming month. They can save a lot of hassle waiting in line to buy tokens.

Metro, Buses and Trolleybuses operate from 6 a.m. to 1 a.m.; Trams 05:30 to 01:30. Metro transfer stations (переходы – *perekhodi*) close at 00:30. Note that these are "official" hours. Given fuel shortages and ever-rising operating costs, expect that many less-busy stations and routes will close down somewhat earlier (and run less often).

TAXIS

If you need to get somewhere fairly quickly, and want to do it above ground and without being crushed by fellow travelers, this is the way to go.

Taxis in Moscow and St. Petersburg are notoriously dirty and dangerous. Courtesy is not a watchword in the Russian hack's lexicon. While there are certainly excellent, good, and poor taxi drivers everywhere, your average Russian taxi driver is ruder to others on the road, more lead-footed, and less concerned with your personal comfort and safety than his counterpart in, say London, Rome, or New York. Every stop light is a drag strip opportunity, and every pedestrian is an open target (making *babushkas* run seems a favorite pastime of most all Russian drivers, who have very different notions of pedestrian right-of-way than you might be accustomed to).

INTERNATIONAL DOCUMENTS
AND PARCELS DOOR TO DOOR
Fastest, most reliable service from and within the C.I.S.

Please call us at:
(095) 956-1000 (Moscow)
(812) 311-2649, 119-6100 (St. Petersburg)

DHL offices in Russia:
Moscow • St. Petersburg • Nizhny Novgorod • Togliatti • Novosibirsk
Khabarovsk • Vladivostok • Nakhodka • Yuzhno-Sakhalinsk

CLUB ROYALE

**Enjoy First-Class Entertainment
in an Atmosphere of
Comfort & Confidence**

Restaurant open from 12 noon to 2 am.
Gaming floor open from 4 pm to 6 am.
Jazz Bar open from 5 pm to 9 am.
Night Club open from 11 pm to 6 am.
Phone 945-1410
Major credit cards accepted.

Some of this is changing as price hikes have caused taxi drivers to compete for a scarcer consumer ruble. It has become much easier since the beginning of 1992 to catch a cab and to get where you want to go. And whereas in times past, passengers had to "beseech" the driver to go where they wanted to go, these changing times are seeing drivers become much more accommodating, quoting the full price of the ride before it begins, and much more frequently charging according to predictable rates (often quoting a per kilometer rate). The little green light in the passenger side of the taxi's windshield, which announces that the taxi is available, is also now a more accurate indicator of the cab's availability.

Gypsy cabs: It should be said that, when speaking of taxi drivers, also included are "gypsy cab" drivers, which means both self-employed drivers, and your average Russian who is just looking for a few extra rubles to meet petrol bills, and is willing to drive you somewhere if it is not too far out of his way (the masculine is accurate usage when speaking about driving, as very few women in Russia drive — rumor has it there are less than a dozen female taxi drivers in Moscow, a city of 9 million). If you ride in cabs regularly, you can count on riding 40-50% of the time in gypsy cabs (where, unlike in official cabs, you are required to wear a seat-belt, or at least drape it across your shoulder; putting on a seat-belt in an official cab, by contrast, is not required and, in fact often viewed by the driver as an insult). In fact, you may occasionally be offered rides in some quite unusual and interesting vehicles. Given the recent rise in crime against foreigners, you are advised to be somewhat wary about riding "gypsy-style."

Meters are never the basis for cab fares. Privatization of taxi parks means all fares are negotiated. As a foreigner, you can expect your negotiating position to be a bit weaker, particularly if you do not speak Russian. If you have a taxi ordered for you by a friend or by the hall lady in your hotel (or if you do it yourself), which you must usually do at least half a day in advance, but theoretically can be done an hour in advance (see Yellow Pages in our *Where in Moscow* or *Where in St. Petersburg* under Taxis), then you will pay a lower ride rate, plus a booking fee.

What to pay? Despite inflation, the rate for taxi rides (for foreigners) has remained pretty constant vs. the dollar, despite dramatic falls in the ruble/dollar exchange rate. Expect a 10-20 minute cab ride to cost you the ruble equivalent of $4-5 or thereabouts.

Being recognizable as a foreigner also opens you to demands of hard-currency payment for rides, particularly late at night, and particularly around foreign tourist hotels and from the airport (from where it is now nearly impossible to get a ride for rubles; in fact, it is **highly** recommended to use a private "limo" service from the airport to your hotel. In Moscow, just go up to one of the taxi counters at the airport or call or fax ahead of your arrival – see the Yellow Pages in our *Where in Moscow* or *Where in St. Petersburg*). If you have to pay with hard currency, it is usually a safe thing to do (although technically illegal, with the Jan. 1994 cash foreign currency ban – see Chapter 5) and a more certain way to get where you want to go. A couple of dollars should get you a good distance in the present cab market (likely about 20-

50% further/longer than the ruble equivalent). In any case, be cautious about flashing lots of dollars or being too "free" with them. As a point of safety, it is wise to put some small bills for cab fares in an easy-to-reach pocket and leave your wallet untouched. See the section on *Crime* in Chapter 5 for some further consideration of this issue.

Riding for rubles: The shrewder (and often more patient) traveler gets rides for rubles by knowing how much to offer. The closer you are to major foreign tourist hotels, the farther away from the center you are asking to be driven, and the later it is in the evening (particularly on weekends), will drive up the price accordingly. As noted above, a 10-15 minute daytime ride around town is worth about $4-5 in rubles and you can get most places you need to go by offering $6-10 in rubles (for gypsy cabs you can count on lower prices). In general, prices for cabs are somewhat lower in St. Petersburg than in Moscow.

You may also want to consider unofficially hiring a cab for the day, the going rate being about $5-10 in rubles per hour for extended periods. If you think you are doing pretty well getting cabs for rubles, remember that even when you can pay rubles, you will generally end up paying much more than a Russian would (although you may have an easier time getting a cab to stop). You can also hire a cab for the day through one of the private cab companies listed in the Yellow Pages in our *Where in Moscow* or *Where in St. Petersburg*.

In general, taxis are a good way to get around, if you are willing to brave excessive speeds and exhaust fumes. It is cheaper, faster and more direct than public transport.

CAR RENTAL

The spread of private enterprise to Russia has widened the alternatives for car rental services. Some good deals can be found, but some real rip-offs also need to be avoided. Most agencies offer cars either with or without drivers.

Two points (warnings?) ought to be to kept in mind when choosing to rent a car to drive yourself. First is the large number of half-crazed taxi and bus drivers you'll be driving among. Second is that neither Moscow nor St. Petersburg are, in any sense, easy cities to navigate. Street signs are sparse and well-hidden, making it very easy to commit traffic violations. Left turns and right turns are often prohibited by an obscure, unlit sign. And your inevitable transgressions of traffic laws are, particularly at intersections, closely monitored by the ubiquitous GAI traffic officers (ГАИ – pronounced "guy-ee"), who, increasingly, look on Western drivers (identifiable by color-coded license plates) in the manner of sharks eyeing wounded prey.

In sum, if you know your way around Moscow or St. Petersburg already, read Russian, and do not mind a bit of added tension on your trip, car rental may be the way for you. Otherwise, stick to taxis or rental cars furnished with a driver. If you do decide to rent a car, here is what you need to know.

License: You must have an International Drivers License (obtained from AAA in the United States) to drive in Russia, and your home country license as well, although GAI rarely get beyond your International License. You can, of course, also drive with a Russian license.

If you do not have an International license, you can get a Russian one (which you must do if you are a resident) by taking your valid license from your home country (along with two passport photos and a nominal fee) to the GlavUPDK Spetsavtotsentr in Moscow at ul. Kievskaya 8, ph. 240-2092. You may have to pass a written test and simulation (complete with model cars), plus a driving test.

Insurance: Most insurance policies can be extended to cover, if they do not already, car rental in Russia. Talk to your insurance agent. Of course, car rental agents also offer insurance when you rent the car, and some may require it. To avoid any problems, you may want to bring proof of insurance coverage. Insurance can also be purchased in Moscow (ul. Pyatnitskaya 12, ph. 231-1677) or St. Petersburg (ul. Kalyaeva 17, ph. 273-0628) from Ingosstrakh. One note: Russian law allows the company to refuse compensation for damage if a driver is pronounced by authorities to have been under the influence of alcohol at the time of an accident. Such determinations can be arrived at without the benefit of documentable tests.

Traffic violations: In the event you are pulled over for a traffic violation, the usual fee is nominal, and can be paid on the spot. More serious violations, such as driving under the influence of alcohol (which is very strictly punished), or inflicting serious human or property damage in an accident can bring heftier fines and land you in jail. Middle range violations, such as driving without a license or not stopping when signalled to by a militia (GAI) officer (this consists of a flick of the baton and signalling you over toward the curb), usually include a lecture and some haggling before payment of a nominal fee. There have been sporadic incidents of harassment of foreign drivers, yet this has been on the decline of late (see the notes on *Crime*, Chapter 5). In general, to avoid difficulties, if stopped for a traffic violation, remind yourself that you are at a distinct disadvantage and opt to pay the nominal cost of roadside justice, taking heart in the fact that you are probably helping to supplement the miserly salary of a public servant.

If you are stopped for suspicion of drinking and driving, GAI will give you a breathalizer test on the spot. If the breathalizer shows green, you can dispute the test (at which point you can be taken in for a blood test) or accept the results on the spot (your license will be confiscated) and agree to show up at the GAI office at a later date, at which time GAI will decide your case.

Accidents: If you should get in an accident, the law is that none of the vehicles in the accident may be moved until a GAI officer comes around and takes measurements and writes up a report. This policy is the cause of most traffic jams. The reality is that, if both parties agree who is at fault in the accident, that person will often offer to settle the situation "directly" (i.e. by paying cash for damages) to avoid a run-in with the bureaucracy and demerits on one's driving record. Be wary, however, of any offer of delayed settlement.

An accident ensures an unhappy and bureaucrat-filled visit, so drive carefully. If you do get in an accident, you will be instructed by the GAI officer where you will need to go to fill out necessary accident report papers. This will depend upon where your vehicle is registered. Take all potentially relevant paperwork (license, registration, insurance papers) and a translator if you need one.

Street signs: Street names are in Russian (Cyrillic) and are usually posted on the corners of buildings. Road signs are mainly in keeping with internationally accepted graphical signage, but there are enough important signs in Russian that you should have a reading knowledge of Russian if you want to drive safely.

Rules of the road: Some important driving rules should be noted. Always wear your seat-belt (you will be stopped if you don't). Horns are for emergencies only. Headlights are never used in city limits except in dimmed position, *even at night* (this is slowly changing, however). The speed limit within the city limits is 60 kph (37 mph); outside the city it is 90 kph (56 mph). Turning right on red lights is prohibited. Even in the daytime, headlights must be turned on (in dimmed intensity) when entering tunnels and turned off when exiting. If there isn't a street sign saying you can turn right or left at an intersection, technically you cannot. Left turns are almost never possible on major roads; you drive on to a U-turn lane, then come back and make a right turn. Drinking and driving is a very serious offence.

Gas Stations: Three types of gasoline are available: 76 octane, 93 octane, and 95 octane. Most stations have the former two. Do not use 76 octane unless you are told the car has been adapted for this, and in this event use only 76 octane. If you are driving a foreign-made car, use only 95 octane. To avoid waiting in line at gas stations, you can buy gas "by the canister" (10-30 liters) from private speculators, who sell gas at prices well above the normal retail price.

Mileage conversion	
US	**Russia**
20 mpg	12 liters/100k
30 mpg	8 liters/100k
40 mpg	6 liters/100k

Beware, however, such vendors often water down the gas they sell, which can immobilize your vehicle without warning.

In the Yellow Pages of our *Where in Moscow,* you will find a list of Moscow city gas stations by region and a list of stores that sell oil and grease for Russian cars. For St. Petersburg gas stations, consult the guide, *Where in St. Petersburg.*

Travel Beyond The Capitals

The same guidelines that apply in Moscow and St. Petersburg are also true for other major cities in Russia. Usually, however, the quality of accommodation and availability of goods and services is better in the two capitals than in other cities. Especially if you are traveling east, it can be much more difficult to make an international phone call or find a competent translator.

With the exception of a few direct international flights to major cities like Tallinn, Vilnius, Riga, Almaty, St. Petersburg and Kiev (and Khabarovsk, Vladivostok and Magadan from Anchorage and Seattle), it is necessary to travel via Moscow to most points within Russia and the former Soviet Union.

As of October 1992, the only areas "closed" to foreign travel are selected "sensitive" military sites. Further, there is no need to notify authorities about one's itinerary for trips throughout Russia (yet it is wise to leave word with friends or your embassy if you are planning extended solo travel in the hinterlands).

It is advised to have your accommodation reserved in advance. The travel agents listed in the Yellow Pages of our *Where in Moscow* can arrange this, as can some of the travel agents listed in Chapter 1 (see also the *Russian City Guide*, Chapter 4). Regarding travel to cities in other states of the Commonwealth, see the notes on *Visas* in Chapter 2.

As a final general note about traveling within Russia and the Commonwealth, it is highly advisable not to bring with you items that you cannot bear to lose, or that are irreplaceable. Remember, you and your luggage will stand out as being clearly "foreign" and will be a more tempting target for thieves. Keep your passport and all valuable documents with you (and not in your luggage) at all times.

GETTING TICKETS

If the organization that is sponsoring your visit does not arrange the booking and purchase of your air/train tickets, and you have not done so from your home country, you can book your internal travel through travel agencies listed in the Yellow Pages of our *Where in Moscow* or *Where in St. Petersburg* or through the travel desk of a major hotel. You can also deal directly with Aeroflot to book a flight, but if you do not speak Russian and do not enjoy waiting in long lines, it is simpler to avoid this.

It is *very* difficult to get tickets for internal travel with less than 72 hours advance booking, so the earlier you submit your request, the better your chances are of traveling. In general, you will have a better chance of getting the flight or train you want if you book through a another travel agency than if you book directly with Intourist or Intourtrans. Travel agencies usually have direct contacts that help speed up the process of confirming bookings.

Aeroflot is dead. Once the world's largest airline, the international division was spun off (now known as Aeroflot Russian International Airlines) and the domestic division is slowly disintegrating into regionally-based airline companies, all flying jets bearing the Aeroflot logo.

At best, what used to be Aeroflot is now a loose confederation of fleets of jets that are irregularly maintained, and offer undependable and wildly under-priced services (by Western standards). Meanwhile, charter agencies are sprouting up, as are some dependable private airlines with scheduled flights (notable among them, Transaero).

What this all means is that the traveler should place a premium on a knowledgeable, savvy local travel agent (see *Where in Moscow* and *Where in St. Petersburg* for listings) who is up on the most recent changes and knows which routes/flights/companies are dependable.

Payment: Foreigners (excepting accredited journalists) are required to pay in hard currency for internal air tickets. An exception may be if you are buying a ticket in a city in the provinces. Often they will not have the ability to accept hard currency and you will be "required" to pay in rubles. Rail tickets can mostly still be purchased for rubles, depending on the linguistic abilities of the passenger and the mood of the ticket salesperson and railcar conductor. It is getting much harder to travel for anything but hard currency on the well-traveled routes (i.e. between Moscow and St. Petersburg). Rail tickets to Helsinki must be paid for in hard currency.

Ruble prices for internal flights (and rail tickets) have skyrocketed with recent price liberalization. The disintegration of the Soviet Union is, needless to say, causing interminable delays with air travel. Planes are often having difficulty refueling in the provinces, making return to Moscow or St. Petersburg somewhat difficult. In sum, if you are flying, expect long delays and unexpected changes in your itinerary.

Book in-country: It is wisest to book tickets for domestic air travel *after* arriving in Russia. Otherwise, you may book a flight from abroad and arrive in Moscow, only to find that your flight has been cancelled or discontinued. Again, rely on a domestic travel agent (see the Yellow Pages in our *Where in Moscow* and *Where in St. Petersburg*) for bookings on internal air travel. If you do book an internal flight from abroad, be certain to reconfirm your reservation upon your arrival in-country.

It is also wise to make a note of the reference number you will be given for your travel reservations, and to keep this with your tickets when they have been issued. This is especially true for flights. There is a chance that when you arrive at the airport with tickets in hand, you will be informed that your name is not on the passenger list and you therefore will not be allowed to board the plane. This occurs because flights are regularly over-booked (especially as fuel shortages have restricted their number). If this happens to you, it is best to simply remain at the counter, present your reference number, and point out that you paid in hard currency for your ticket. A bit of obstinacy may be required on your part, but in the end "hard currency passengers" are rarely bumped off of flights.

It used to be that for air and rail travel within the former USSR, arrival and departure times were given in Moscow time. This convention has shattered with the assertion of the former republics' independence. Even Russian cities have begun discarding this admittedly odd standard. More and more it is the exception, rather than the rule, that the Moscow time is used to denote local arrival and departure times. In any case, check the time differences chart on the map at the front of the book (or the city-by-city clocks in the section following) to calculate local arrival and departure times *vis-a-vis* Moscow time. Then check locally to see which standard is being used.

AIR TRAVEL

Moscow has four airports, Sheremetevo I and II, Domodedovo and Vnukovo, so it is very important to find out from which airport your flight is scheduled to leave. Sheremetevo I is for flights to the North and West, including St. Petersburg; Sheremetevo II is for international flights; Domodedovo (Russia's largest airport) is for Eastern destinations; Vnukovo is for southern destinations. All of the airports are quite a distance outside the city; allow one hour traveling time to get to the airport by car or taxi; allow one and a half hours to get to Domodedovo (a 46 km drive).

St. Petersburg has two airports, Pulkovo and Rzhevka. Pulkovo has two terminals. Pulkovo I services domestic flights, Pulkovo II services international flights. Rzhevka handles short distance domestic flights.

Be sure to arrive at the airport at least one hour before your flight is scheduled to depart, and be warned that if you do not allow yourself that much time you stand a chance of not getting on the flight. Check-in and boarding take longer in Moscow or St. Petersburg than in most Western cities.

When you arrive at the airport, keep in mind that foreigners often still must go to a separate check-in desk, usually located somewhat apart from the main check-in hall. You usually locate this desk by looking for a blue and white "Intourist" sign. Your taxi driver or your Russian hosts will almost certainly know where it is located. After you have presented your ticket and checked your baggage (weight limit is 44 lbs.), you will be directed to a waiting room until it is time to board the plane.

When the plane is ready for boarding, an airline representative will escort you to the plane. Often foreigners are driven out to the plane and seated in the front of the forward cabin before the other passengers come aboard – this is considered First Class. Do not expect to be extremely comfortable during the flight. "First class" and "club class" as you may know them do not exist for internal flights. All of the seats are very close together and there is little room for carry-on luggage. The cabins are also generally not as clean or well-maintained as they are on other airlines. Overcrowding (one step beyond over-booking) flights is a common occurrence.

Unless the flight is more than several hours long, food and drink may not be served. If you suspect that you will be hungry or thirsty during the flight, it is best to bring your own provisions (bottled water is highly advised).

It is essential to always reconfirm the next flight on your itinerary as soon as possible at the Intourist or other travel desk of your hotel.

TRAIN TRAVEL

Many foreigners find that travel by train is easier, more comfortable and more convenient than air travel if the destination is relatively close to Moscow or St. Petersburg. For example, a common way for a business person to travel between Moscow and St. Petersburg is by the night train, which leaves either city at just before or after midnight and arrives in the other city between 8:00 and 9:00 am. In the summer months, it is even light early enough to allow for a view of the countryside.

One of the advantages of traveling by train is that you depart and arrive in the center of a city, instead of 30-40 minutes outside of it. And, unless you have more than 77 lbs. of luggage with you, you do not need to wait to collect it when you arrive at your destination. Train travel can also be more relaxing because you have more room to move around and stretch out than you have on a plane. In the winter months, when airports are often closed due to bad weather conditions, train travel is also more reliable. And with recent fuel shortages causing huge delays with air travel, train travel, while slower, is a more certain mode of transport.

If you plan to eat on the train, it is advisable to bring your own food. Dining cars are showing more plentiful supplies of food these days, but this is relatively speaking, and it is best to pack what suits your tastes. *Definitely bring your own supply of water* (bottled water can now be bought in most major Moscow and St. Petersburg hotels), even for brushing your teeth. It is advisable to bring your own toilet paper or tissues. If you travel "soft class" (see below), sheets, blankets and towels will be provided, but you must pay a small ruble fee for these after you board the train or when you buy your ticket.

Which class? Several different classes are available for train travel, and you must specify what you want when you request your reservation. *By all means travel first class.* There are two types of cabins available. A *coupé* cabin has four berths, two up, two down. A soft class cabin has two berths and is a hair bigger. If you do not buy the whole compartment for yourself (which you should always try to do), you will share it with others. If you buy out a whole cabin and travel alone (or as a twosome in a four-berth cabin) the train conductor, if she finds out, will insist you cannot do this, and will say they must put someone else in your cabin. This problem can usually be resolved with a small "gift."

If you do not buy out a whole compartment, be forewarned that it is not a convention to assign persons of the same sex to a sleeping compartment, so if you do not already have a traveling companion, be prepared to share a compartment with either males or females.

A first class compartment has cushioned berths, a small table, reading lamps and a radio. Restroom facilities are located at the end of the car. In no case should you agree to ride by *platzcar*, which is an open bunk car. There are also sitting (*sideniye*) cars, which are acceptable only for short rides. It is preferable to have a cabin in the middle of the train car as they are less noisy.

You can buy train tickets through Intourist or other travel agencies if you want to pay hard currency. You can also simply go to the train station where the train will leave from (or to the Advance Ticket Sales office – or the Intourtrans office in Moscow at ul. Petrovka 15 and nab. Kanala Griboyedova in St. Petersburg) and buy a ticket, if it is more than 48 hours or less than 24 hours before the train leaves. See the Yellow Pages in our *Where in Moscow* or *Where in St. Petersburg* for telephone numbers you can call to order tickets from your home/office and have them delivered to you there. Usually if you order tickets 3-4 days in advance you will not have trouble with availability. *One caveat:* given the steep hikes in air fares, which will continue, expect relative overcrowding of rail transport for the foreseeable future.

At the end of 1992 a new regulation was put in place to combat speculation and black marketeering in train tickets. The upshot is that passengers must now have their name printed on the ticket they use, and must show identification both when buying the ticket and when boarding. Since the beginning of 1993, foreigners are also 'supposed' to pay for rail tickets in hard currency. The reality is that, as noted above, linguistic ability, the mood of train officials (to say nothing of train station cashiers' ability to deal with currency payments), and the amount of foreigner traffic on a route tends to determine how consistently this is enforced. Despite the regulations, there is still a booming business in platform sales of tickets (usually for twice the list price), and train conductors frequently sell empty spaces (or even their own sleeping space) to ticket-less passengers just before the train gets underway.

Crime on trains has been on the rise of late. See the notes on how to protect yourself when traveling by train in Chapter 5.

Both Moscow and St. Petersburg have more than one train station, so be sure to find out from which station your train will leave. As a general guide:

In Moscow: Byelorusskiy Station serves Belarus, Poland and the West; Kievskiy Station is for the Ukraine; Leningradskiy Station is for the North and St. Petersburg and Helsinki; Riga Station is for the Baltics; Yaroslavskiy Station serves the East and North Russia; Kurskiy Station serves the Caucausus and the Crimea; Paveletskiy Station serves Southeastern Russia; Kazanskiy Station serves the Urals, Central Asia, and Western Siberia.

In St. Petersburg: Finlandskiy Station serves trains to Vyborg, Repino, Razliv and to and from Finland; Varshavskiy Station is for trains to Tallinn and Riga; Baltiyskiy Station is for trains to the southern outskirts of the city and Petrodvorets; Moskovskiy Station serves Moscow, the North East and South of Russia; Vitebskiy Station handles trains to Pushkin, Pavlovsk and Belarus and Ukraine.

It is best to be at your train at least 30 minutes before departure time – trains tend to leave more promptly than planes. The conductor will ask for your ticket (and identification) before you will be allowed to board the train. Be sure you get the ticket booklet, including the cover, back if you have other tickets in it. Once the train is underway, the conductor will usually serve hot tea before you leave and in the morning on overnight trains. At various train stops budding capitalists will board the train selling food; on well-traveled routes, vendors will walk the train pretty much constantly, selling everything from colas to ice cream to *buterbrody* (open-faced sandwiches).

TRAVEL BY CAR

It would be a severe understatement to say driving conditions in Russia and the former USSR are rugged. Fuel and service stations are few and far between (and poorly stocked these days) and only major highways are well paved. Bring a heating pad.

Still, should you decide to get about between cities by car, read the section earlier in this chapter on *Car Rental*. Adhere strictly to local driving regulations. If you are bringing a car in, you may be required to sign a statement guaranteeing re-export of the car, or to pay a hefty import duty. This statement is not obviated by damage to a vehicle, by the way.

Russian City Guide

From Astrakhan to Yuzhno-Sakhalinsk

What follows is a listing of important addresses and phone numbers in the 77 largest cities (most have over 150,000 inhabitants) of Russia. As such, it may serve as a starting point for arranging business meetings, accommodations and travel to these cities. While there may be other hotels, restaurants and travel agencies in these cities, the existence of those given below was verified just prior to publication and are thus your most reliable contacts. Still, keep in mind that this type of contact information changes frequently. Corrections and additions are enthusiastically encouraged.

The number listed for information is the local directory information number, which can be called from Moscow, St. Petersburg or other cities which allow direct inter-city dialing. This number can be used to call to get the number of locally-based enterprises or of individuals living in that city.

KEY

☾ City code for dialing this city

✈ Air miles to this city from Moscow

🕐 Local time when 12 noon in Moscow

NOTES ON DIALING:

❶ If the number for information for the city is 990-9111 (i.e. as with Omsk),then after dialing 8 and waiting for a second dial tone (see *Long Distance Dialing Within Russia and the CIS*, Chapter 7), dial only the first three numbers of the city code, then 990-9111.

❷ If the number of digits in the phone number you are dialing (city code plus the local phone number) is less than 10, you will likely not be able to place that call without an operator, but you can try filling in the extra digits with 2's or 0's first (dialed between the city code and the local number) to get ten digits. If the number of digits is 11 or 12, try leaving out the final zero(es) or two(s) of the city code when dialing.

ARKHANGELSK ✆ 818-00 ✈ 621

Information: 300-00
Hotel(s): *Purnavolok*, ul. Lenina 88, ph. 323-89; *Dvina*, pr. Pavlina Vinogradova 52, 955-02
Restaurant(s): *Yubileiny*, pr. Pavlina Vinogradova 52, ph. 318-80
Intourist: ul. Lomonosova 209, ph. 359-25; **Other travel agent(s):** ul. Svobody 6, ph. 396-18
Aeroflot: ul. Engelsa 116, ph. 626-49
Telegraph office: ul. Engelsa 5, ph. 320-11
Bank(s): ul. K. Libknekhta 3, ph. 375-93
City Council/Administration: ul. Lenina 5, ph. 386-84
Hospital: ul. Suvorova 1. ph. 753-71

ASTRAKHAN ✆ 851-00 ✈ 777

Information: 265-21
Hotel(s): *Lotos*, ul. Kremlevskaya 4, ph. 295-00; *Atrakhansky Gostiny Dvor*, ul. Ulyanovykh 6, ph. 229-88
Restaurant(s): *Secret*, Komsomolskaya nab. (in steamboat), ph. 530-76 (open 19-24); *Lotos*, ul. Kremlevskaya 4, ph. 498-89 (11-23)
Intourist: ul. Sovetskaya 21, ph. 297-30; **Other travel agent(s):** pr. Molodyozhny 8, ph. 299-39
Aeroflot: ul. Pobedy 54, ph. 547-49
Telegraph office: ul. Chernyshevskovo 10/27, ph. 238-09
Bank(s): ul. Sovetskaya 14, ph. 282-15
City Council/Administration: ul. Sovetskaya 15, ph. 217-67
Hospital: ul. Tatishcheva 2, ph. 567-18

BARNAUL ✆ 385-2 ✈ 1818

Information: 256-683
Hotel(s): *Barnaul*, pl. Pobedy 3, ph. 252-581; *Tsentralnaya*, ul. Lenina 57, ph. 253-449
Restaurant(s): *Barnaul*, pl. Pobedy 3, ph. 252-435, 252-440
Intourist: ul. Pushkina 78, ph. 232-872
Aeroflot: ul. Sovetskaya 4, ph. 243-301, 254-511
Telegraph office: ul. Internatsionalnaya 74, ph. 236-688
Bank(s): ul. Gornoaltayskaya 14, ph. 774-712
City Council/Administration: pr. Lenina 18, ph. 233-295
Hospital: ul. Dimitrova 62, ph. 221-466

BELGOROD ✆ 072-22 ✈ 357

Information: 222-22
Hotel(s): *Tsentralnaya*, ul. Kommunisticheskaya 86, ph. 21-755; *Belgorod*, pl. Revolyutsii 1, ph. 22-512

Restaurant(s): *Tsentralniy*, ul. Kommunisticheskaya 86, ph. 20-470, 20-596; *Yuzhniy*, ul. Vatutina 2A, ph. 59-624

Intourist: ul. Vorovskovo 60, ph. 78-600, fax 71-370; **Other travel agent(s):** *Turburo*, ul. Vatutina 2A, ph. 74-762; *Sputnik*, ul. Narodnaya 135, ph. 29-403, 26-340

Aeroflot: ul. Lenina 32, ph. 34-951, 40-928

Telegraph office: ul. Lenina, ph. 22-054

Bank(s): *Belgorodpromstroibank*, ul. Frunze 72, ph. 21-363, 21-517

City Council/Administration: pr. Lenina 38, ph. 77-206

Hospital: ul. Nekrasova 8, ph.60-483; Polyclinc #1, ul. Litvinova 95A

Other useful information: *Oblast Art Museum*, ul. Pobedy 77, ph. 22-001; *Museum of Local Culture*, ul. Kommunisticheskaya 86, ph. 23-582, 21-678; *Representation of the Ministry of Foreign Economic Relations*, pr. Lenina 38, Oblispolkom

BLAGOVESCHENSK   ① 416-22   ✦ 3433

Information: 990-9111

Hotel(s): *Zeya*, ul. Kalinina 8, ph. 21-100

Restaurant(s): *Druzhba*, ul. Kuznechnaya 1, ph. 90-510

Intourist: ul. Lenina 108/2, ph. 45-772, 93-326; **Other travel agent(s):** *Bureau for Tourism and Excursions*, ul. Shevchenko 34, ph. 21-230, 26-914; *Sputnik*, ul. Krasnogvardeyskaya 124, ph. 28-391

Aeroflot: ul. Lenina 193, ph. 25-902, 25-002

Telegraph office: *Post office*, ul. Pionerskaya 27, ph. 25-660, 25-673, 22-425

Bank(s): *Bashprombank*, ul. Sovetskaya 2, ph. 22-902

City Council/Administration: ul. Lenina 133, ph. 21-238

Hospital: *Polyclinic #1*, ul. Kalinina, ph. 27-538

Other useful information: *Museum of Local culture*, per. Internatsionalny 6, ph. 24-149

BRYANSK   ① 083-22   ✦ 202

Information: 990-9111

Hotel(s): *Turist*, ul. Duki 62a, ph. 47-711, 47-492

Restaurant(s): in the *Turist* hotel, ph. 47-556

Travel agent(s): *Council for Tourism and Excursions*, ul. Pionerskaya 33, ph. 65-451, 61-792, 65-313

Aeroflot: pr. Lenina 57, ph. 48-430, 48-482

Telegraph office: *Main Post Office*, ul. K. Marksa 9, ph. 63-296, 42-704

Bank(s): *Bryansksotsbank*, ul. Fokina 121, ph. 61-677, 61-625

City Council/Administration: pr. Lenina 35, ph. 43-013, 42-109

Hospital: *Hospital #4*, ul. Fokina 40, ph. 44-852

Other useful information: *Graphic Arts Museum*, ul. Yelyutina 39, ph. 41-503, 60-864; *Museum of Local Culture*, ul. Oktyabrskaya 86, ph.17-053

CHEBOKSARY   ① 835-0   ✈ 373

Information: 222-222
Hotel(s): *Druzhba*, ul. Tsivilskaya 11, ph. 234-248; *Rossiya*, pl. Gagarina 34, ph. 230-525
Restaurant(s): *Moskovskiy*, ul. Elgera 11, ph. 248-963; *Rossiya*, pl. Gagarina 34, ph. 231-176
Intourist: Egerskiy bulv. 59, ph. 253-914; **Other travel agent(s):** ul. Konstantina Ivanova 7, ph. 420-041
Aeroflot: pr. Lenina 32, ph. 221-471
Telegraph office: pr. Lenina 2, ph. 222-232
Bank(s): ul. K. Marksa 25, ph. 220-848
City Council/Administration: pl. Lenina 2, ph. 220-996
Hospital: Moskovskiy pr. 11, ph. 496-208

CHELYABINSK   ① 351-2   ✈ 917

Information: 990-9111
Hotel(s): *Malakhit*, ul. Truda 153, ph. 335-478; *Yuzhny Ural*, pr. Lenina 52, ph. 335-382
Restaurant(s): *Uralskiye Pelmeni*, ul. Engelsa 28, ph. 653-065; *Yuzhny Ural*, pr. Lenina 52
Intourist: pr. Lenina 52, ph. 334-305, 335-360; **Other travel agent(s):** ul. Tsvillinga 51A, ph. 346-234
Aeroflot: pr. Lenina 28, ph. 361-234
Telegraph office: ul. Kirova 161, ph. 361-533
Bank(s): ul. Elkina 61, ph. 367-960
City Council/Administration: pl. Revolutsii 2, ph. 333-805
Hospital: ul. Vorovskovo 16, ph. 346-234

CHEREPOVETS   ① 817-36   ✈ 233

Information: 52-222
Hotel(s): *Leningrad*, bulvar Domenschikov 36, ph. 75-616, 75-620
Restaurant(s): *Leningrad*, bulvar Domenschikov 36, ph. 71-176
Travel agent(s): *Meridian*, pr. Stroitelei 1, ph. 24-872
Aeroflot: Pr. Pobedy 78, ph. 57-619
Telegraph office: *Otdeleniye Svyazi #27*, pr. Stroitelei 6, ph. 75-128
Bank(s): *Cherepovetskiy*, pr. Sovetski 57, ph. 53-403
City Council/Administration: pr. Stroitelei 2, ph. 72-629
Hospital: *Polyclinic #2*, ul. Belyaeva 24, ph. 37-565

CHITA   ① 302-22   ✈ 2921

Information: 990-9111
Hotel(s): *Obkomovskaya*, ul. Profsoyuznaya 18, ph. 65-270
Restaurant(s): *Maran*, ul. Bogomyadgova 23, ph. 33-292

Intourist: ul. Lenina 56, ph. 31-246; **Other travel agent(s):** *Council for Tourism and Excursions*, ul. Babushkina 42a, ph. 27-270, 31-718; *Sputnik*, ul. Kalinina 68, ph. 32-985, 38063
Aeroflot: ul. Leningradskaya 36, ph. 34-381, 42-924
Telegraph office: ul. Chaikovskovo 22, ph. 33-939
Bank(s): *Chitakompromstroibank*, ul. Petrovskovo 37, ph. 32-858
City Council/Administration: ul. Chaikovskovo 8, ph. 32-407
Hospital: *Polyclinic #8*, ul. Chaikovskovo, ph.34-879
Other useful information: *Regional Art Museum*, ul. Chkalova 120a, ph. 32-750, 33-223

ELISTA   ① 847-22   ✦ 715

Information: 556-40
Hotel(s): *Elista*, ul. Lenina 237, ph. 54-170; *Rossiya*, ul. Lenina 241, ph. 54-000
Restaurant(s): *Rossiya* (in hotel of the same name), ph. 54-080; *Styep*, ul. Khomutnikova 107, ph. 61-085
Travel agent(s): *Bureau for Tourism and Excursions*, ul. Lenina 251, ph. 56-498
Aeroflot: ul. Gorkovo 11, ph. 54-296, 53-312
Telegraph office: ul. Rozy Luxemburg 31, ph. 62-903
Bank(s): *Natsionalny Bank*, ul. Krupskoy 3, ph. 57-850, 53-275
City Council/Administration: ul. Lenina 249, ph. 52-314
Hospital: *Republican Hospital*, ul. Pushkina, ph. 58-566, 27-897
Other useful information: *Information Office of Railway Station*, ph. 50-926; *Museum of Local Culture*, Teatralny per., ph. 62-488; *Art Gallery*, Pervy Mikrorayon 33, ph. 50-112

GROZNY   ① 871-2   ✦ 932

Information: 234-502
Hotel(s): *Kavkaz*, pr. Pobedy 27, ph. 222-038
Restaurant(s): *Kavkaz*, pr. Pobedy 27
Intourist: ul. Taimieva 16, ph. 235-019; 236-621
Aeroflot: pr. Avtorkhanova 6, ph. 223-608
Telegraph office: ul. Krasnykh Frontovikov 9, ph. 220-198
Bank(s): ul. Komsomolskaya 112, ph. 227-384
City Council/Administration: ul. Gvardeyskaya 103, ph. 220-142
Hospital: ul. Pervomayskaya 3, ph. 227-647
Other useful information: This muslim city works on Sunday and does not work on Friday and Saturday.

IRKUTSK   ① 395-2   ✦ 2578

Information: 244-311
Hotel(s): *Intourist*, bulvar Gagarina 44, ph. 295-335, 296-338; *Angara*, ul. Sukhe Batora 7, ph. 241-631; *Sibir*, ul. Lenina 8, ph. 937-51; *Baikal*,

(on lake Baikal), ph. 296-234
Restaurant(s): *Angara,* ul. Sukhe-Batora 7, ph. 293-481; *Sibirsky Traktir,* 296-329; *Chingiz,* ph. 296-297; *Irkutskiy,* ph. 296-341; *Pekin* (Chinese cuisine), ph. 296-325; *Japanese bar,* ph. 296-305; *Sibir,* ph. 293-861, *Tsentralny,* ph. 344-167
Intourist: bulvar Gagarina 44, ph. 296-315; **Other travel agent(s):** ul. Sverdlova 35, ph. 243-888
Aeroflot: ul. Gorkovo 29, ph. 242-535
Telegraph office: ul. Proletarskaya 12, ph. 244-801
Bank(s): ul. Lenina 16, ph. 336-952
City Council/Administration: ul. Lenina 14, ph. 336-504
Hospital: ul. Yubileynaya 100, ph. 466-507
Other useful information: *Sprint office,* ph. 336-116 (Access Number: 433-496); *Japan-Russia Trade Association,* ul. Gorkovo 31, ph. 245-444; *Mongolian Consulate,* ul. Lapina 11, ph. 242-370; *Regional Center for Trade and Commerce,* ul. Sukhe-Batora 16, ph. 271-409, fax 272-387

IVANOVO   ① 093-2   ✦ 155

🕐 **Information:** 990-9111
Hotel(s): *Intourist,* ul. Yermaka 20, ph. 37-6519; *Sovietskaya,* pr. Lenina 64, ph. 37-2547; *Ivanovo,* ul. Karla Marksa 46, ph.3 7-4024
Restaurant(s): *Intourist,* in the hotel of same name, ph. 37-0391; *Atlant,* pr. Lenina 64, ph.34-2378
Intourist: pr. Engelsa 1/25, ph. 32-3292; **Other travel agent(s):** *Bureau for Travel and Excursions,* ul. Ermaka 20, ph. 32-0651; *Sputnik,* ul. Stepanova 14, ph. 32-6048, 32-8256
Aeroflot: pr. Stroitelei 24, ph. 61-617
Telegraph office: *Post office,* pr. Lenina 17, ph. 32-5451
Bank(s): *Tekstil,* pr. Lenina 18, ph. 32-6562, 32-7603
City Council/Administration: pl. Revolyutsii 4, ph. 32-7020
Hospital: *Regional Hospital,* ul. Lyubimova, ph. 26-9566
Other useful information: *Regional History Museum,* ul. Baturina 6/40; *Rep. of the Ministry of Foreign Economic Relations,* ul. Baturina 5

IZHEVSK   ① 341-2   ✦ 590

🕐 **Information:** 223-881
Hotel(s): *Kama,* ul. Sovetskaya 3, ph. 781-542; *Tsentralnaya,* ul. Pushkinslaya 223, ph. 233-090
Restaurant(s): *Otdykh,* ul. Sovetskaya 18, ph. 787-017; *Izhevsk,* in *Tsentralnaya* Hotel, ul. Pushkinskaya 223
Intourist: ul. Sovetskaya 16, ph. 787-120
Aeroflot: ul. Pushkinskaya 138, ph. 757-376
Telegraph office: ul. Pushkinskaya 278, ph. 228-372
Bank(s): Izhkredobank, Zavod plastmass, ph. 768-510
City Council/Administration: ul. Pushkinskaya 276, ph. 228-487
Hospital: Botkinskoye shosse 17, ph. 265-483

KALININGRAD ① 011-2 ✈ 668

🕐 **Information:** 070 or 990-9111
Hotel(s): *Turist*, ul. A. Nevskovo 53, ph. 460-801, 432-332; *Kaliningrad*, Leninskiy pr. 81, ph. 469-440, 469-683
Restaurant(s): *Olsztin*, ul. Olstinka 1, ph. 444-635; *Tourist*, ul. A. Nevskovo 53, ph. 431-237
Intourist: ul. Ozernaya 25A, ph. 27-5265; **Other travel agent(s):** *Sputnik*, Prospekt Mira 15, ph. 214-507, 216-225; Leninskiy pr. 28, ph. 431-031
Aeroflot: ph. 460-483, 439-426, 460-828
Telegraph office: ul. Kosmonavta Leonova 22, ph. 219-270
Bank(s): *Kredobank*, ul. Bagryamyana, ph. 430-483
City Council/Administration: pl. Pobedy 1, ph. 215-395, 214-898
Hospital: ul. Klinicheskaya 74, ph.461-405
Other useful information: *Representation of the Ministry of Foreign Economic Relations*, ul. Dm. Donskovo 1, Oblispolkom; *Regional Chamber of Trade and Commerce*, pr. Pobedy 55, ph. 187-15; *Free Economic Zone Administration*, ul. D. Donskovo, ph. 467-545.

KALUGA ① 084-22 ✈ 93

🕐 **Information:** 22-222
Hotel(s): *Kaluga*, ul. Kirova 1, ph. 49-740
Restaurant(s): *Kaluga*, ph. 49-677
Intourist: ul. Lenina 81, ph. 78-763, 76-454; **Other travel agent(s):** *Bureau for Travel and Excursions*, ul. Engelsa 14, ph. 78-142
Aeroflot: ul. Lenina 35, ph. 23-345, 23-550
Telegraph office: pl. Lenina, ph. 73-996
Bank(s): *Promstroybank*, ul. Dostoevskovo 20, ph. 74-859
City Council/Administration: ul. Lenina 74, ph. 73-125
Hospital: ul. Vishnevskovo 1, ph. 49-049

KAZAN ① 843-2 ✈ 451

🕐 **Information:** 760-095
Hotel(s): *Tatarstan*, pl. Kuybysheva 2, ph. 326-979; *Molodyozhny Tsentr* (Youth Center), ul. Dekabristov 1, ph. 327-954; *Kazan*, ul. Baumana 9/10, ph. 200-91; *Volga*, ul. Said Galiyeva 1a, ph. 321-894
Restaurant(s): *Kazan*, ul. Baumana 9, ph. 327-054; *Nauruz*, ul. Kuybysheva 7, ph. 324-815
Intourist: ul. Baumana 9/10, ph. 210-212, 324-195
Aeroflot: Stary Aeroport Kazan-2, ph. 768-035
Telegraph office: ul. Rakhmatulina 3, ph. 367-143
Bank(s): ul. Dekabristov 1, ph. 578-346
City Council/Administration: ul. Lenina 1, ph. 327-060
Hospital: ul. Chekhova 1a, ph. 384-176
Other useful information: *Sovam Teleport office:* ph. 762-366 (Access number: 763-688)

KEMEROVO   ① 384-2   ✦ 1864

Information: 990-9111
Hotel(s): *Kuzbass*, ul. Vesennyaya 20, ph. 250-254; *Ton*, ul. Pritonskaya nab. 7, ph. 259-902
Restaurant(s): *Kuzbass*, 250-254 (in hotel of same name); *Ton*, 267-209 (in hotel of same name)
Intourist: ul. Vesennyaya 20, ph. 257-821
Aeroflot: 551-788 (airport), booking office, Oktyabrskiy pr. 1
Telegraph office: Oktyabrskiy pr. 1, ph. 523-812
Bank(s): ul. Kirova 4, ph. 265-745, 265-734
City Council/Administration: Sovetskiy pr. 54, ph. 264-610
Hospital: ul. N. Ostrovskovo 22, ph. 264-531

KHABAROVSK   ① 421-0   ✦ 3790

Information: 331-524
Hotel(s): *Lyudmila*, ul. Muravieva-Amurskovo 33, ph. 388-665; *Intourist*, Amurskiy bulvar 2, ph. 336-507; *Sapporo*, ul. Komsomolskaya 79, ph. 332-702; *Tsentralnaya*, ul. Pushkina 52, ph. 336-731; *Amur*, ul. Lenina 49, ph. 335-043; *Dalny Vostok*, ul. Karla Marksa 18, ph. 335-093; *Vassily Payarkov* (boat), City Pier, ph. 398-201
Restaurant(s): Hotel Restaurants; *Sapporo* (Japanese), ul. Komsomolskaya 79, ph. 330-882; *Krasny Zal*, 339-081; *Niigata* (Japanese), ul. Lenina; *Utes Cafe*, Central Park of Culture, ph. 339-352; *Harbin*, ul. Volochayevskaya 118, ph. 331-558; *Rus*, ul. Muravieva-Amurskovo 5, ph. 330-912; *Unikal* (Japanese), Amursky bulvar 2, ph. 399-315
Intourist: Amurskiy bulv. 2, ph. 337-634; **Other travel agent(s):** *International Travel Associates*, ph. 223-528
Aeroflot: Amurskiy bulv. 5, ph. 348-521
Telegraph office: Amurskiy bulv. 2, ph. 399-536
Bank(s): ul. Kim-Yu-Chena 45, ph. 210-327
City Council/Administration: ul. Karla Marksa 66, ph. 335-346
Hospital: Amurskiy bulv. 2. Room 125, ph. 399-188
Other useful information: *Sprint office*, ul. Muravieva-Amurskovo 58, ph. 214-937 (Access Number: 218-799); *DHL Office*, ul. Muravieva-Amurskovo 4, ph. 330-857, 338-478, 338-498, fax 330-949; *TNT Worldwide Express*, ul. Krasnodarskaya 31/8, ph. 378-033; *Japan Air Lines* (at airport), ph. 370-686; *Korean Airways* (at airport), ph. 348-024, 373-204; *Regional Chamber of Trade and Commerce*, ul. Sharnova 113, ph. 330-311, fax 330-312; *US Foreign Commercial Service*, ul. Turgeneva 69, ph. 337-923; [Alternative international direct dial to 6-digit Khabarovsk numbers via Sprint: use city code 50931 instead of 4210 after the country code (if Sprint is not your carrier, dial 10333 first, i.e. 10333-011-7-50931, then the local number)]

KOSTROMA   ☎ 094-22   ✈ 186

🕐 **Information:** 094 or 990-9111
Hotel(s): *Volga,* ul. Yunosheskaya 1, ph. 54-6262; *Motel* (Intourist), ph. 53-3661
Restaurant(s): *Rus,* Yunosheskaya 1, ph. 59-4298
Travel agent(s): *Bureau for Tourism and Excursions,* ul. Sovetskaya 6, ph. 7-34-31, 7-20-26; *Sputnik,* ul. Lenina 54A, ph. 55-0523
Aeroflot: pl. Sovetskaya 3, ph. 57-4213
Telegraph office: ul. Podletayeva 1, ph. 57-5112
Bank(s): *Tsentrobank,* ul. Knyazeva 5, ph. 57-5112
City Council/Administration: ul. Sovetskaya 1, ph. 57-6515
Hospital: *Hospital #1,* ul. Sovetskaya, ph. 55-4832
Other useful information: *Kostroma Graphic Arts Museum,* pr. Mira 5, ph.74-678; *Representation of the Ministry of Foreign Economic Relations,* ul. Dzerzhinskovo 14

KRASNODAR   ☎ 861-2   ✈ 761

🕐 **Information:** 550-333
Hotel(s): *Intourist,* ul. Krasnaya 109, ph. 558-897; *Motel Yuzhny,* ul. Moskovskaya 40, ph. 559-442
Restaurant(s): *Burgis,* ul. K. Libknekhta 175, ph. 356-925; *Yuzhny,* ul. Moskovskaya 40, ph. 551-684
Intourist: ul. Krasnaya 109, ph. 553-450, 576-697
Aeroflot: ul. Krasnaya 129, ph. 576-007
Telegraph office: ul. Sverdlova 68, ph. 522-663, 522-056
Bank(s): ul. Krasnaya 76, ph. 575-008, ul. Krasnaya 129, ph. 545-901
City Council/Administration: ul. Krasnaya 122, ph. 554-348
Hospital: ul. Krasnaya 103, 577-290
Other useful information: *Regional Center for Trade and Commerce,* ul. Kommunarov 8, ph. 523-754

KRASNOYARSK   ☎ 391-2   ✈ 2066

🕐 **Information:** 275-959
Hotel(s): *Krasnoyarsk,* ul. Uritskovo 94, ph. 273-769; *Turist,* ul. Matrosova 2, ph. 361-470; *Oktyabrskaya,* ul. Mira 15, ph. 271-916
Restaurant(s): *Yenisey-Batyushka,* ul. Dubrovinskovo 1a, ph. 225-228; *Turist,* ul. Matrosova 2, ph. 366-912; *Krasnoyarsk,* ul. Uritskovo 94, ph. 273-536
Intourist: ul. Uritskovo 94, ph. 273-715, 273-643
Aeroflot: ul. Matrosova 4, ph. 222-156, 261-931
Telegraph office: ul. Karla Marksa 80, ph. 222-555
Bank(s): ul. Semafornaya 243a, ph. 364-937
City Council/Administration: ul. Karla Marksa 93, ph. 222-231
Hospital: ul. Mira 35, ph. 270-570

Other useful information: *TNT Worldwide Express* (at airport), ph. 236-418; *Regional Center for Trade and Commerce*, ul. Kirova 26, ph. 239-613

KURGAN   ① 352-22   ✦ 1057

Information: 24081
Hotel(s): *Moskva*, ul. Krasina 49, ph. 55-774, 55-309
Restaurant(s): *Moskva*, ul. Krasina 49, ph.55-333
Intourist: pr. Mashinostroiteley 33A, ph. 33-756; **Other travel agent(s):** *Bureau for Travel and Excursions*, ph. 49-830, 49-896
Aeroflot: ul. Lenina 9, ph. 25-345, 23-965
Telegraph office: ul. Gogolya 44, ph. 22-416
Bank(s): *Kredobank*, ul. Uritskovo 102, ph. 30-375, fax 30-567, 75-244
City Council/Administration: pl. Lenina, ph. 22-452, 21-192
Hospital: *Central Hospital*, ul. Gogolya 42, ph. 21-194, 21-545
Other useful information: *Sovam Teleport office*, ph. 71-637 (Access number: 36-869)

KURSK   ① 071-00   ✦ 280

Information: 21-313
Hotel(s): *Kursk*, ul. Lenina 2, ph. 29-9389; *Solovinaya Roshcha* (Intourist), ul. Engelsa 142A, ph. 51-562, 59-394
Restaurant(s): *Kursk* (in hotel of same name), ph. 29-9389; *Oktyabrskaya*, ul. Lenina 72, ph. 29-9840
Intourist: ul. Engelsa 142A, ph. 59-255, 35-9213
Other travel agent(s): *Bureau for Travel and Excursions*, pl. Krasnaya 6, ph. 20-460, 26-055; *Sputnik*, pl. Krasnaya 6, ph. 22-168, 21-300, 22-163
Aeroflot: ul. Karla Marksa 12, ph. 25-682
Telegraph office: ul. Krasnaya Ploshchad 8, ph. 25-006
Bank(s): *Kurskbank*, ul. Gorkovo 34, ph. 56-6518, 56-6444
City Council/Administration: ul. Lenina 1, ph. 26-363
Hospital: *Hospital #1*, ul. Dimitrova 61, ph. 23-453
Other useful information: *Art Gallery*, ul. Sovetskaya 3, ph. 23-936, 23-946; *Museum of Local Culture*, ul. Lunacharskovo 6, ph. 26-474

LIPETSK   ① 074-2   ✦ 233

Information: 77-2222
Hotel(s): *Lipetsk*, ul. Lenina 11, ph. 24-7217; *Metalurg*, ul. Lenina 36, ph. 24-1311
Restaurant(s): Cafe in the Hotel Metalurg, ph. 24-1311; *Yakhont*, pr. Pobedy 8, ph. 77-3220
Intourist: ul. Plekhanova 1, Dom Pechati, ph. 246761, 7194; **Other travel agent(s):** *Council for Tourism and Excursions*, ul. K. Marksa 1, ph. 77-4555; *Sputnik*, ul. Lenina 23, ph. 72-0546, 77-8537, 24-4900
Telegraph office: ul. Plekhanova 1a, ph. 24-1307
Bank(s): *Lipetskkombank*, pl. Plekhanova 4, ph. 24-5327

City Council/Administration: ul. Sovetskaya 5, ph. 77-6524
Hospital: *Regional Hospital #2*, ul. Lenina 35, ph. 24-2297, 24-0164
Other useful information: *Lipetsk Museum of Local Culture*, pr. Lenina 4, ph. 24-2293, 24-0478; *Representation of the Ministry of Foreign Economic Relations*, pl. Lenina 1, Dom Sovetov

MAGADAN ① 413-00 ✦ 3791

🕐 **Information:** 209-99

Hotel(s): *Magadan*, ul. Proletarskaya 8, ph. 210-14, 259-86; *Biznes-Tsentr*, ul. Proletarskaya 84-Ve, ph. 589-44, 588-23

Restaurant(s): *Avgust*, pr. Karl Marksa 60a, ph. 517-93; *U Maksa*, ul. Proletarskaya 84-Ve, ph. 582-55; *Primorskiy*, ul. Kommuny 14, ph. 272-07, ph. 272-09

Intourist: ul. Proletarskaya 30A, ph. 210-32

Aeroflot: ul. Naberezhnaya 7, ph. 288-91

Telegraph office: ul. Proletarskaya 10, ph. 230-05, 225-72

Bank(s): pr. Proletarskaya 25/1, ph. 266-97

City Council/Administration: pl. Gorkovo 1, ph. 250-47

Hospital: 2nd proyezd Gorkovo 5, ph. 261-77

Other useful information: *Bus station*, pr. Lenina 1, ph. 288-97

MAKHACHKALA ① 872-00 ✦ 980

🕐 **Information:** 703-62

Hotel(s): *Leningrad*, ul. Lenina 57, ph. 771-54

Restaurant(s): *Kavkaz*, ul. Sovetskaya 18, ph. 762-65; *Smolyan*, ul. Gagarina, ph. 242-49

Intourist: ul. Buinakskovo 8, in the Hotel *Kaspiy*, ph.795-88; **Other travel agent(s):** *Dagtur*, ul. Kalinina 35, ph. 253-98, 574-63

Aeroflot: ul. Lenina 119, ph. 794-72, 794-12

Telegraph office: pr. Kalinina, ph. 721-78

Bank(s): *Kavkaz-Kredobank*, ul. Chernyshevskovo 115, ph./fax 535-49

City Council/Administration: pl. Lenina, ph. 726-70, 724-82

Hospital: *Zheleznodorozhnaya*, pr. Kalinina 32, ph. 720-10

Other useful information: *Dagestan Historical and Architectural Museum*, pl. Lenina 43, ph. 733-64

MURMANSK ① 815-00 ✦ 917

🕐 **Information:** 514-70

Hotel(s): *Polyarniye Zori*, ul. Knipovicha 17, ph. 502-82; *Arktika*, pr. Lenina 82, ph. 579-88

Restaurant(s): *Dary Morya*, pr. Lenina 72, ph. 723-35; *Polyarniye Zori*, ul. Knipovicha 17; *Arktika*, pr. Lenina 82, ph. 543-60; *International Seamans' Club*, ul. Karla Marksa 1, ph. 591-26

Intourist: ul. Knipovicha 17, ph. 543-85

Aeroflot: pr. Lenina 19, ph. 605-08

Telegraph office: pr. Lenina 82a, ph. 556-13
Bank(s): ul. Profsoyuzov 11, ph. 563-48
City Council/Administration: pr. Lenina 75, ph. 551-60
Hospital: ul. Pavlova 6, ph. 662-60
Other useful information: *TNT Worldwide Express,* per. Lenina 46, ph.
693-201; *Regional Center for Trade and Commerce,* ul. Papanina 9, ph.
512-86, fax 484-00
Diplomatic Missions: *Finnish Consulate,* ul. Karla Marksa 17, ph. 576-35,
fax 560-49; *Norwegian Consulate,* ul. Pushkina 10, ph. 507-08

NABEREZHNIYE CHELNY   ① 843-9   ✦ 575

Information: 53-5095
Hotel(s): *Tatarstan,* ul. Gidrostroiteley 18a, GES district, ph. 42-1028
Restaurant(s): *Druzhba,* Moskovskiy pr., ph. 54-1847, 54-2335
Travel agent(s): *Sputnik,* Novy Gorod 2/07, ph. 53-5217, 53-7036
Aeroflot: pr. Musy Dzhalilya 2/10, ph. 42-4491
Telegraph office: pr. Druzhby Narodov, ph. 58-5710
Bank(s): Avtogradbank, ul. Pervomaiskaya 12, ph. 46-3191
City Council/Administration: ul. Khasana Tufana 23, ph. 53-9227, 53-
6643
Hospital: *Polyclinic #2,* ul. Musy Dzhalilya 19, ph. 42-1432
Other useful information: *Post Office,* ul. Gidrostroiteley, ph. 42-4174

NAKHODKA   ① OPERATOR   ✦ 4039

Information: 550-09
Hotel(s): *Vostok,* Tsentralnaya pl., ph. 65-02; *Nakhodka,* Shkolnaya ul. 3,
ph. 471-88; *Hotel Pyramid,* Vladivostokskaya ul. 2, ph. 598-94, satellite
fax 7-504-915-2207
Restaurant(s): *Nakhodka hotel, pyh. 45-307; Taidongon* (Korean), Mys
Astafeva 20, ph. 414-33; *Zaliv Amerika,* at Rybny port, corner of
Nakhodkinskiy pr. and ul. Gagarina, ph. 207-22
Intourist: Nakhodinskiy pr. 11, ph. 448-85; Other Travel agent(s):
Turburo, ul. Pogranichnaya, ph. 592-90.
Aeroflot: Morskoy vokzal, ph. 552-25
Telegraph office: per. Nizmenny, ATS-4, ph. 475-03
Bank(s): *Vneshtorgbank,* ul. Shkolnaya 19, ph. 475-55, fax 458-59
City Council/Administration: Nakhodinskiy pr. ph. 553-25
Hospital: *Polyclinic #1,* Pochtovy per. 3, ph. 552-67
Other useful information: *Casino Spartak,* Nakhodkinskiy pr., ph. 557-
59; *Sprint office,* ph. 427-10, 467-20 (Access Number: 447-72); *SeaLand
Transport,* ph. 915-1101; *DHL Office,* Nakhimovskaya ul. 30; Represen-
tative of the Ministry of Foreign Economic Relations, ul. Portovaya 4;
(City Code is 423-66 if you are in direct-dial range)
Diplomatic Missions: *North Korean Consulate,* ul. Vladivostokskaya 1, ph.
552-10; *Vietnamese Trade Mission,* ul. Gorkovo 18a, ph. 570-34, 563-09

NIZHNEVARTOVSK   ① 346-6   ✈ 1429

🕐 **Information:** 235-222
Hotel(s): *Venetsiya,* ul. Internatsionalnaya 39, ph. 220-682
Restaurant(s): in *Venetsiya* hotel, ph. 224-407
Other travel agent(s): *TurBuro,* ul. Mira 54A, ph. 224-314
Aeroflot: ul. Sportivnaya 17, ph. 237-404, 251-168
Telegraph office: ul. Lenina 16, ph. 235-230, 231-906
Bank(s): *Samotlor-Kredobank,* pr. Pobedy 18A ph. 349-76, 236-68
City Council/Administration: ul. Tayezhnaya 24, ph. 237-347, 239-776
Hospital: ul. Mira 68, ph. 234-859; *Polyclinic,* ph. 223-244
Other useful information: *Hospital #1,* ul. Neftyanikov, ph. 234-708,
    Kapital bank, ul. Medeleyeva 13, ph. 238-653

NIZHNY NOVGOROD   ① 831-2   ✈ 249

🕐 **Information:** 362-222
Hotel(s): *Tsentralnaya,* ul. Sovetskaya 12, ph. 444-270; *Rossiya,* Verkhne-
    Volzhskaya nab. 2a, ph. 391-971; *Oktyabrskaya,* Verkhne-Volzhskaya
    nab. 9a, ph. 320-670
Restaurant(s): *U Shakhovskovo,* ul. Piskunova 10, ph. 367-264; *Okhotnik,*
    ul. Belinskovo, Pushkin garden, ph. 339-324; *Russkiy Club,* ul. Markina,
    river station, ph. 313-476
Intourist: ul. Sovetskaya 12, ph. 444-692
Aeroflot: pr. Lenina 7, ph. 443-976
Telegraph office: pl. Gorkovo, Dom Svyazi, ph. 339-815
Bank(s): ul. Sverdlova 26, ph. 335-922
City Council/Administration: Kremlin, Dom Sovetov, ph. 391-506
Hospital: ul. Rodionova 190, ph. 361-723
Other useful information: *DHL Office,* Oktyabrskaya pl. 1, office 37-8,
    ph. 322-599; *Regional Center for Trade and Commerce,* ul. Lyadova 21A,
    ph. 366-358

NIZHNY TAGIL   ① 343-5   ✈ 854

🕐 **Information:** 22-3009
Hotel(s): *Tagil,* ul. Sadovaya 5, ph. 29-8219
Restaurant(s): *Severny Ural,* ul. Lenina 6, ph. 25-2265
Travel agent(s): *Sputnik,* pl. Lenina 28a, ph. 22-6800
Aeroflot: pr. Stroiteley 4, ph. 22-3723
Telegraph office: ul. Pervomaiskaya 52, ph. 25-5488
Bank(s): *Nizhnetagilskiy Uralkombank,* ul. Uralskaya 2, ph. 22-4970
City Council/Administration: ul. Lenina 1a, ph. 22-5264, 22-6813
Hospital: *Polyclinic #2,* ul. Goroshnikova 31, ph. 22-0838, 25-4265

Ⓣ **Information:** 93-011
Hotel(s): *Beresta (Marco Polo)*, Rayon 3, ph. 34-747; *Sadko*, Gagarina pr. 16, ph. 95-170, 95-174; *Rossiya*, nab. A. Nevskovo 19/1, ph. 99-385
Restaurant(s): *Kafe Posad*, ul. Bolshevikov 14, ph. 94-849
Intourist: ul. Dmitrievskaya (Velikaya) 16, ph. 74-644
Other travel agent(s): *Bureau for Travel and Excursions*, ph. 32-311, 34-612
Aeroflot: ul. Oktyabrskaya 26, ph. 74-002, 75-446, ph. 74-242 (airport)
Telegraph office: ul. Lyudogoschaya 2, ph.77-281
Bank(s): *Novgorodskiy*, ul. Mira 17, ph. 21-909
City Council/Administration: ul. B. Vlasievskaya (Chernyshevskovo) 4, ph. 72-540
Hospital: *Polyclinic #1*, ul. Plavnaya, ph. 34-163, 34-043
Other useful information: *Kremlin, Novgorod Museum of History and Architecture*, ph. 73-608, 73-691, 75-021; *Vitoslavskiy Museum of Ancient Art*, Poselok Yurievo, ph.72-062; *Representation of the Ministry of Foreign Economic Relations*, pl. Pobedy 174

NOVOKUZNETSK   ① 384-3   ✦ 1864

Ⓣ **Information:** 409-111
Hotel(s): *Novokuznetskaya*, ul. Kirova 53, 465-155; *Metallurg*, pr. Metallurgov 19, ph. 446-185
Restaurant(s): *Otel*, ul. Kirova 53, ph. 465-088
Travel agent(s): Sputnik, pr. Metallurgov 37, ph. 441-341
Aeroflot: ul. Tsiolkovskovo 57, ph. 472-935, ph. 453-501 info
Telegraph office: pr. Metallurgov 21, ph. 447-917, 18, 19
Bank(s): pr. Metallurgov 39, ph. 463-225
City Council/Administration: ul. Kirova 71, ph. 462-455
Hospital: pr. Bardina 36, ph. 440-365

NOVOSIBIRSK   ① 383-2   ✦ 1740

Ⓣ **Information:** 990-9111
Hotel(s): *Sibir*, ul. Lenina 21, ph. 237-870; *Tsentralnaya*, ul. Lenina 3, ph. 221-366; *Novosibirsk*, Vokzalnaya Magistral 1, ph. 201-120; *Soran*, ul. Ilyicha 10, ph. 356-609
Restaurant(s): *Druzhba*, ul. Lenina 3, ph. 227-244; *Sibir*, ul. Lenina 21, ph. 231-348, 231-792; *Okean*, Krasny pr. 92, ph. 251-738; *Sadko*, Krasny pr. 96, ph. 269-933
Intourist: ul. Lenina 21, ph. 237-870; **Other travel agent(s):** ul. Shamshurina 10, ph. 297-177
Aeroflot: ul. Pyatovo Goda 83, ph. 291-999
Telegraph office: ul. Sovetskaya 33, ph. 297-959
Bank(s): Krasny pr. 27, ph. 220-809
City Council/Administration: Krasny pr. 34, ph. 224-932

Hospital: ul. Zalezhskovo 6, ph. 250-719
Other useful information: *Sprint office*, ph. 298-861 (Access Number: 227-006); *DHL Office*, Krasny pr. 28 (Centre of Russia Hotel), ph. 980-203, fax 233-735; *TNT Worldwide Express*, ul. Tereshkovoy 30, ph. 356-001; *Regional Center for Trade and Commerce*, pr. Marksa 1, ph. 464-150

OMSK ☎ 381-2 ✈ 1383

Information: 990-9111
Hotel(s): *Omsk*, Irtyshskaya nab. 30, ph. 310-721; *Mayak*, ul. Lermontova 2, ph. 315-431; *Irtysh*, ul. Krasny Put 155, korpus 1, ph. 232-702
Restaurant(s): *Omsk*, Irtyshskaya nab. 30, ph. 310-731; *Mayak*, ul. Lermontova 2 (in hotel of same name)
Intourist: pr. Marksa 4, ph. 311-490
Other travel agent(s): *Turist*, ul. Gagarina 2, ph. 250-624
Aeroflot: River terminal, ph. 312-266
Telegraph office: ul. Gertsena 1, ph. 251-572
Bank(s): Bankovsky per. 1, ph. 242-195
City Council/Administration: ul Gagarina, ph. 34, ph. 243-554, 246-626
Hospital: ul. Berezova 5, ph. 235-285

ORENBURG ☎ 353-2 ✈ 761

Information: 990-9111
Hotel(s): *Fakel*, Parkovy pr. 32, ph. 471-728; *Orenburg*, ul. Vystavochnaya 30, ph. 418-185; *Ural*, ul. Kirova 32, ph. 472-919
Restaurant(s): *Orenburg*, ul. Vystavochnaya 30, ph. 410-512; *Fakel*, Parkovy pr. 32, ph. 471-701
Intourist: ul. Chkalova 16/2, ph. 416-181; Other travel agent(s): Solyanoy proyezd 22, ph. 473-130
Aeroflot: ul. Turkestanskaya 9, ph. 411-555
Telegraph office: ul. Kirova 16, ph. 478-165
Bank(s): ul. Devyatovo Yanvarya 48, ph. 473-150
City Council/Administration: ul. Sovetskaya 60, ph. 475-055
Hospital: ul. Aksakova 23, ph. 414-722

ORYOL ☎ 086-00 ✈ 202

Information: 62-523
Hotel(s): *Oryol*, ul. Pushkina 5, ph. 50-589; *Rossiya*, ul. Gorkovo 37, ph. 74-550
Restaurant(s): *Orlik*, ul. Komsomolskaya 228, ph. 23-152; *Oka*, ul. Lenina 16, ph. 65-701
Intourist: ul. Gorkovo 39, ph. 65-909, 31-520; Other travel agent(s): *Travel Bureau*, ul. Lenina 36, ph. 65-038; *Sputnik*, ul. Saltykova-Schedrina 19/21, ph. 65-532, 63-634, 65-635
Aeroflot: ul. Moskovskaya 14, ph. 53-412
Telegraph office: ul. Lenina 43, ph. 63-934

Bank(s): *Sotef,* ul. Gurtyeva 2, ph. 95-060, 93-923, fax 9-57-71
City Council/Administration: Proletarskaya Gorka, ph. 62-212
Hospital: Bulvar Pobedy 30, ph. 93-852
Other useful information: *State Literature Museum named for I. S. Turgeneva,*
ul. Turgeneva 11, ph. 65-500, 65-574; *Orlov Museum of Local Culture,*
ul. Moskovskaya 1/3, ph. 56-791, 56-793; *Orlov Oblast Art Gallery,* ul.
Saltykova-Schedrina 33, ph. 60-587, 63-870

PENZA   ① 841-2   ✈ 342

Information: 664-895
Hotel(s): *Penza,* ul. Slavy 10, ph. 668-209; *Lastochka,* ul. Mira 35, ph. 634-396
Restaurant(s): *Penza,* ul. Slavy 10; *Lastochka,* ul. Mira 35, ph. 637-350
Intourist: ul. Karla Marksa 26, ph. 665-118; Other travel agent(s): ul.
Lermontova 34, ph. 666-203
Aeroflot: ul. Bakunina 30, ph. 663-762
Telegraph office: Teatralny proyezd 5, ph. 550-250
Bank(s): ul. Uritskovo 127, ph. 553-245
City Council/Administration: pl. Tsentralnaya 4, ph. 631-463
Hospital: ul. Lermontova 28, ph. 664-820

PERM   ① 342-2   ✈ 700

Information: 990-9111 or 333-420
Hotel(s): *Ural,* ul. Lenina 58, ph. 344-417; *Turist,* ul. Ordzhonikidze 43,
ph. 342-494; *Prikamiye,* Komsomolsky pr. 27, ph. 348-662, 349-428
Restaurant(s): *Yevropeisky,* ul. Lenina 72B, ph. 338-716
Intourist: ul. Popova 9, ph. 333-843; Other travel agent(s): ul. Gorkovo
14A, ph. 325-028, 327-757
Aeroflot: ul. Krisanova 19, ph. 334-668; 333-547
Telegraph office: ul. Dvadtsat Pyatovo Oktyabrya 9, ph. 328-418
Bank(s): *Permkombank,* bul. Gagarina 65, 483-357, 481-622
City Council/Administration: ul. Lenina 23, ph. 324-084
Hospital: ul. Sovetskoy Armii 17, ph. 272-593
Other useful information: *Sovam Teleport office,* ph. 391-500 (Acces no.:
391-259); *Sprint office,* ph. 488-341 (Access Number: 659-636); *Regional Center for Trade and Commerce,* ul. Lenina 56A, ph. 333-170, fax
338-971; *Sota Store,* ul. Popova 25, ph. 343-630 (cash advances)

PETROPAVLOVSK-KAMCHATSKIY   ① 415-00   ✈ 4288

Information: 91-909
Hotel(s): *Petropavlovsk,* pr. Karla Marksa, ph. 50-374, 50-911; *Avacha,* ul.
Leningradskaya 61, ph. 27-333
Restaurant(s): *Geyzer,* ul. Toporkova 10, ph. 56-393
Intourist: PO box (a/ya) #272, ph. 23-200, 28-442; Other travel agent(s):
Bureau for Tourism, ul. Partizanskaya 15, ph. 28-303, 24-606

Aeroflot: pr. Karla Marksa 31, ph. 54-950
Telegraph office: Post office, ul. Sovetskaya 65, ph. 24-800, 23-003
Bank(s): *Kamchatbiznesbank*, ul. Leninskaya 24, ph. 21-917, fax 22-482
City Council/Administration: ul. Sovetskaya 22, ph. 21-000
Hospital: *Polyclinic #3*, ul. Sovetskaya 32, ph. 55-381
Other useful information: *Tourist Center Taratunka*, ul. Tushkanova 3;
  Oblast Museum for Local Culture, ul. Leninskaya 20, ph. 22-244, 25-411,
  25-690; *Representation of Ministry of Foreign Economic Relations*, ul.
  Sovetskaya 22; *Polyclinic #5*, ul. Leningradskaya 114, ph. 23-745

PETROZAVODSK   ☎ 814-00   ✦ 435

Information: 51-201
Hotel(s): *Severnaya*, pr. Lenina 21, ph. 76-354; *Karelia*, nab. Gyullinga 2,
  ph.58-897, 52-306
Restaurant(s): *Severnaya*, in hotel of same name, ph. 73-491; *Petrovskiy*,
  ul. Andropova 1, ph. 70-992
Intourist: ul. Lenina 21, ph. 71-903, 76-306; **Other travel agent(s):**
  Sputnik, ul. Engelsa 5, ph. 75-861, 71-281, fax 76-470; *Council for
  Tourism and Excursions*, nab. Gyullinga 2, ph. 73-891
Aeroflot: ul. Antikainena 20, ph. 74-486, 74-566
Telegraph office: ul. Maksima Gorkovo 4, ph. 72-091
Bank(s): *Tekobank*, ul.Sovetskaya 22, ph. 49-352, 47-393
City Council/Administration: pr. Lenina 2, ph. 74-941
Hospital: *Republic Hospital*, ul. Pirogova 3, ph. 74-035
Other useful information: *Graphic Arts Museum*, pr. K. Marksa 8; *Museum
  of Local Culture*, ul. Uritskovo 22; *Rep. of the Ministry of Foreign Economic
  Relations*, pr. Lenina 19, room 17; *Ben & Jerry's Ice Cream Shop*, Pioneer
  Palace; *Sovam Teleport office*, ph. 51-189 (Access number: 72-071)

PSKOV   ☎ 811-22   ✦ 373

Information: 22-145
Hotel(s): *Oktyabrskaya*, Oktyabrskiy pr. 36, ph. 25-593; *Rizhskaya*,
  Rizhskoye shosse 2-6, ph. 33-243
Restaurant(s): *Kavkaz*, Oktyabrskiy pr. 10, ph. 24-637; *Pskov*, ul. Yana
  Fabritsiusa 5a, ph. 28-758
Intourist: pr. Rizhski 25, Hotel *Rizhskaya*, k. 214, ph. 62-254; **Other
  travel agent(s):** *Sputnik*, Oktyabrskiy pr. 36, Hotel *Oktyabrskaya*, room
  201, ph. 38-581, 22-119, 25-423, fax 38-581
Aeroflot: Rizhskiy pr. 29, ph. 26-262, 22-215
Telegraph office: ul. Nekrasova 17, ph. 25-454
Bank(s): *Pskovbank*, pr. Oktyabrskiy 8, ph. 23-670, 23-680
City Council/Administration: ul. Nekrasova 22, ph. 22-666
Hospital: *Polyclinic #1*, ul. N. Ostrovskovo 19, ph. 25-357, 25-352
Other useful information: *Pskov State Museum for History, Architecture and
  Art*, ul. Nekrasova 7, ph. 22-518, 23-568; *Mirozhskiy Monastyr*, ph. 33-

ncil/Administration: ul. Sovetskaya 26, ph. 92-22-57
Polyclinic #4, ul. Dogomyskaya 42, ph. 91-41-40, 91-41-75
ful information: *Museum of the Tourist City Sochi,* ul. Ordzhon-
9, ph.92-31-57

① 865-22   ✈ 760

: 25-252
el Complex Intourist, ph. 37-755, 37-510;
: *Intourist* (in hotel of same name), ph. 59-196; *Kavkaz,* ul.
16, ph. 42-520
yleeva 5, ph. 24-525, 35-218; **Other travel agent(s):** *Travel*
Dobrolyubova 18, ph. 32-075, fax 37-413; *Sputnik,* pr.
h. 30-749, 26-439, 29-841
ootekhnicheskiy 13, ph. 45-926, 55-545, 230-50
e: ph. 30-587, 30-608
lpromstroibank, ul. Pushkina 4A, ph. 27-730, fax 27-230
ministration: pr. Karla Marksa 94, ph. 30-310
l Hospital, ul. Semashko 1, ph. 97-231
rmation: *Graphic Arts Museum,* ul. Dzerzhinskovo 115,
5; *Regional Center for Trade and Commerce,* ul. Lenina
), ph. 60-756

① 821-22   ✈ 621

Kommunisticheskaya 67, ph. 301-43; *Tsentralnaya,*
3, ph. 242-80
(restaurant, bar, casino), ul. Gorkovo 2, ph. 223-
ul. Kommunisticheskaya 67; *Tsentralny* (hotel),

8, ph. 201-24, 211-65
86, ph. 222-22
ina 60, ph. 211-50
h. 215-48
ion: ul. Babushkina 22, ph. 210-04
heskaya 41, ph. 358-37
rian Consulate, ul. Babushkina 10, ph. 235-

① 075-22   ✈ 249

2, ph. 222-013, 210-100; *Tambov,* ul.
227-502
ternatsionalnaya 14, ph. 227-106; *Tolna*
, ph. 210-140, 210-141

340; *Representation of the Ministry of Foreign Economic Relations,* ul. Kommunalnaya 54a, room 742

ROSTOV   ① 085-36   ✈ 109

Information: 370-80
Hotel(s): *Intourist,* ul. Engelsa 115, ph. 659-066; *Rostov,* ph. 391-818; *Moskovskaya,* ul. Engelsa 62, ph. 388-700; *Mezhdunarodny Molodyozhny Tsentr,* Rostov Kremlin, ph. 318-54
Restaurant(s): *Pogrebok Alyoshi Popovicha,* Kremlin, ph. 318-54
Intourist: Kremlin, ph. 312-44; **Other travel agent(s):** ul. Okruzhnaya 64, ph. 319-47
Aeroflot: ul. Karla Marksa 17, ph. 317-43
Telegraph office: ul. Severnaya 44/2A, ph. 325-78
Bank(s): ul. B. Sadovaya 188, ph. 536-918
City Council/Administration: Sovetskaya pl. 7, ph. 322-29
Hospital: ul. Leninskaya 37, ph. 336-36

ROSTOV-ON-DON   ① 863-2   ✈ 590

Information: 326-609
Hotel(s): *Intourist,* Bolshaya Sadovaya 115, ph. 659-065; *Rostov,* Budyonnovskiy pr. 53, ph. 391-670; *Turist,* pr. Oktyabrya 19, ph. 325-427; *Petrovskiy Prichal,* left bank of the Don, ph. 631-354; *Yakor,* ul. Beregovaya 10, ph. 620-158
Restaurant(s): *Intourist,* B. Sadovaya 115, ph. 659-080; *Rostov,* 321-202; *Kazachiy Khutor,* left bank of the Don, ph. 631-822
Intourist: B. Sadovaya 15, ph. 655-049; **Other travel agent(s):** Voroshilovskiy pr. 66, ph. 329-315
Aeroflot: Sotsialisticheskaya ul. 144-146, ph. 659-112
Telegraph office: ul. Serafimovicha 62, ph. 662-584
Bank(s): B. Sadovaya 70, ph. 666-777; pr. Sholokhova 43, ph. 539-656; pr. Semash 102, ph. 544-788
City Council/Administration: Bolshaya Sadovaya 47, ph. 666-263
Hospital: ul. Pushkinskaya 133, ph. 662-231
Other useful information: *Sprint office,* ph. 696-911 (Access Number: 344-722); *TNT Worldwide Express,* ph. 522-831

RYAZAN   ① 091-2   ✈ 110

Information: 726-920
Hotel(s): *Lovich,* pl. Dimitrova 4, ph. 726-920; *Priokskaya,* ul. Kalyaeva 13E, ph. 771-257
Restaurant(s): *Lovich,* pl. Dimitrova 4, ph. 726-935
Travel agent(s): *Sputnik,* ul. Lenina 35, ph. 773-925; pl. Dimitrova 4, office 223, ph. 726-309
Aeroflot: ul. Dzerzhinskovo 69, ph. 764-110
Telegraph office: ul. Svobody 36, ph. 411-341

Bank(s): ul. Griboyedova 24/5, ph. 444-720; ul. Podbelskovo 43, ph. 772-328
City Council/Administration: ul. Podbelskovo 64, ph. 774-882
Hospital: ul. Internatsionalnaya 3A, ph. 534-608
Other useful information: *International Communications Center*, ul. Lenina 35, ph. 772-590

SAMARA ① 846-2 ✈ 528

Information: 334-583
Hotel(s): *Rossiya*, ul. Maksima Gorkovo 82, ph. 390-311; *Volga*, Volzhskiy pr. 29, ph. 338-796; *Oktyabrskaya*, ul. Avrory 209, ph. 222-985
Restaurant(s): *Parus*, ul. Krasnoarmeyskaya 1A, ph. 324-768; *Tsentralny*, ul. Frunze 91, ph. 330-744
Intourist: ul. Kuybysheva 109, ph. 333-411; Other travel agent(s): ul. Kuybysheva 44, ph. 325-728, 332-778
Aeroflot: ul. Molodogvardeyskaya 223, ph. 338-105
Telegraph office: ul. Krasnoarmeiskaya 17, ph. 333-760
Bank(s): ul. Kuybysheva 112, ph. 320-325
City Council/Administration: ul. Kuybysheva 135, ph. 323-044
Hospital: ul. Karla Marksa 165, ph. 663-814
Other useful information: *Sprint office*, ph. 330-021 (Access Number: 332-690); *Regional Center for Trade and Commerce*, ul. A. Tolstovo, ph. 331-159, fax 327-662

SARANSK ① 834-22 ✈ 311

Information: 42-222
Hotel(s): *Saransk*, ul. Kommunisticheskaya 35, ph. 17-8882; *Tsentralnaya*, ul. Sovetskaya 49, ph. 40-671
Restaurant(s): *Saransk*, in the hotel of same name, ph. 17-8846; *Natsionalniy*, ul. Sovetskaya 47, ph. 17-5438
Travel agent(s): *Sputnik*, ul. Razina 42, ph. 42-513, 46-779, 48-587
Aeroflot: ul. Razina 42, ph. 44-655, 76-223
Telegraph office: ul. Bolshevitskaya 31, ph. 17-3026
Bank(s): *Mordovskiy Finist-bank*, ul. Sovetskaya 35, ph. 17-6394
City Council/Administration: ul. Sovetskaya 30, ph. 17-6836
Hospital: *Hospital #3*, ul. Kommunisticheskaya 86, ph. 17-6493
Other useful information: *Mordovskiy Museum of Local Culture*, ul. Moskovskaya 48; *Graphic Arts Museum*, ul. Sovetskaya 29; *Representation of the Ministry of Foreign Economic Relations*, ul. Sovetskaya 26, Dom Sovetov, room 501

SARATOV

Information: 245-300
Hotel(s): *Slovakia*, ul. Lermc Chernyshevskovo 57, ph. 2'
Restaurant(s): *Slovakia*, ul. L(
Travel agent(s): *Sputnik*, Ner 166B, ph. 242-445
Aeroflot: per. Mirny 17, r
Telegraph office: ul. Per
Bank(s): ul. Sovetskaya ʃ
City Council/Administ'
Hospital: ul. Lizunovɘ
Other useful informɑ 640-498; *Regional* ph. 911-757, fax

SMOLENSK

Information: 5'
Hotel(s): *Rossi* Lenina 2/' 397
Restaurant/ 7, ph. (
Intourist *Sputn*
Aerofl
Teleg
Bank
City (
H (
SO
(

STAVROPOL
Informatio
Hotel(s): *H*
Restaurant(s
Sovetskaya
Intourist: ul. *Bureau*, ul. Marksa 76,
Aeroflot: per. Telegraph offic
Bank(s): *Stavrop*
City Council/*
Hospital: *Regiona*
Other useful info ph. 30-052, 30-0 (in Dom Sovetov

SYKTYVKAR
Information: 236-09
Hotel(s): *Syktyvkar*, ul. ul. Pervomayskaya
Restaurant(s): *Fortuna* 96, 281-26; *Syktyvkar*, ul. Pervomaiskaya 8
Intourist: ul. Pushkina 8
Aeroflot: ul. Sovetskaya Telegraph office: ul. Le
Bank(s): ul. Lenina 45, r
City Council/Administra
Hospital: ul. Kommunisti
Diplomatic Missions: *Bulg*
44, 211-10

TAMBOV
Information: 224-474
Hotel(s): *Tolna*, pl. Tolstovc Maksima Gorkovo 2/90, pl
Restaurant(s): *Tsentralny*, ul. In (in the hotel of same name)

Russian City Guide

Intourist: pl. Tolstovo 2, ph. 10-105; **Other travel agent(s):** *Sputnik*, ul. Internatsionalnaya 30G, ph. 222-017, 226-691, 223-774, fax 222-017
Aeroflot: ul. Kooperativnaya 10, ph. 28-636, 70-770
Telegraph office: *Post office,* ul. Oktyabrskaya 1, ph. 222-400, 220-440
Bank(s): *Tambovkreditprombank,* ul.Sovetskaya 118, ph. 220-508, fax 222-664
City Council/Administration: ul. Sovetskaya 106, ph. 223-300
Hospital: *Regional Hospital,* ul. Moskovskaya 29, ph. 222-606
Other useful information: *Tambov Travel Bureau,* ul. Internatsionalnaya 29, ph.25-054, 25-680; *Art Gallery,* ul. Sovetskaya 59, ph.25-679; *Tambov Museum of Local Culture,* pl. Oktyabrskaya 11, ph. 26-313, 27-072

TOLYATTI ② OPERATOR ✈ 513

Information: 8-15
Hotel(s): *Zhiguli,* ul. Mira, ph. 222-643
Restaurant(s): *Zhiguli,* in the hotel of same name, ph. 296-245
Intourist: ul. Zhilina 24, ph. 235-292; **Other travel agent(s):** *Sputnik,* ul. K. Marksa 38, ph. 260-026, 260-126, 224-549, 222-301, 269-361
Aeroflot: Bulvar Lenina, ph.284-215
Telegraph office: *Post office of Central region,* ul. Mira, ph. 232-058
Bank(s): *Avtovazbank,* ul. Voroshilova 33, ph. 303-518, 263-395, 245-201
City Council/Administration: pl. Svobody, ph. 261-444
Hospital: ul. Banykina, ph. 280-222
Other useful information: *DHL Office,* ul. Karla Marksa 46, ph. 234-354, 225-473

TOMSK ② 382-2 ✈ 1771

Information: 223-894
Hotel(s): *Rubin,* pr. Akademicheskiy 16, ph. 259-689; *Oktyabrskaya,* ul. Karla Marksa 12, ph. 222-151
Restaurant(s): *Rubin Hotel,* 259-177; *Beryozka* (bar), ul. Krasnoarmeyskaya 122, ph. 444-414
Intourist: ul. Belinskovo 15, ph. 232-537, fax 232-447
Aeroflot: ul. Nakhimova 13, ph. 441-466
Telegraph office: ul. Lenina 93, ph. 223-715
Bank(s): ul. Belinskovo 54, ph. 445-570
City Council/Administration: pr. Lenina 73, ph. 233-450
Hospital: *Medical University Hospital,* pr. Lenina 38, ph. 230-581, 234-316

TULA   ② 087-2   ✦ 109

⏱ **Information:** 258-403
Hotel(s): *Moskva,* pl. Moskovskovo vokzala, ph. 208-952
Restaurant(s): *Moskva,* pl. Moskovskovo vokzala, ph. 208-963; *Druzhba,*
  pr. Lenina 78, ph. 256-407
Intourist: ul. Sovetskaya 52, ph. 272-766, 272-774
Aeroflot: Krasnoarmeyskiy pr. 9, ph. 205-457
Telegraph office: pr. Lenina 22, ph. 314-978
Bank(s): ul. Sovetskaya 88, ph. 313-089
City Council/Administration: pl. Lenina 2, ph. 278-085
Hospital: ul. Pervomayskaya 13, ph. 318-540

TVER   ② 082-22   ✦ 93

⏱ **Information:** 37-474
Hotel(s): *Motel Tver,* Sankt-Peterburgskoye sh. 130, ph. 556-92; *Volga,*
  ul. Zhelyabova 1, ph. 381-00
Restaurant(s): *Tsentralny,* Novotorzhskaya ul. 3/8, ph. 361-50; 380-82;
  Motel Tver, Sankt-Peterburgskoye sh. 130, ph. 549-49, 596-98
Intourist: Sankt-Peterburgskoye shosse 130, ph. 557-68
Aeroflot: pr. Chaykovskovo 17, ph. 277-16
Telegraph office: ul. Novotorzhskaya 23/35, ph. 343-32
Bank(s): ul. Volodarskovo 34, ph. 27-217
City Council/Administration: ul. Sovetskaya 11, ph. 301-31
Hospital: Sankt-Peterburgskoye shosse 103, ph. 558-78

TYUMEN   ② 345-22   ✦ 1041

⏱ **Information:** 252-096
Hotel(s): *Tourist,* ul. Respubliki 156, ph. 73-573; *Prometei,* ul. Sovetskaya
  20, ph. 251-423
Restaurant(s): *Prometei,* ul. Sovetskaya 20, ph. 250-027
Intourist: ul. Gertsena 74, ph. 250-810, 242-371; **Other travel agent(s):**
  Sodruzhestvo, ul. Geologorazvedchikov 2, ph. 228-777, fax/ph. 226-
  250; *Sputnik,* ul. Respubliki 19, ph. 240-713
Aeroflot: ul. Respubliki 156. ph. 23-252, 62-946, 33-503
Telegraph office: ul. Respubliki 12, ph. 261-398
Bank(s): *Tyumenprofbank,* ul. Khokhryakova 50, ph. 246-780
City Council/Administration: ul. Pervomaiskaya 20, ph. 246-526
Hospital: *Regional Hospital,* ul. Kotovskovo 53, ph. 226-258
Other useful information: *Museum for Local Culture,* ul. Respubliki 4,
  ph. 61-159, 68-071

UFA ☾ 347-2 ✚ 715

Information: 225-720
Hotel(s): *Bashkiria*, ul. Lenina 25/26, ph. 223-347; *Rossiya*, pr. Oktyabrya
81, ph. 343-181
Restaurant(s): *Sakmar* (restaurant & casino), ul. Pervomayskaya 46, ph.
421-412
Intourist: ul. Lenina 25, ph. 231-204
Aeroflot: ul. K. Marksa 26, ph. 233-656
Telegraph office: ul. Chernyshevskovo 6, ph. 236-287
Bank(s): ul. Tsuryupy 5, 236-426
City Council/Administration: pr. Oktyabrya 120, ph. 312-816
Hospital: Lesnoy proyezd 3, ph. 325-279
Other useful information: *Central Post Office*, ul. Lenina 28, ph. 232-612;
Sovam Teleport office, ph. 224-927 (Access number: 284-296)

ULAN-UDE ☾ 301-22 ✚ 2719

Information: 990-9111
Hotel(s): *Barbuzin*, ul. Sovetskaya 28, ph. 21-958, 20-809
Restaurant(s): *Barbuzin* (in the hotel of same name), ph. 26-823
Intourist: ul. Ranzhurova 12, ph. 29-267, teletype 219268
Other travel agent(s): *Council for Tourism*, ul. Sovetskaya 28, ph. 22-411,
21-958; *Sputnik*, pr. Pobedy 9, ph. 20-834, 21-862, 23-991
Aeroflot: ul. Yerbanova 14, ph. 22-248, 32-110
Telegraph office: *Main Post Office*, ul. Lenina 61, ph. 23-520, 22-703
Bank(s): Mosbiznesbank, ul. Lenina 28, ph. 25-401
City Council/Administration: ul. Lenina 54, ph. 25-323, 26-902
Hospital: *Urgent Medical Aid*, 45th kvartal, Oktyabrskiy rayon, ph. 71-
555, 70-544
Other useful information: *Museum of Eastern Art*, ul. Profsoyuznaya 29,
ph.22-170; *Ethnographic Museum of Baikal Peoples*, ul. Kuibysheva 29

ULYANOVSK ☾ 842-2 ✚ 435

Information: 322-222
Hotel(s): *Venets*, ul. Sovetskaya 19, ph. 394-880, 70; *Oktyabrskaya*, ul.
Plekhanova 1, ph. 314-282
Restaurant(s): *Venets*, ul. Sovetskaya 19, ph. 394-897
Intourist: ul. Sovetskaya 19, ph. 319-735
Aeroflot: ul. K. Libknekhta 28A, ph. 314-442
Telegraph office: ul. Lva Tolstovo 60, ph. 312-072
Bank(s): ul. Goncharova 26, ph. 325-254
City Council/Administration: ul. Kuznetsova 7, ph. 313-080
Hospital: ul. Orenburgskaya 3, ph. 251-611

⏰ **Information:** 32-222

Hotel(s): *Zolotoye Koltso*, ul. Chaikovskaya 27, ph. 48-807, 48-819; *Klyazma*, ul. Sudokhodskoye shosse 15, ph. 24-483; *Zarya*, ul. Pushkina, ph. 91-441; *Vladimir*, ul. Tretyevo Internatsionala 74, ph. 23-042

Restaurant(s): *Zolotoye Koltso*, ph. 47-853; *Vladimir*, ul. Tretyevo Internatsionala 74, ph. 24-741; *Lada*, ul. pr. Lenina 23, ph. 23-274

Intourist: ul. Tretyevo Internatsionala 74, ph. 24-262, 27-514; **Other travel agent(s):** *Bureau for Travel and Excursions*, ul. Kremlevskaya 5A, ph. 26-414, 22-322, fax 22-428

Aeroflot: pr. Lenina 7, ph. 43-716, 24-736

Telegraph office: ul. Gorokhovaya 20, ph. 31-859

Bank(s): *Menatep*, ul. Tretyevo Internatsionala 49, ph. 24-138

City Council/Administration: ul. Gorkovo, ph. 32-817

Hospital: *Regional Polyclinic*, Sudogodskoye shosse 41, ph. 29508, 26179

Other useful information: *Museum of Crystal and Lacquer Miniatures*, ul. Moskovskaya, ph. 24-872; *Vladimir-Suzdal Museum of History, Architecture and Art*, ul. Tr. Internatsionala 43, ph. 22-515; *Representation of the Ministry of Foreign Economic Relations*, Oktyabrskiy pr. 21, room 419

⏰ **Information:** 250-269

Hotel(s): *Hotel Versailles*, Svetlanskaya 10, ph. 264-201; *Hotel Acfes Seiyo*, pr. 100-letiya Vladivostoka 103, ph. 318-760; *Vladivostok*, ul. Naberezhnaya 10, ph. 222-208, 222-246; *Ekvator*, ul. Naberezhnaya 20, ph. 212-260; *Amurskiy Zaliv*, ul. Naberezhnaya 9, ph. 225-520; *Vlad Motor Inn*, kilometer 19 (on way to airport), 215-829, satellite fax, 7-509-851-5116

Restaurant(s): *Vladivostok-Sakura* (Japanese, in Hotel Vladivostok), ul. Naberezhnaya 10, ph. 260-305; *Nagasaki*, ul. Svetlanskaya 115, ph. 265-043; *Ekvator*, ul. Naberezhnaya 20, ph. 212-873

Intourist: Okeanskiy pr. 90, ph. 256-210, fax 258-839

Aeroflot: ul. Posietskaya 14, ph. 260-880

Telegraph office: Okeanskiy pr. 24/2, ph. 222-806

Bank(s): *ATR-Credobank*, ul. Aleutskaya 16, ph. 222-264; ul. Svetlanskaya 71, ph. 228-791; *Dalnevostochny*, Okeanskiy pr. 19, ph. 228-005

City Council/Administration: Okeanskiy pr. 20, ph. 224-229, 223-800

Hospital: ul. 25 Oktyabrya 57, ph. 257-553; *Health Asia Clinic*, contact via Vlad Motor Inn (see above), ph. 215-829

Other useful information: *US Peace Corps*, c/o Institute for Marine Biology, ul. Palkevskiy 17, ph. 228-271; *Regional Chamber of Commerce and Trade*, Okeansky pr. 13A, ph. 684-23; *Sovam Teleport*, ul. Krasnovo Znameni 10, ph. 252-598 (Access number: 254-643); *DHL Office*, Khabarovskaya ul. 27, ph. 255-252, ph./fax 255-226; *TNT Worldwide Express*, ul.

Uborevicha 24/1, ph. 224-552, 237-087. *Alaska Airlines* (at airport), ph. 227-645

Diplomatic Missions: *US Consulate* (and Business Center), ul. Mordovtseva 12, ph. 268-458, fax 268-445, ph. tlx 213206; *Indian Consulate,* Hotel Vladivostok, room 7002, ph. 229-669, 228-536, 228-110; *South Korean Consulate,* ul. Aleutovskaya 45, 5th floor, ph. 227-729, 227-765, fax 229-9471; *Australian Consulate,* ul. Uborevicha 17, ph. 228-628; *Japanese Consulate,* ul. Mordovtseva 12

VOLGOGRAD ① 844-2 ✦ 559

Information: 330-301

Hotel(s): *Intourist,* ul. Mira 14, ph. 364-553; *Volgograd,* ul. Mira 12, ph. 361-772; *Oktyabrskaya,* ul. Kommunisticheskaya 5A, ph. 338-120

Restaurant(s): *Volgograd,* ph. 336-324 (in hotel of same name); *Intourist,* 361-117 (in hotel of same name); *Ostrava,* ul. Krasnoznamenskaya 25, ph. 339-561; *Drakon* (Chinese), pr. Lenina 10, ph. 367-746

Intourist: ul. Mira 14, ph. 361-468, 364-552, 337-512; **Other travel agent(s):** *Sputnik,* ul. Chuykova 65, ph. 347-242

Aeroflot: Alleya Geroyev 5, ph. 335-305

Telegraph office: ul. Mira 9, ph. 336-743, 336-152

Bank(s): ul. Mira 12, ph. 335-598

City Council/Administration: ul. Volodarskovo 5, ph. 335-010

Hospital: ul. Zemlyachki 74, ph. 351-782

VOLOGDA ① 817-22 ✦ 249

Information: 22-222

Hotel(s): *Oktyabrskaya,* ul. Oktyabrskaya 25, ph. 20-145

Restaurant(s): *Oktyabrskiy,* ul. Oktyabrskaya 25, ph. 63-138

Intourist: ul. Klary Tsetkin 26, ph. 24-281, 26-063; **Other travel agent(s):** *Travel Bureau,* Kremlevskaya pl. 8, ph. 26-090, 24-389

Aeroflot: ul. Gertsena 45, ph. 23-302, 90-799

Telegraph office: ul. Pushkinskaya 16, ph. 20-620, 20-622, 22-340

Bank(s): *Skombank,* ul. Kremlyovskaya pl. 12, ph. 22-557, 22-025

City Council/Administration: ul. Kamenny Most 4, ph. 20-042

Hospital: *Polyclinic #3,* ul. Blagoveschenskaya 39, ph. 23-705

Other useful information: *Oblast Museum of Local Culture,* ul. S. Orlova 15; *House-Museum of Peter I,* pr. Sovetskiy 47; *Representative of the Ministry of Foreign Economic Relations,* ul. Uritskovo 6, room 319

VORONEZH ① 073-2 ✦ 280

Information: 522-222

Hotel(s): *Brno,* ul. Plekhanovskaya 9, ph. 509-247; *Tsentralnaya,* pr. Revolutsii 43, ph. 550-418; *Rossiya,* Teatralnaya ul. 23, ph. 555-898

Restaurant(s): In hotels of same name: *Brno,* 553-453; *Rossiya,* 565-037; *Tsentralny,* 554-631

Intourist: ul. 9 Yanvarya 12, ph. 553-746; Other travel agent(s): ul. Plekhanovskaya 2, ph. 556-884
Aeroflot: ul. Plekhanovskaya 22a, ph. 526-470
Telegraph office: pr. Revolutsii 35, ph. 553-790
Bank(s): ul. Ordzhonikidze 25, ph. 555-374
City Council/Administration: ul. Plekhanovskaya 10, ph. 550-427
Hospital: pr. Patriotov 23, ph. 336-960
Other useful information: *Regional Center for Trade and Commerce*, ul. Plekhanovskaya 53, ph. 521-374, fax 522-995

VYATKA ☎ 833-2 ✦ 482

Ⓨ Information: 622-222
Hotel(s): *Administratsii Oblasti*, ul. Gertsena 49, ph. 69-1018; *Vyatka*, Oktyabrskiy pr. 145, ph. 64-8396
Restaurant(s): *Vyatka* (in the hotel Vyatka); *Rossiya*, ul. Moskovskaya 5, ph. 62-7827
Intourist: ul. Volodarskovo 127, ph. 90-949; Other travel agent(s): *Lyukon*, ul. R. Lyuksemburg 30, ph. 24-134; *Tourist Council*, ul. K. Marksa 79, ph. 25-748, 22-538
Aeroflot: ul. Gorkovo 56, ph. 44-472, 25-287
Telegraph office: *Post office*, ul. Drelevskovo 39, ph. 62-5565
Bank(s): *Mezhkombank*, ul. Komsomolskaya 43, ph. 45-232, 41-911
City Council/Administration: *Meriya*, ul. Vorovskovo 39, ph. 62-8940
Hospital: *Polyclinic*, ul. K. Marksa, ph. 69-2375, 62-1558
Other useful information: *United Historical Archive and Literary Museum*, ul. Lenina 82, ph. 23-738, 27-896; *Rep. of the Ministry of Foreign Economic Relations*, ul. K. Libknekhta 69, Oblispolkom, room 69

VYBORG ☎ 812-78 ✦ 466

Ⓘ Information: 225-02
Hotel(s): *Druzhba*, ul. Zheleznodorozhnaya 5, ph. 257-44; Vyborg, Leningradskiy pr. 19, ph. 223-83
Restaurant(s): *Druzhba*, ph. 944-64 (in hotel of same name); *Kruglaya Bashnya*, Rynochnaya pl. 678-38; *Sever*, pr. Lenina, ph. 201-13
Intourist: (in Druzhba hotel), ph. 247-60
Telegraph office: Moskovskiy pr. 26, ph. 225-40
Bank(s): ul. Zheleznodorozhnaya 5 (in Druzhba hotel), ph. 943-51
City Council/Administration: ul. Sovetskaya 12, ph. 221-75
Hospital: ul. Onezhskaya 8, ph. 223-75

YAKUTSK ☎ 411-22 ✦ 3075

Ⓘ Information: 22-141
Hotel(s): *Lainer*, ul. Bykovskovo 1, ph. 52-227; *Lena*, pr. Lenina 8, ph. 44-890; *Yakutzoloto*, pr. Lenina 11, ph. 24-351

Restaurant(s): *Volna,* pr. Lenina 1, ph. 28-628; *Kristal,* ul. Kirova 15, ph. 21-239; *Kytylyk,* ul. Ammosova 16, ph. 43-590

Intourist: ul. Oktyabrskaya 20/1, ph. 54-090, 53-820; **Other travel agent(s):** *Sputnik,* pr. Lenina 30, ph. 23-731, 23-741, ph./fax 23-737; *Turburo,* ul. Lomonosova 25, ph. 23-104, 24-921

Aeroflot: ul. Ordzhonikidze 8, ph. 20-203, 22-460

Telegraph office: pl. Ordzhonikidze, ph. 23-847, 20-352

Bank(s): *Aeroflotbank,* ul. Ordzhonikidze 10, ph. 42-756, 41-344

City Council/Administration: pr. Lenina 28, ph. 23-092

Hospital: *Healing Center* (Lechebny Tsentr), ph. 68-982 (in suburbs)

Other useful information: *Yakutsk State Museum of History and Culture of the Northern Peoples,* pr. Lenina 5/2, ph. 34-734; *Regional Center for Trade and Commerce,* ul. Kirova 15, ph. 203-82

YAROSLAVL   ① 085-2   ✈ 155

Information: 225-766

Hotel(s): *Yubileynaya,* Kotoroslennaya nab. 11A, ph. 224-159; *Yaroslavl,* ul. Ushinskovo 40/2, ph. 221-275; *Kotorosl,* ul. B. Oktyabrskaya 87, ph. 212-415

Restaurant(s): *Kotorosl,* 211-536 (in hotel of same name); *Medved,* ul. Svobody 40/2, ph. 223-638

Intourist: Kotoroslennaya nab. 11A, office 230A, ph. 221-613, 229-306

Aeroflot: ul. Svobody 20, ph. 222-420

Telegraph office: ul. Pobedy 36, ph. 253-584

Bank(s): ul. Sverdlova 34, ph. 220-216

City Council/Administration: Sovetskaya pl. 3, ph. 220-212

Hospital: ul. Zagorodny Sad 11, ph. 231-993

YEKATERINBURG   ① 343-2   ✈ 870

Information: 990-9111

Hotel(s): *Yubileynaya,* pr. Lenina 40, ph. 578-028; *Oktyabrskaya,* ul. Sofii Kovalevskoy 17, ph. 445-146; *Sverdlovsk,* ul. Chelyuskintsev 106, ph. 536-261

Restaurant(s): *Okean,* pr. Lenina 40, ph. 578-042; *Kharbin* (Chinese), ul. Kuybysheva 38, ph. 226-325; *Kosmos* (with casino), ul. Dzerzhinskovo 2, ph. 516-455; *Sverdlovsk,* ul. Chelyuskintsev 106, ph. 536-461; *Staraya Krepost,* ul. Chelyuskintsev 102, ph. 536-273

Intourist: ul. Lenina 40, ph. 513-898, 519-102; **Other travel agent(s):** ul. K. Marksa 43, ph. 240-098; *Adams and Ruffle Travel,* ph. 515-289, 517-423

Aeroflot: ul. Bolshakova 99A, ph. 299-298, 299-122

Telegraph office: pr. Lenina 39, ph. 517-222, 512-537

Bank(s): ul. Generalskaya 7, ph. 573-869; ul. Mamina-Sibiryaka 58, ph. 558-370

City Council/Administration: prosp. Lenina 24A, ph. 515-546

Hospital: ul. Volgogradskaya 185, ph. 283-459

Other useful information: *Sprint office*, ph. 519-949 (Access Number: 414-368); *Regional Center for Trade and Commerce*, ul. Vostochnaya 6, ph. 530-449, fax 557-351; *Sovam Teleport office*, ph. 605-175 (Access number: 491-032)

Diplomatic Missions: *Mongolian Mission*, ul. Furmanova 45, ph. 445-453

YOSHKAR-OLA   ☼ 836-22   ✈ 388

Information: 62-222

Hotel(s): *Yubileinaya*, Leninskiy pr. 26, ph. 54-936

Restaurant(s): *Yubileiny*, in the hotel of same name, ph. 92-557

Intourist: Leninskiy pr. 29, ph.56-272, 98-068; Other travel agent(s): *Sputnik*, ul. Palatnaya 77, ph. 65-278; *Bureau for Tourism and Excursions*, ul. K. Marksa 109, ph. 61-348, 64-350

Aeroflot: ul. Volkova 164, ph. 98-809, 52-370

Telegraph office: ul. Sovetskaya 138, ph. 56-118

Bank(s): *Marprombank*, ul. Pushkina 30, ph. 11-5251, fax 11-1021

City Council/Administration: Leninskiy pr. 27, ph. 56-434, 56-401

Hospital: *Polyclinic #1*, pr. Gagarina 15, ph. 53-577

Other useful information: *Art Gallery*, ul. Sovetskaya 153; *Scientific Museum of Local Culture*, ul. Sovetskaya 153

YUZHNO-SAKHALINSK   ☼ 424-00   ✈ 4178

Information: 561-21

Hotel(s): *Sakhalin-Sapporo*, ul. Lenina 181, ph. 366-29; *Lada*, ul. Komsomolskaya 154, ph. 331-45

Restaurant(s): *Sakhalin-Sapporo*, ul. Lenina 181, ph. 327-90; *Lada*, ul. Komsomolskaya 154, ph. 316-39; *Casino*. ul. Komsomolskaya 154, ph. 329-58

Intourist: Kommunisticheskiy pr. 32, ph. 232-39; Other travel agent(s): *Sakhalin-Tourist*, ul. Sakhalinskaya 2, ph. 361-05

Aeroflot: ul. Lenina 198, ph. 356-88

Telegraph office: ul. Lenina 220, ph. 221-06

Bank(s): Kommunisticheskiy pr. 47, ph. 226-66

City Council/Administration: ul. Lenina 173, ph. 229-36

Hospital: ul. Mira 430, ph. 553-41

Other useful information: *Sprint office*, ph. 290-91 (Access number: 223-99); *DHL Office*, Sakhincenter, office 228, Kommunisticheskiy pr. 32, ph. 298-451

5

Money & Crime

The Ruble

For decades the Soviet/Russian ruble was a wholly-non-convertible currency. It had no value beyond Soviet borders and had a fairly warped value within those borders. Since the ruble was not directly convertible to foreign currencies, the Soviet government had to, for the purposes of international trade and tourism, create artificial rates (i.e. the commercial ruble, the gold ruble, the tourist ruble), which were nothing more than accounting tools for changing between different foreign currencies at world market rates. It was impossible to turn an everyday ruble into, say, a gold ruble.

Four actions taken by the Russian government since the collapse of the Soviet Union served, together, to fundamentally alter this situation. As a result, the nature and value of the Russian ruble have been changed irretrievably, and with them the Russian economy.

First, in December 1991, by Presidential decree, virtually all bureaucratic barriers to the conduct of foreign trade through private channels were abolished. The centralized system of foreign trade, necessitated by the Soviet planned economy and artificial internal pricing, had, since the late 1980s, been increasingly challenged by the growing private sector and joint ventures. The Soviet government had attempted to exercise control at various times through the use of licensing, quotas and other customs controls. But now all bets are off. Any legally-registered company could trade in any legal commodity.

Second, in January 1992, the Russian government freed prices on nearly all goods. Prices soared. And, as expected, the shops began to fill with goods. Wages and pensions were also unleashed, setting in motion an inflationary spiral that escalated throughout 1992, slowing somewhat during 1993. Yet, still, in early 1994, prices were growing at a rate of 20% per month.

Third, in July 1992, the government eliminated all artificially-created exchange rates for the ruble. This forty-year-old practice (begun by Stalin) had contributed to the ruble's "soft," or inconvertible, status by grossly overvaluing it for foreign trade operations. At the time of this change, at least four different artificial ruble rates were used for trade, tourist and banking operations. Now there was to be just one "official" ruble exchange rate, and this would be set through a currency auction mechanism (the Moscow Interbank Currency Exchange – MICE). Commercial banks would, further, be allowed to set exchange rates for individuals independent of this official rate. But, since MICE was the major mechanism for large-scale currency conversion, banks would become very attentive to activity on this exchange. Before this move, the ruble was valued at 125R to the dollar. By early 1993, commercial banks were buying dollars for in excess of 700 rubles, and by early 1994, this rate had slid to over 1500R/$1 (see chart below).

Finally, also in mid-1992, the Russian government began to take steps to stem the "dollarization" of the Russian economy. All stores selling goods for cash hard currency were required to offer their goods at ruble prices as well, which meant goods would be (and still are) tagged with dollar prices and the store would set a "house rate" of exchange into rubles at which goods could be bought, usually set well above the current average dollar sell rate.

A year and a half later, in January 1994, the government brought into force a ban on the use of foreign cash currency for the purchase and sale of goods and services in Russia. All commercial transactions for cash must now use rubles. Credit card purchases are still valued in dollars or DM, as are foreign trade contracts. But, inside Russia, the ruble is the only legal tender that may be used in cash operations.

The result of these four measures is an abundance of consumer goods. Almost any good is available in Russia, and certainly in Moscow. And all goods are available for rubles, usually lots of them (often more than the average person can afford). This includes a wide assortment of imported Western goods, from Snickers to Reebok sneakers. Thus, whereas a couple of years ago, the Russian consumer market was typified by crippling shortages and excess liquidity, now it is characterized by a wealth of consumer goods and high inflation.

The Ruble's fall   **February 1993 – February 1994**

Weekly ruble/dollar exchange rates
(rubles per dollar, based on average of MICE, black market and bank rates)

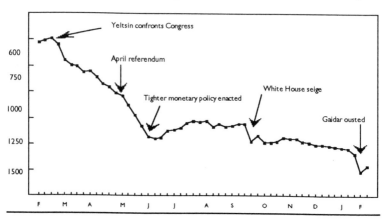

Internal convertibility and inflation: The ruble is now, for all intents and purposes, internally convertible. The trade-off is that the ruble is also seriously devalued, because the Russian Central Bank has continued printing money to support state enterprises, rather than rapidly privatize them or let them fail. And the economy has become seriously destabilized by the resulting inflationary cycle. Most experts agree that only a tighter monetary policy and acceleration of privatization will be able to break this cycle in the near term. Barring these actions or some unforeseen serious government intervention, the value of the ruble will continue its steady decline.

The implication for travelers is that it is not wise, or necessary, to change large amounts of money into rubles. Bank exchange rates continue to be somewhat volatile, and longer-term visitors will want to pay fairly close attention to exchange rate trends. Inflation in the consumer sector has tended to keep pace with market exchange rates to the dollar, so expect prices to rise while the value of the ruble against the dollar falls.

For Western traders, the obvious implication is to avoid the inflationary and convertibility problems of the domestic economy by selling to Russian companies for hard currency, paid up front and on irrevocable letters of credit, rather than through consignment or installments. Russian law also allows barter operations, and many Western firms have succeeded in overcoming payment problems by taking it in-kind.

WHAT THE RUBLE IS WORTH

What the ruble is actually worth is a somewhat difficult question to answer. As an individual unit, a single ruble is worth very little in relation to other currencies (i.e. just a fraction of a cent). But, as a currency, the ruble is stronger than it was five or ten years ago, in the sense of guaranteeing access to goods and services. Certainly hyperinflation has meant a swift devaluation of the ruble's buying power. But it is significant that, if one has the requisite number of rubles to pay the stated price of a good, that good is more readily available than it was a few years ago, and without having to tack on additional costs, such as bribery, *blat* or barter. Of course, if inflation is not slowed, the ruble will become so utterly devalued that it will be simpler to engage in barter operations (it would also be naive to assert that *blat,* or influence, has lost sway – particularly in the provinces – but it certainly has lessened greatly).

Equivalent dollars: An instructive demonstration of the ruble's value is shown in the chart on the page following, which is based on a methodology first published in 1992 by the Institute of World Affairs. By converting dollars into rubles at the MICE (Moscow Interbank Currency Exchange) exchange rate, the ruble is shown to be very weak. The resulting prices on the goods cited is much lower than what one would expect to pay in the US (which makes export of goods bought for rubles a potentially quite profitable venture, some have found). Conclusion: the ruble is worth very little.

On the other hand, if the ruble prices for these same goods are represented in terms of the share of average Russian monthly income required to purchase them, and if we factor this by the US average monthly

Comparative value of the ruble

Product	Average ruble price*		Market dollar rate**		Equivalent dollars+	
	1993	1994	1993	1994	1993	1994
Beef (1 kilo)	600	6,000	$1.07	$3.87	$85.00	$42.50
Butter (1 kilo)	912	2,400	$1.63	$1.54	$129.20	$17
Sugar (1 kilo)	243.2	800	$0.44	$0.52	$34.45	$5.67
Potatoes (1 kilo)	53.2	500	$0.10	$0.32	$7.53	$3.54
Vodka (1 liter)	938.5	6,000	$1.68	$3.87	$132.95	$42.50
Eggs (10)	179.2	1,200	$0.32	$0.77	$25.39	$8.50
Color TV	60,000	1,300,000	$107.33	$838.71	$8500	$9208

*Moscow, February 16, 1993 and February 1, 1994; **Based on 2/18/93 and 2/1/94 MICE rates of 559R:$1 and 1550R/$1, respectively; + Based on average current Russian salaries of R12,000 (1993). R240,000 (1994) and average current US salary of $1,700.

income, the picture is slightly different. This "equivalent dollar" rate highlights the currently warped nature of the ruble, begat by hyperinflation. Commodities that are relatively inexpensive when bought for dollars sold for rubles, are expensive when considered as a share of the average Russian's income (though the equivalent dollar rates clearly show that the ruble's buying power over the last year has increased significantly).

Ruble flight: As one might expect, this economic reality has led entrepreneurs and private citizens to hedge inflation by turning rubles into dollars or stable-valued commodities, converting them back to rubles only as necessary. The net effect is further devaluation of the ruble.

The government has responded to this (and to its need to service its foreign debt), by imposing stiff taxes on currency earnings and restricting some dollar operations. This has resulted mostly in the flight of currency to hidden (i.e. non-taxable) foreign bank accounts.

Denominations

The ruble (at the time of publication) comes in denominations of 100, 200, 500, 1000, 5,000, 10,000, 50,000 and 100,000 rubles.

Inflation has led the Soviet, and now Russian government to introduce higher and higher ruble notes. In 1991, 200 and 500 ruble notes were introduced. In 1992, notes of 5,000 and 10,000 denominations were printed. In 1993, the 50,000R and 100,000R notes began circulating, while lower denomination notes (1, 3, 5, 10, 25, 50) began being taken out of circulation.

The ruble consists of 100 kopeks. Yet, due to the steep and steady devaluation of the ruble, kopeks are becoming obsolete. There are 1, 5, 10, 20, and 50 ruble coins. Both telephones and metros have been or are being shifted over to accept only tokens (жетони – *zhetoni*), so that prices can be changed more easily. In some cities (including Moscow and St. Petersburg), a 1R coin (and sometimes the similarly-sized 15k pieces) still works on phones that have not yet been converted to zhetoni.

WARNING: In 1993 the Russian government banned use of all bills and coins printed or minted prior to 1993. *Do not accept as change any bills that are not dated 1993 or 1994.*

Currency Questions

CHANGING MONEY

The loosening of controls on the ruble's exchange rate has been accompanied by a loosening of exchange restrictions for individuals. While you must fill out a customs declaration upon entering and exiting the country (in which you note the amount of currency in your possession), this has become something of a pointless formality. You may legally change dollars into rubles and rubles into dollars at any licensed commercial bank or exchange point, and are not required to show any identification for either transaction, nor to have either type of operation noted on your declaration (as was the case a few years ago).

Banks change their rates of exchange daily and there are some significant differences in exchange rates among banks, so it does bear shopping around a bit if you are exchanging large sums of money. Most banks charge a fee (usually a percentage of the amount being exchanged) for exchange transactions and thus "hide" a less advantageous rate of exchange in such fees. Be sure to find out all fees before handing over your cash.

You are advised to only exchange money through officially licensed banks, not at kiosks and not on the street (see section below on Crime).

Precautions: If you have a good contact in Moscow or St. Petersburg, you may want to tell them to change some rubles for you ahead of your arrival. With the devalued ruble exchange rate, exchange points are often out of cash early in the day and, paradoxically, the cheaper the ruble gets, the harder it is to find them.

PURCHASING

Effective January 1, 1994, all cash transactions in Russia must be effected in Russian rubles. It is illegal to pay in cash foreign currency for goods or services in stores, restaurants, or on the street.

It is legal, however, to pay for transactions with a credit card (VISA, MC and AMEX are all widely accepted). In this instance, your credit card will be debited in dollars or deutschemarks, or whatever currency the establishment is using as its currency for pricing.

Beware the house rate: It is a widely-used practice for foreign-produced goods to be tagged in stores with dollar or DM prices, and for the ruble total of the purchase (if done in cash, vs. a credit card) to be calculated according to a "house rate" of exchange, which is usually changed daily. These house rates can be quite usurious – find out what they are before you buy. House rates are usually pegged just above the rate at which the store must purchase dollars (the commercial bank *dollar selling rate*). And since you likely obtained rubles at the lower (usually by 5-10%) *dollar buying rate*, it usually makes more sense to purchase goods with a credit card in these stores. *If you have exchanged foreign currency for rubles at a rate lower than the store's house rate, use your credit card.* You will save at least 5-10% on your purchase.

Leave home without them: In general, travelers checks are a hassle in Russia and are only readily accepted without objections when exchanging money in better-established banks. Cash and credit cards are the best form of hard currency to carry – in fact credit cards rank above cash in terms of their ease and safety of use. It is now even possible at several venues to obtain cash (dollars or rubles) with your VISA or AMEX card (see below, *Dealing with a Cash Crunch*). If you bring cash, small bills (e.g. $20 or less) are preferable to large ones because making change will be easier and it will be more convenient for tipping, cab rides, etc. Non-American visitors would be wise to change their intended hard currency spending money into dollars, as the relative value of pounds, deutschemarks, yens or francs is not widely known in this 'dollarizing' economy.

DEALING WITH A CASH CRUNCH

Time was, if you ran out of cash while traveling in Russia, you were in something of a quandary. But, thanks to some advances in consumer services in this area, travelers and business people in Russia now have a few options for dealing with a cash crunch.

Wire transfers

Electronic wire transfers have long been the preferred mode of getting money into and out of accounts in Russia. And it is now possible to use this means to send cash to (Western) contacts in Russia or to receive it when sent by the home office.

The easiest channel is through DialogBank, which has a very service-oriented office on the ground floor of Moscow's Slavyanskaya-Radisson hotel. From the US or any other Western country you can transfer any amount of money to DialogBank's correspondent account in New York. In the transfer, you designate the full name of the individual who is to receive the money in Moscow and his/her passport number (a Russian citizen cannot be the recipient). The wire takes about 2-3 days to arrive after it is sent, and can be picked up in cash at the DialogBank office.

The minimum acceptable transfer amount is $1000. There is a 3% service charge on the receiving end for the transfer, plus a $15 fee. The bank you send the wire from will also likely take a $10-30 fee. You will want to add the full amount of any anticipated fees to the total amount you would like to have received in Moscow. You must indicate that the beneficiary is DialogBank. Contact DialogBank (see below) for account information prior to effecting a transfer.

Immediate cash with plastic

You may use your American Express (Amex) card to obtain a small amount of cash at the ATM machines in the Amex Moscow office (see below) or in the lobby of Moscow's Hotel Mezhdunarodnaya. But this, of course, requires that you have registered a PIN for your card. You can also obtain larger cash advances off your Amex card at any Amex office. The commission is 4%.

DialogBank offers a slightly better commission on a different type of transaction. You, in effect, carry out a remote-transfer from your bank account in the West, using your Amex card to secure a check written off that account (i.e., if the check bounces, you'll see the charge show up on your next Amex statement). This is a good reason to bring along your personal

---

If you lose your credit card...
(here are the numbers to call)

AMEX, Moscow ph. 956-9000, St. Petersburg ph. 311-5215 (or via AT&T USA Direct to the US, call 919-333-3211 collect)
Other cards: Moscow ph. 284-4873 or 284-4802, St. Petersburg, ph. 312-6015

---

and/or business checkbook when you travel to Moscow. You can undertake this operation once every 21 days. If you have a regular Amex card (green), the limit during this period is $1000, with a gold card $5000, and with a platinum card $10,000. The cost of conducting such a remote-transfer is 3% of the total amount or $30, whichever is greater.

Cash advances off VISA cards are also available. Credobank is the leader on this front. Normal cash advance interest charges apply, plus Credobank charges a 4% commission. Several Credobank and other bank offices in Russia which can effect cash advances are listed below. Elbim Bank, with a convenient office in the lobby of the Mezhdunarodnaya office building, can also effect cash advances on a VISA card. They also take a 4% commission.

Western Union

This is essentially a wire transfer without the bank. Cash may be directly transferred from a Western Union (WU) office outside Russia (most US and major European cities have one) or by calling (having your home office call) WU (800-325-6000) and drawing the money off your VISA or MC. There is no limit on the amount you may transfer. There is a commission on the sending end which decreases proportionally the more money you send.

The money is available within minutes in Russia. WU serves many large Russian cities, including Moscow, St. Petersburg, Novosibirsk, Omsk, Rostov-on-Don, Saratov, St. Petersburg and Volgograd. Other cities are steadily being added. To get a current list of cities and banks where money can be received, call either the WU Moscow office (*Sberbank,* ul. Yunosti 5/1, ph. 119-8250) or WU in the US, at the 800 number given on the previous page. Tell them the city you want to send to, and they will let you know if there is a WU office there yet.

Money can be picked up in dollars or rubles at the current WU rate (which is near the MICE rate). A processing fee of 5% is taken out at the receiving end for receipt of dollars. A smaller fee is taken for receipt of rubles. The receiving party can be notified by phone or telegram upon the money's arrival (not the most reliable of alternatives), or may call the WU number in Moscow (see above) to find out where to pick the money up (better). When you send the money, you can also find out from the WU agent the address of banks in the city where the money can be picked up.

Fast cash: In at least Moscow and St. Petersburg (and later in other cities), the WU offices are also "outgoing" WU branches, which means money can be sent as well as received there. Thus, from Moscow you could effect a transfer to a colleague in Novosibirsk. In a pinch you could also use a credit

---

Useful Addresses in a Cash Crunch:

American Express: *Moscow,* ul. Sadovaya-Kudrinskaya 21a, ph. 956-9000, 956-9004; *St. Petersburg:* Grand Hotel Europe, ph. 315-7487

Credobank: Main office: ul. Stanislavskovo 10, 229-7788, ; **For CredoCard** (oversees cash advances): 956-3456

Credobank cash advance facilities in Russia:

    MOSCOW: Mezhdunarodnaya hotel (24 hours), Krasnopresnenskaya nab. 12 , 252-6481; **Manezh Exhibition Hall,** Manezhnaya Pl. 1, ph. 202-4836, 202-8556, 9:30 am-7 pm; **NGSBank,** Zhitnaya ul. 14, ph. 238-7210, 10 am-3 pm; **Inkombank,** Telegrafny per. 12/8, ph. 923-3810, 9am-4pm; **Belgrade Hotel,** Smolenskaya pl. 4, ph. 248-1268, 10am-7pm; **Olympic-Penta Hotel,** Olimpiysky prosp. 18/1, ph. 235-9003 (ext. 26-60), 9am-9pm; **Pullman-Iris Hotel,** Korovinskoye shosse 10, ph. 488-8102; **Pekin Hotel,** ul. B. Sadovaya 5, ph. 209-2317 (Roskredit)

    ST. PETERSBURG: Hotel Peterhof, nab. Makarova, ph. 219-9417; **Promstroibank,** ul. Mikhailovskaya 4, ph. 110-4909; **Astoria Hotel,** ul. Gertsena 39, ph. 210-5878; **Moskva Hotel,** ph. 274-2127; **Pribaltiyskaya Hotel,** ph. 356-3803.

    KALININGRAD: Credobank, ul. Bagryamyana 4, ph. (0112) 43-0483

    PERM: Permkombank Main office, bulvar Gagarina 65, ph. (3422) 483-357, 9 am-7 pm; **SOTA Store,** ul. Popova 25, ph. (3422) 343-630, 9am-1pm

    TVER: Tveruniversalbank Main office, ul. Volodarskovo 34, ph. (08222) 272-17, 9 am-1 pm

    YEKATERINBURG: Uralvneshtorgbank Main office, ul. Generalskaya 7, ph. (3432) 573-844

    VLADIVOSTOK: ATR-Credobank Main office, ul. Aleutskaya 16, ph. (4232) 222-264.

DialogBank: Moscow, Slavyanskaya-Radisson Hotel, ph. 941-8434

Elbim Bank, Mezhdunarodnaya hotel, phone 205-6560

Western Union: (Sberbank), ul. Yunosti 5/1, ph. 119-8250

---

card to send money to yourself or a colleague in Moscow or St. Petersburg. The commissions on both ends (plus credit card cash advance fees) could easily top 10%, however, and this is much less desirable than a simple cash advance, which is widely available (see above).

Midnight Express

If you need fast cash in the middle of the night and all the banks are closed, here is a "midnight-express" option. Visit a local casino, which Moscow and St. Petersburg now have many of, use your credit card to get cash at a teller (paying only your card's cash advance charges in most cases) for use in betting. Play a few slots, drink a few drinks, then head for the door. Not all casinos offer cash advances, and, if this option is exercised by too many people too often, expect on-again, off-again availability of cash by this means.

Crime

The 'golden days' when Russia was about the safest place in the world to travel to (with respect to crime) are gone. As a foreigner in Moscow or St. Petersburg (more so in Moscow), you stand out as a person with hard currency, by both the way you dress and act, and by the places you frequent. While there is no significant dislike for foreigners (in fact the opposite is usually true), some foreigners have experienced local resentment for reminding Russians "of all they do not have." And in times of heightened unemployment, inflation and desperation, foreigners are an obvious target for crime. This is not to say that Moscow and St. Petersburg have become dangerous, just that they are no longer as safe as they used to be and some precautions are in order. With this in mind, here is a compilation (with thanks to many fellow travelers, the US Department of State and the Russian Interior Ministry) of some of the most useful tips for avoiding becoming a victim.

PROTECT VALUABLES. Don't bring valuables with you to Russia that you don't really need. Do not leave money in your hotel room or apartment, and carry it with you in a secure place. There has been an increased incidence of burglary of hotel rooms, seemingly with the collusion of staff. Use hotel safes for highly valuable items or, better yet, leave them at home.

TRAIN WISELY. When you travel by train, always buy tickets for the entire cabin, even if you are traveling alone. Do not let the conductor put other passengers in your cabin, even if he insists that this is "the required procedure." Pay the conductor a modest "fee," if you must, to quiet him. There have been cases of theft from sleeping cars on overnight trains (particularly between Moscow and St. Petersburg). Always lock your train cabin door and the little flip-out *sekretka*, and secure it with a rope or belt when you sleep.

MIND THE COMPANY YOU KEEP. Avoid beggars, prostitutes, black market dealers, and groups (especially bands of gypsies). These people are often pickpockets as well. Do not give donations to "suspicious looking" beggars and avoid making eye contact with gypsies. There also have been incidents where a deaf-mute approaches a foreigner for assistance, distracting him while cohorts pick their pockets or worse. Gangs of adolescent thieves are also on the rise. *Do not be afraid to defend yourself aggressively if you are accosted openly. Swing your bags and yell.* Wrapping rubber bands around your wallet is a good way to make it harder to pick from your pocket.

AVOID BAD SECTIONS. Be wary of black marketeers, money changers and gypsies in front of tourist hotels, and, in Moscow, in front of the Bolshoy Theater, on Red Square, on the Arbat, and on Kalininskiy Bridge (leading to the Ukraine hotel). In St. Petersburg, avoid the square in front of Gostiny Dvor and be wary in Klenovy (Maple) alley. Other areas of heightened criminal activity are: train stations, flea markets, food markets, airports, large public gatherings, cheap hotels or hostels, casinos and nightclubs, parking lots where cars are sold and areas with lots of "unofficial" commercial activity or kiosks.

BE CAREFUL WHERE AND HOW YOU BUY. It is easy to be distracted during the purchase of souvenirs and to be ripped off in the process. Be sure that the goods you buy are the ones you get. If you think you are getting a deal that is too good to be true, you probably aren't – look for a set up. Don't flash a lot of cash around during a purchase – you can bet your actions will be under some scrutiny during this part of a transaction, and it is wise not to openly display the location of your money, passport or other valuables. Don't place convenience over personal safety. And don't allow yourself to be rushed. Always be sure to get your credit card back after each transaction. *Exchange money only at officially-registered exchange points.*

DRINK WISELY. The incidence of foreigners being slipped a "mickey" has reached anecdotal levels, but is not widespread. Still, it is wise to drink only with a trusted friend, and for one of you to remain sober. Even slight intoxication alters your judgement and responses significantly, a fact professional thieves prey on. Do NOT purchase drinks from opened bottles except in a reputable bar.

KEEP YOUR OWN COUNSEL. Do not tell strangers where you are staying or what your travel or evening entertainment plans are. Do not open your door to unknown individuals. Be cautious about accepting invitations to first-time acquaintances' apartments. Be careful who you visit and what cars you get into. There have been cases of harassment of foreign motorists by militia officers, but this is very rare and declining. If you suspect this is about to happen to you, be polite, do not speak Russian, and be "accommodating." Look for a badge number.

TAXI RULES. Use only an official "limo" service from the airport. And at night, stick to official taxis, versus gypsy cab rides, which are not recommended in any case. *Never, never get in a cab that already has a rider.* If your luggage is put in the trunk, do not exit the car until the driver gets out and proceeds to open the trunk, and leave the passenger door open until all your luggage is removed from the vehicle.

DON'T BE FLASHY. Keep a low profile. Dress and act conservatively. Be polite and low-key. Avoid loud conversations and arguments. Showing lots of dollars around in restaurants and other semi- or fully-public places is not advisable. Don't keep all of your money in one place – put smaller amounts in different pockets and recall what is where, and take out only the money you need. Keep your wallet pocketed (in your front pocket, preferably) in public places.

USE THE BUDDY SYSTEM. If you want to walk the streets at night, stick to main avenues and, when possible, take along a friend. Do not use short cuts or poorly-lit streets. Do not stop at night for strangers or people who need a cigarette lit. Before going into a pedestrian underpass, be alert to who is already in or going into the underpass. *Stay away from parks at night.*

WHAT TO YELL. If you are in trouble, and there are people near who may help, yell 'pozhar' (fire) to attract attention.

IF YOU ARE MUGGED OR ASSAULTED. While this is unlikely if you heed the tips above, it is always a possibility. If you are victimized, get in touch with the militia or service bureau in your hotel, and/or with your embassy. It will only serve to help others. Never resist giving up valuables to armed attackers. Never carry items around with you that you cannot do without.

6

Food & Health

Food

OPTIONS

The restaurant business was at the forefront of the Soviet Union's first tentative steps toward the market in the late 1980s. Cooperative restaurants sprang up in sidestreets around Moscow, St. Petersburg and larger cities, offering a welcome alternative to the sluggish service and mediocre meals of state-owned restaurants. Now, after seven years, the number of privately-owned restaurants and cafes in larger cities of Russia is rivaled only by the explosive growth of stores selling imported Western goods.

From the beginning, dining out at private restaurants has been a luxury reserved for those with an abundance of rubles: Russia's *nouveau riche* and foreigners. Indeed, a recent poll in Moscow showed that just 1% of average Muscovites went out for an evening meal at a restaurant during 1993. Lunches out are more common.

Yet, even for those with plenty of rubles, dining out in Moscow and St. Petersburg is getting more and more expensive. With the devaluation of the ruble and hyperinflation, foreigners are less often able to eat better and more for the equivalent of a few dollars changed into rubles, and more and more of the finer restaurants are accepting credit card payment only.

Your best bet is to learn the ground rules before ordering your meal. Find out whether payment is in rubles or by credit card. If prices are in a foreign currency, both options will be open, but, as with shopping, the "house rate" of exchange (see Chapter 5) will determine whether it is in your best interest to pay with credit card or cash.

Below is a list of types of restaurants to try, in order of preference:

Private and Cooperative Restaurants

When coops (as cooperative restaurants are commonly known) first began operating, it was scandalous when they charged five rubles for a meal (then about 50¢ to a dollar at the black market rate of exchange). Now prices for dinner at preferred venues can easily top 10-20 thousand rubles per person. Lunches are slightly less than dinners, but not much. Despite inflation, the value of the dollar, in terms of what kind of meal it can buy when converted to rubles, is holding pretty constant. Thus, at good restaurants, expect to pay the dollar equivalent of $10 a person for lunch and twice that for a good dinner. Drinks are extra.

Reservations are recommended for evening meals, particularly at popular coops. Popular state restaurants and some cooperatives require a week's advance notice for reservations, but at most places, calling in the morning or the day before assures you a table. When making your reservation (best to have a Russian speaker do this), ask about the availability of liquor. Most coops offer liquor or wine only for hard currency (credit card). If they do not offer liquor or wine, they usually will not frown on you bringing your own bottle of wine (but may charge a corking fee).

Recall the saying that there is no free lunch. If, when you arrive at a restaurant, a table full of *zakuski* (appetizers) are laid out to greet you, check into the cost of this welcome, as many restaurants will try to pad your bill with zakuski. Find out ahead of time if the coop has live music or a floor show, which can mean an extra charge on your bill and *very* loud music. Avoid coops with floor shows if you want to converse with your dinner companions (this goes for all types of restaurants). See the list of restaurants in the yellow pages of our *Where in Moscow* and *Where in St. Petersburg.*

Joint Venture Restaurants

These figure below coops because their prices are quite high by American or European standards (a notable exception being McDonalds Moscow). The majority of such restaurants are in newly-refurbished hotels like the Metropol, Slavyanskaya-Radisson, Savoy, Olympia, Baltschug, Palace and Pullman Hotels in Moscow and the Astoria Hotel and Grand Hotel Europe in St. Petersburg. Still, there are plenty outside hotels as well, as in the Sadko Arcade in Moscow or the Chaika and Sankt-Peterburg restaurants in St. Petersburg. Check the listings in our *Where in Moscow* and *Where in St. Petersburg* for the best spots. The food at these restaurants (and at some of the non-hotel based joint venture restaurants) is generally of a consistently high quality, and you usually can't go wrong. Lunch prices tend to start at around $20 per person. Dinners at $30-40 per person. As with restaurants the world over, check into the reputation for quality and pricey-ness to avoid surprises. Again, see our afore-mentioned yellow pages.

State Restaurants and State-owned Hotel Restaurants

A godsend of privatization is that it may succeed in eradicating these dinosaurs and turning them into more efficient, amenable and service-oriented private restaurants. But this is not going to happen overnight, so expect to encounter these types of restaurants for some time to come, particularly outside Moscow and St. Petersburg.

The food is generally fair to lackluster, and the service abysmal. But the prices are lower than at cooperative restaurants. Here you can sometimes get alcohol at reasonable prices, and quite a bit of food for your money. Always ask the waiter for his/her recommendations, and *always order with an eye to freshness*. Pates can be dangerous, and beef is usually a safer bet than pork or chicken. *Do not eat any meat that is not fully cooked, especially seafood.* Chicken Kiev is usually a safe bet anywhere you go, however, and a good *kapusta* (marinated cabbage salad) or stolichny salad (potato and meat salad) are usually on the menu, as is fresh cheese, herring and caviar.

Your waiter will likely warm up to you if you order plenty of alcohol and caviar, as there is then the prospect of something like a real tip in it for him. Even if a service charge is included in the bill, tip generously but not ostentatiously, i.e. about 10%.

Stolovayas (Cafeterias) in Enterprises

Your visit may offer you the opportunity to eat in the cafeteria of your host organization. Depending upon the priorities and influence of the enterprise, you could see cafeteria cooking in Russia at its worst or best.

Almost every large enterprise and organization has its own *stolovaya* (столовая) to counteract the shortage or high prices of private eating establishments (as well, new, successful private enterprises have adopted this penchant for in-house cooking and can offer some tasty meals). Prices are heavily subsidized. Some of these stolovaya can be very good (i.e. government *stolovayas*). Follow the recommendations of those you are eating with.

Other Stolovayas and Restaurants

Public *stolovayas* are available for your patronage throughout Russia, but without a strong recommendation and/or a staggering hunger, these places are to be avoided. The prices are low, as are generally the health standards. They have long depended on subsidies and most are going out of business or privatizing.

The food and service are generally not worth mentioning, but there are a few places that offer pleasant surprises in both categories. Many of these places are stand-up affairs, and many are, in fact, not a bad place to go for tea and a pastry (пирожное – *pirozhnoe*) if they offer that. Meats should be avoided in these establishments. However a sidewalk grill (шашличная – *shashlichnaya*), if the meat is thoroughly cooked, can offer a pleasant and quick meal on the go. You can consider your visit well-rounded if, upon the recommendation of a trusted Russian, you try the *pelmeni* (пельмены – a Siberian meat dumpling) or *blini* (блины – pancakes) offered in such specialized stolovayas. Prices, again, are low.

SOME GENERAL TIPS FOR DINING OUT

❶ **Do not drink the water.** Moscow water is fairly harmless, but not if your system is not used to it. St. Petersburg water should not be drunk on any condition, unless it is boiled; it harbors the *giardia lamblia* bacterium, which is harmless if your system is used to it, debilitating if not (see the *Health* section below). Tea and coffee are safe if the water has been adequately boiled. Water in the provinces is generally unpredictable. Bring bottled water.

If you get desperate, the safest water is probably that in the newest hotels. What goes under the name of mineral water in Russia is very salty and carbonated. *Mors, sok* and *napitok,* the ubiquitous (and usually quite tasty) fruit beverages of infinite variety are made from water, but few people have problems with them (in Moscow). Bottled water is available in most major hotels and in hard currency grocery stores. Avoid bottled water from St. Petersburg. Be careful of melons which may have been injected with water to increase their size.

❷ **Always make reservations.** Larger hotel restaurants cater to groups. Thus, individuals are not welcomed without reservations, and even in that event do not expect red carpet treatment.

❸ **Tipping** is increasingly expected. 10-15% is adequate.

❹ **Take your time.** When you go out for lunch in a Russian restaurant, expect it to take at least an hour to hour and a half. When you go out to dinner, it is a night-long engagement. Most Russian restaurants do not try to turn tables every 45 minutes as Western restaurants do. You will not be hurried along; sit back and relax. When a Russian goes out to dinner, it is for a night of entertainment. Eating and running, particularly at someone's home, is considered rude.

❺ **Share the costs.** When dining with Russian guests or hosts, the rule is usually that the host pays for the meal. If you are eating out with persons whose organization will probably not pay for the meal, insist on paying or at least going dutch. While you can joke about the low value of the ruble over dinner, do not ever be ostentatious or throw a lot of money around when it comes time to pay the check. Remember, most Russians do not eat out that often. The prices have just gotten too high.

❻ **Always carry a cotton handkerchief** for dining out, as Russian cities are dirty, and you will probably want to wash your hands before eating, and often restaurant restrooms lack clean towels (although hot air dryers are some-times available). The handkerchief will also come in handy for wiping off silverware in some of the greasier of greasy spoons.

❼ **If it is on the menu, it is not necessarily available.** Russian restaurants are subject to radical fluctuations in food supplies. The items that are available will have prices next to them or be indicated in some way. Some items may, at first request (in state and large hotel restaurants) be unavail-able. But often a little 'encouragement' helps uncover forgotten stashes.

Health

For the uninitiated, travel in Russia can be physically taxing at the least and exhausting at the worst. This is particularly true for elderly persons and persons with special health concerns or problems. The air quality in major cities, while tolerable, can cause problems for people with asthma or other lung problems. Pharmacies which stock basic cold and influenza or other over-the-counter drugs are few and far between. Balanced meals, i.e. with healthy portions of fruits and vegetables, are not readily available, so vegetarians or persons with special dietary needs may find satisfying their requirements quite difficult. On top of this, the general situation with health care, be it emergency medical services, hospitals, or the supply of medicines and disposable needles, is well below the accepted standards in most Western nations. Even basic health care services may be totally unavailable outside major metropolitan areas (see the *Russian City Guide*, Chapter 4).

This said, most or all of these and other potential health-related problems can be avoided by gaining a proper understanding of the environment one is traveling into and by taking proper precautions.

PRECAUTIONS

Business and independent travelers will ensure a more enjoyable and successful trip by checking/updating their health insurance status, getting necessary inoculations, bringing required medicines and taking certain precautions before and during travels.

Health Insurance

Before you depart for Russia for travel or residency, check with your health insurance carrier or overseer (whether private or state, as in the case of the UK or Canada) to understand the nature and extent of coverage they extend to a policyholder traveling to Russia or the former Soviet Union. If your provider does not cover you for travel to this region, you are strongly advised to either purchase a rider to your policy expressly granting this coverage or seek a temporary insurance provider which specializes in travel insurance (see below or ask your travel agent).

You may also wish to consider insurance covering the eventuality of medical evacuation from Moscow to Finland, New York or Germany. The minimum cost for such an evacuation by normal air carrier can be over $10,000, or nearly $100,000 if by special hospital aircraft. A few US companies that insure against this eventuality are listed below.

Third, study up ahead of time on the health care facilities available in the cities/regions you will be visiting. Recommended facilities for Moscow and St. Petersburg are listed below. Also find out where your country's nearest embassy or consulate is located. They are there to serve you in the event of emergencies, including medical emergencies.

SPECIALIZED TRAVEL INSURANCE PROVIDERS

American Medical Center, 1055 Washington Blvd., Stamford, CT 06901, ph. (800) 393-2833, fax (203) 325-3127. Offers a Traveler's Medical Access Plan for $40 that guarantees full access to American-staffed and run medical centers in Moscow and St. Petersburg.

Medicine, Inc., 105 James Way, Southampton, PA 18966, ph. (800) 551-1311. Offers a travel insurance package for Moscow that entails 30 days of coverage and costs $66. Treatment is at the former Kremlin Hospital to the North of the city center.

Traveler's Emergency Network, 103 West Main St., Durham, NC 27702, ph. 800-ASK-4TEN. Offers a $30 traveler's insurance policy covering evacuation, physician referral, prescription delivery and more.

Aero Ambulance International, Executive Airport, Philadelphia, PA, ph. (800) 443-8042, (305) 776-6800

Air Ambulance of America, ph. (800) 323-4444

Euro-Flite, Box 187, 01531 Vantaa, Finland, ph. (358-0) 174-644, fax (358-0) 870-2507. Offers quick bedside-to-bedside evacuation with certified medical staff from anywhere in Russia to Finland (also cargo and charter services).

International SOS Assistance, ph. (800) 523-8930

Medicines

Bring your own. This includes not just any prescription medicines you would need for your trip (including the eventuality that it might be extended), but also non-prescription, over the counter items which you might consider necessary. While Western-style pharmacies have been opening up in Moscow and St. Petersburg, it is best not to count on the availability of something easily obtainable in your home country. Chapter 2 lists the bare essentials any traveler or short-term resident should take: disposable syringes, Pepto-Bismol or medicine containing bismuth, antacids, ibuprofen, prescription drugs, and iodine tablets for disinfecting water. In addition, you may wish to consider taking some or all of the following: flu or influenza medicine, cold medicine, cough drops, antibiotics, bandages and antibiotic creme. Carry wash-n-dry towelettes for when you can't wash up.

Immunizations

Check with your physician and consider updating your immunizations, particularly for the "childhood diseases": diphtheria, measles, mumps, rubella and polio. An alarming trend has been the rise of diphtheria in Moscow in recent years, due to vaccine shortages. Some 1100 cases were reported in Moscow last year. You need three boosters over a period of 6-12 months to have adequate protection, so get started as soon as possible. A tetanus update can't hurt while you are at it.

If you are planning on traveling to the provinces, you should be immunized against hepatitis A and typhoid, and receive immunoglobulin injections. Tick-borne encephalitis (which can also be transmitted via unpasteurized milk) and lyme disease (transmitted by tick bites) have also been reported in Siberia. You can, and should, get a vaccination against the former. This can be done in Europe or upon arrival in Moscow.

If you decide belatedly (i.e. after you arrive in Moscow or St. Petersburg) to travel East or North in Russia, almost all of these immunizations can be obtained at the American Medical Center or European Medical Center (see addresses below) and from some embassy medical services.

Finally, the US Center for Disease Control operates a special International Travelers Hotline that summarizes the most prevalent diseases and health risks of different regions. Call (404) 332-4559 – includes a Fax-back service where you can order printed medical reports of travel destinations.

Checklist of Health Precautions for Travel to Russia and the CIS

ITEMS TO BRING:

☑ Aspirin, Tylenol or acetominophen *(for fevers, colds, pain, headaches and flu)*

☑ Cold medicine, cough drops, flu medicine

☑ Pepto-Bismol and/or Immodium, antacids *(for diarrhea, food poisoning and indigestion)*

☑ Disposable syringes, general antibiotic *(in the event of an accident)*

☑ Iodine tablets or chemical water purifier *(to purify water and prevent giardia, diarrhea and other drinking-water-related problems – conventional water filters may also do the job)*

☑ Condoms, tampons and sanitary pads

☑ Benadryl, cortisone creme *(for allergic reactions and rashes)*

☑ Prescription medicines and a copy of eyeglass/ contact lens prescriptions

TO GET BEFORE DEPARTURE:

☑ A full medical check-up if going for a long stay.

☑ Immunization updates for diphtheria, tetanus and polio – DTP *(the US Center for Disease Control says that diphtheria boosters must be recieved three times to be effective, and spread out over 6-12 months, so get started early)*

☑ Immunization against Hepatitis B

☑ A gamma globulin injection *(to prevent contracting Hepatitis A)*

☑ Update of any immunizations for "childhood diseases"

☑ A health insurance rider or separate policy covering evacuation and emergency medical services

☑ The latest health report on the region from the CDC, phone (404) 332-4559.

A pound of cure

Prevention is your most reliable means to ensuring a problem-free trip. Here is a list of some tips from seasoned travelers and doctors:

❶ **Drink on the plane.** Take in lots of water or fluids (alcohol doesn't count) during the flight over, if it is over 5-6 hours in length. Otherwise you will find yourself dehydrated for several days. Caffeinated drinks and alcohol will also dry you out.

❷ **Don't drink the water.** To repeat, St. Petersburg water carries the *giardia lamblia* parasite, the cure for which is painful and/or unsure. While Moscow water is usually safe, the city water in Siberian cities is notoriously polluted from industrial wastes. Don't take risks. Bottled water is now available in most Western hotels and almost all hard currency food stores. For a complete listing, see our *Where in Moscow* or *Where in St. Petersburg*. If traveling beyond these cities, take along what you will need and boil any water for five minutes before drinking. Avoid ice cubes, use bottled water for brushing your teeth, and avoid uncooked fruits and vegetables that cannot be peeled.

❸ **No sushi.** With price rises, food is sitting on the shelves longer than it used to in Russia. And refrigeration is not widespread or dependable. Salmonella can be found in chicken, eggs and cheese that is insufficiently cooked. Pork and game meat should also be cooked thoroughly to avoid trichanosis. Raw fish, a delicacy in some regions (particularly in the Far East, where cold fish soup is common) can be dangerous. Many fish have been contaminated with opisthorchiasis which affects the liver and other vital organs. So abstain from raw fish and make sure all fish is thoroughly cooked through.

❹ **Fruits too.** Bigger has always been better in Russia/the USSR. This goes too for fruits. One way to achieve this is to inject fruit (i.e. watermelon, melons) with water while it is growing. The sensitive traveler will way want to avoid such fruits (see above on drinking water). Also, when possible, peel fresh fruit or wash it off *very* well.

❺ **Problem salt.** Long term residents will want to buy Western-made salt, fortified with iodine. Russian salt is not and this has caused some problems for expatriates.

❻ **Get documented.** If you have a preexisting medical condition, you should carry a letter from your physician describing the condition and including any information on prescription drugs, including the generic name for them, that you may need to take. Any prescription drugs you bring in should be kept in their original containers, to avoid customs problems.

❼ **Just to be safe.** Diarrhea does not just come from what you may eat or drink. Avoid use of reusable towel machines in public restrooms. Use only disposable paper towels or wipes to dry off your hands.

WHEN PRECAUTIONS FAIL

If you do come down with something serious that you do not have medicine for and/or need to seek medical attention, consult the list of facilities and services listed below.

Diarrhea: This is the most common traveler's ailment and can be debilitating in extreme cases. If you develop diarrhea that is bloody or lasts longer than five days, consult a physician immediately. If you run out or forgot to bring your Pepto Bismol or Immodium, here is an alternative cure that may work (if you can find the ingredients):

DIARRHEA HOME REMEDY*

Prepare in one glass 8 ounces of orange, apple or other fruit juice, a half teaspoon of honey or corn syrup, and a pinch of salt. In a second glass, prepare 8 ounces of boiled or bottled water and a quarter teaspoon of baking soda. Drink alternately from each glass until your thirst is quenched. Supplement this as desired with carbonated beverages, water or tea made with boiled or carbonated water. Avoid solid foods and dairy products until recovery occurs.

Courtesy of the US National Institutes of Health

Medical Services: Below is a list of medical service providers in Moscow and St. Petersburg. Also contact your consulate or embassy for any other facilities they may recommend or have experience with. Medical facilities in the 77 largest Russian cities are listed by city in Chapter 4.

MOSCOW

Ambulance: 03
American Medical Center, Shmitovskiy proyezd 3, ph. 956-3366, 256-8378, fax 973-2142 {full medical staff and services}
European Medical Center, Gruzinskiy per. 3, ph. 253-0703
Diplomatic Polyclinic, 4th Dobryninskiy per. 4, ph. 237-8338
Tourist's Clinic, Gruzinskiy proyezd 2, ph. 254-4396
American Embassy Medical Clinic, ph. 252-2451
British Embassy Doctor, ph. 231-8511
French Embassy Doctor, ph. 237-4655
Moscow Medical International Center, ul. Obukha 14, ph. 297-1848
Evacuation services: **Euromedical Emergency Service,** ph. 432-1616

ST. PETERSBURG

Emergency Medical Assistance: 278-0025
Ambulance: 03
American Medical Center, nab. Reki Fontanka 77, ph. 119-6101, fax 119-6120 {full medical staff and services}
Polyclinic #2, Moskovskiy pr. 22, ph. 292-5904

Communication & Shipping

Telecommunications

The Russian phone system is still arguably the worst in any industrialized country. Line quality is poor to abysmal. Cutoffs and crossed-lines are frequent. International phone lines are difficult if not impossible to access. In general, be prepared to be frustrated by the Russian phone system.

PHONES

This said, it bears noting that some huge strides have been made by Russo-Western joint ventures to, in effect, leapfrog the limitations of the antiquated Russian phone system, parts of which date to before the 1917 revolution. Cellular overlays, microwave transmitters and innovative satellite patches are providing some temporary and valuable solutions for direct international dialing. Mobile phones can be leased for car or home. AT&T and Sprint have both introduced direct-dial (USA Direct and World Connect) services from Moscow. There are now more lines into and out of Russia; whereas just a few years ago there were a total of twelve circuits, there are now over 1,000.

Still, the domestic phone system remains founded on a decaying copper wire system (some Moscow phone lines laid in 1905 are still in use) which, along with mechanical switching is noisy and enervating. The aim of this section, therefore, is to help you make the best of this situation and to take advantage of the new high-tech solutions.

Placing a Call

Phoning from a phone booth on the street in Moscow or St. Petersburg requires use of a token (жетон – *zheton*). A token, at the time of publication costs 30-50 rubles. Tokens are available at newspaper stands, in some stores and many kiosks. This zheton system is still being phased in and you can still find booths requiring a one ruble coin (15k coins will also work on these phones, as the 15k and 1R coins are similar in size and weight). In other cities, the cost of a phone call from the street varies widely, since phone booths belong to the city and each city is implementing price hikes in its own way.

For directory assistance in getting a local phone number, dial 09.

Long Distance Dialing within Russia and the CIS

To dial long distance direct within Russia and the Commonwealth, you must first dial 8, wait for the dial tone, then dial the city code (see the table on page 5), then the local phone number. For example, if you needed to dial the Nizhny Novgorod number 78652, you would dial 8-8312-78652.

From some cities, you will need to order intercity calls with the operator, depending upon the capabilities of the local network. But in major cities you can direct dial to most other major cities. From Moscow you can dial most anywhere (Nakhodka and Tolyatti being notable exceptions). From some provincial cities, however, you cannot direct dial Moscow.

Connection times can be very long, due to the fact that Russia still relies on mechanical telephone switching systems. If your call has not connected within one minute, hang up and try again.

Other problems: You will often need to add zeroes or twos between the city code and the local portion of a phone number. *There must be ten digits for you to complete an intercity call by direct dialing.* If adding 2's or 0's does not work, you will need an operator to put the call through.

From some phones, you must dial the number of the phone you are calling from after dialing the number you are calling. In Moscow, to find out your line's ability to dial intercity calls and what extra numbers you may need to add, call 271-9118; in St. Petersburg, you dial 07. These are also the numbers to dial if you have any problems with intercity dialing.

To get the city codes for cities not listed in the table on page 5, find out the local directory assistance phone number from your hotel desk (or call the information number listed for the city in Chapter 4). It differs from city to city; in Moscow or St. Petersburg it is 07.

Dialing Internationally from Russia

To dial internationally, you must dial 8, wait for the dial tone, then 10, then the country code, then the city or area code (without the zero which may often precede it), then the number within the country you are dialing. See the table on page 6 for a listing of international country and city codes.

Since 1993, it has been possible to dial international calls directly any time of the day from Moscow and St. Petersburg, subject to the amount of other traffic on the lines (which is steadily declining with continual hikes in the cost of making international calls). Most, but not all, apartment phones in these cities have this capability. If your phone does not have a direct dial capability, or if you cannot get through, you have at least four options.

Operator assisted calls: You can book a call with an international operator any time of the day or night. To book an international call while in Moscow or St. Petersburg, dial 8, wait for a dial tone, then dial 194 or 196. From a hotel in Moscow dial 333-4101, in St. Petersburg 315-0012. There are operators who speak English; when the operator answers the phone, say clearly and slowly: "Pah angleesky." They ought to understand and hook you up with the right operator. Tell the operator what you want. If you want the next possible available line, be prepared to wait several hours to get a call back from the operator. You can set a specific time for the operator to call you back with the call connected, but do not be surprised if you do not get called back or get called back later than requested. It happens.

With inflation, international call rates are being increased every month or two. Still, the cost for calling Europe is holding at about $1 per minute in rubles (depending on the time of day). For calls to the US, the price is a bit higher (around $1.50-2 per minute), for Australia and Japan higher still. If

---

Calling with your card:
AT&T USA Direct (Moscow): **155-5042**
Sprint Express (Moscow): **155-6133**
MCI Call USA (Helsinki): **8-10-358-9800-102-80**

---

you are staying in a hotel, be sure to ask ahead of time what the per minute rates are. If you are quoted a ruble price, be sure to get the exchange rate at which you will be paying. If you wish, you can connect up and have your party call you back (find out your hotel's switchboard number, or your room's direct number – the caller may also have to give your hotel room number).

Put it on your card: If you have an AT&T or Sprint calling card, you can now call an AT&T USA Direct (which also has Russia-speaking operators) or Sprint Express number in Moscow (see above) and be immediately connected with a US operator. The connect charges are not cheap. You pay $3.25 for the first minute and $2.50 for each additional minute, plus a $2-2.50 service charge per call. If you have an MCI card, you can call the MCI Call USA number in Helsinki and pay about the same charges, plus the cost of the call to Helsinki. All three services also allow you to call non-US numbers through the US operator. *You may now also dial 800 numbers via USA Direct, MCI or Sprint international access numbers, although the call will not be toll-free.*

Call collect: You can use the AT&T, Sprint and MCI numbers above to place a collect call. For this you don't need a card (the call recipient will be billed the above charges, plus a hefty fee, about $5).

Leapfrogging: For persons setting up offices or staying in Russia longer term, there are a number of companies offering different technological fixes to leapfrog the bottleneck in international dialing: everything from installation of local and international direct lines, to cellular phones, to independent Inmarsat direct links via satellite from any location in Russia. A common solution is to have a "satellite phone" or fax number, which allows one to bypass the Russian phone system altogether. In such instances, this satellite number has a different city code from "local" phones (i.e. 501, 502, 509). For a complete city-specific listing of telecommunications service companies, see the Yellow Pages in our *Where in Moscow* or *Where in St. Petersburg*. The only service which is not city-specific is that provided by the US company BelCom. They provide portable single and multichannel satellite telephone systems that allow direct communication (voice, fax, telex and data) from remote locations in the CIS. Contact (in the US): BelCom Communications, 515 Madison Ave., New York, NY 10022, ph. (212) 371-2335, fax (212) 755-0864.

Communicating with Russia from Abroad

Since the fall of 1989, it has been possible to direct dial Moscow from the United States. It has long been possible to do this from most European countries. It is now theoretically possible to dial direct to most any Russian city which you can direct dial from Moscow, but you must contend with low capacity lines. In practice, poor line quality and congestion make calling direct to anywhere but Moscow something of a trial. Often, the costlier variant of dialing via an operator can help speed the call and secure better line quality.

To dial Russia, dial 011-7, then the city code (see table page 5), then the local number.

The best time to call Moscow from the US is during US non-business hours (i.e. nights and weekends). At any time, your ability to dial successfully will depend upon where in the US you are calling from. New York and Washington are best placed on the US network and Western cities like Houston and San Diego are much farther down on the electronic totem pole and will, regardless of the time, find direct dialing much more difficult. Calling from Europe is usually much easier than from the US.

The cost of a call from the United States to Russia, with any of the major carriers, is about $2 a minute (less on weekends). From the US, Sprint offers the greatest number of lines into Russia, as it has its own circuits, plus it uses AT&T circuits for overflow traffic, whereas the reverse is not true. You can access Sprint, regardless of your carrier, by dialing 10333, then the complete number (beginning with 011, as above). You can access AT&T, regardless of your carrier, by dialing 1028801, then the country code and number. MCI can be accessed from any phone by dialing 10222.

FAX

Sending faxes to and from Russia is usually guaranteed to end in frustration. Line quality is not consistently sufficient to sustain a quality transmission, and business hours are the most difficult time to get through. And at $2-3 per minute, the costs can be astronomical. From Europe, the situation is, of course, somewhat better.

Still, a growing number of Russian businesses now have fax machines (vs. the old telex standby), and it is becoming as much a mainstay of business activity there as in the West. A fact is worth noting in this context. A fax machine (or modem) in Russia must be registered with the local authorities (in this instance the local telephone network), and its hookup inspected by them (to make sure it complies with Russian standards). There is an initial hookup fee and an annual "service charge." Of late, there have been campaigns to "catch" unregistered fax machines, with "offenders" paying fines which basically amount to the hookup and annual fees, plus a factoring.

For places in Moscow or St. Petersburg to send a fax to or from (service bureaus), see the Yellow Pages in our *Where in Moscow* or *Where in St. Petersburg*.

FAX FORWARDING

Through the use of electronic mail services (see below) and satellite technology, some companies are providing what is known as fax forwarding services to Russia and the CIS. The procedure involves either sending an electronic mail message for conversion into a fax and transmission within Russia, or faxing a message to a Western fax relayer, who stores the fax and sends it on electronically, for retransmission within Russia. In either case, the sender's hassle is greatly reduced and, in most cases, the quality of transmission is greatly improved. The current providers of this service are:

Sovam Teleport: Through the electronic mail link (see below) the user merely specifies that the message is to be delivered by fax, and the message is forwarded and faxed electronically from a machine in Moscow. This improves the quality (and ease) of transmission by sending a digital message by data link to Moscow, and a fax message from Moscow to other points in Russia. For more info, call Sovam Teleport at 415-931-8500.

Global SprintFax: US Sprint offers a service called Global SprintFax. When you subscribe to this service (start-up fees of about $500, plus a $100 monthly minimum), you can send a fax to a local number in the West or Russia, it is digitized and sent electronically over dedicated lines to or from Russia, and then faxed out from the location closest to your fax's destination. This means no hassle with direct-dialing to Moscow, and greatly improved transmission quality. The cost between Europe and Russia is about $1.50, between the US and Russia, about $3 a page. Contact your local Sprint sales representative, or Sprint in Moscow (see *Electronic Mail*). Since Sprint has set up fax servers throughout Russia and the former USSR, your fax will often be un-digitized and sent from a server quite close to your recipient's number. Sprint's Email service (see below) uses these same servers to turn text Email messages into faxes at the user's request.

Email carriers: All other major email carriers (i.e. Compuserve, Prodigy, MCI Mail, see below) also allow you to send electronic mail messages to a fax machine, including faxes in Moscow. This tends to be a bit more expensive than sending it yourself (and more expensive than the Sovam alternative), but it does take the task off you hands; typically the number is tried repeatedly by the service until it gets through. These services will send your fax from a US-based server (vs. a Moscow-based one) and use direct dial international phone lines, which means the quality will be a bit less reliable. In any case, the limitation of any Email-based fax system (including Sovam and Sprint) is that you can only send text messages.

ELECTRONIC MAIL

One way any business or individual can circumvent communications difficulties (i.e. relying on phone and fax communications with Moscow or outlying areas) is to tap into an electronic mail (Email) service. Because this requires only local calls at either end of a communication channel and not a direct link between communicating parties, it is a much simpler, more flexible, and a much less expensive means of communication.

What you need. To use Email, aside from a computer, you need communications software, a modem and an account on an Email system, which together should not cost more than $200.

To use Email in Russia, the user *must* have either a modem with error correction capability (to compensate for the bad lines), often known as **MNP5 or V.42 bis Error Correction**, or telecommunications software which can effect the same type of correction (we recommend WordPerfect Communications, formerly MTEZ, which costs $99, call 800-451-5151 or 801-225-5000).

To connect your modem (or fax) to Russian phone lines, you will also need an adaptor that converts a US RJ-11 phone plug to the flat, four-pronged Russian phone plug. To get one in the US, call 800-639-4301 and ask for item A710. They are also available at selected stores in Moscow. To convert from European plugs to Russian plugs, call TeleAdapt in the UK at 44-81-421-4444, fax 44-81-421-5308.

What Email is. Email is an electronic, often instantaneous, postal service. You write your mail in a word processing program on your computer, then save it as a text file (which strips out text formatting codes like bold, italic and font sizes). You then use your communications software to connect (log-on) to your Email service by modem and transmit (upload) your text message onto the system, providing an address of the recipient that the system understands (i.e. risvt@sovusa.com). The Email system then forwards your message intact through a network of servers (X.25 pads) and satellite connections, to land in your intended recipient's mailbox and await her next log-on to the service at that end. Mail sent to you from colleagues and friends also sits in your Email "in-box" until you log-on to retrieve (download) it.

The beauty of using Email to communicate with Russian partners is that, like faxes, it lets you communicate freely regardless of wide differences in time zones. But, unlike fax communication, Email requires only local phone calls on both ends and, thanks to error-correcting technology, communications rarely get garbled the way a fax bouncing off satellites can.

But the value of Email only begins with the ability to send text messages in and out of Russia effortlessly. Because Email systems also allow you to send and receive *binary* files (formatted word processing files – including documents in Russian, spreadsheets, graphics files, etc.), you can easily exchange complex reports, publications and files. And it can be done quite inexpensively, particularly if you use compression software to decrease the size of your binary files (often to 10-25% of their original size) – needless to say, both the sender and the receiver must be using the same software. Software called PKZIP/PKUNZIP is the standard and can be obtained on most any Email/bulletin board network, such as Compuserve.

Another advantage of Email is that you can very easily send and receive telexes right from your computer. This is particularly important since most larger Russian enterprises and factories still use telex (not fax) as a primary means of communication. This puts you in easy touch with all points of Russia and the Commonwealth with a simple keystroke.

Corporate Forwarding
Your partner in the former USSR

A further permutation of Email is possible. If you purchase a fax modem instead of an ordinary modem (indeed, most all modems these days are fax modems), you can use the fax modem to receive faxes (even those sent to yourself, if you have two lines), then save the file as a bitmapped image (which can be viewed or printed by most any graphics or word processing software), compress it, and send it as a binary file to or from Russia.

How to get started. Several companies operate Email services which are primarily Russian-Western services. And most of the major Email services that can be accessed in the West can be accessed from Moscow, St. Petersburg and from anywhere else in the former Soviet Union where a call can be placed directly to one of these cities.

Most Email systems are inexpensive to use on the Western side (i.e. sending from the US to Russia or receiving in the US from Russia). The most expensive part of the equation in any case is sending and receiving on the Russian end. Prices between services vary, as do the services and features each provides.

To get started in the West, you can contact any of the offices below to set up an Email account. If you are already using an Email service, chances are, if a Russian partner can get hooked up on a system there, they can communicate with you via Internet addressing (ask your Email service's customer service department about this).

Electronic Mail Services

Compuserve, PO Box 20212, Columbus, OH 43220, ph. 800-848-8990
This well-known electronic mail and bulletin board system can be accessed from Moscow via the VNIIPAS host (contact Sovam Teleport JV in Moscow for a host account – ph. 095-229-9663), from many large Russian cities via Sprint/Telenet servers, or via the Moscow Infonet host (least expensive, a separate local account is not required for either the Telenet or Infonet hosts) and offers the best alternative for speedy transfer of binary files, because it supports the Compuserve B transfer protocol. While reasonably priced on the Western end, going through the VNIIPAS or Telenet hosts makes access pricey in Russia. The Infonet host is cheaper, but we have not found it to be as reliable.

Glasnet, 437 Mundel Way, Los Altos, CA 95072, phone 415-948-5753; fax 415-948-1474
This system cuts costs to users by using packet sending, whereby messages are stored up and sent every couple of hours in batches. Costs in Moscow are competitive and often negotiated on contract. If you don't require immediate delivery of messages, this may be your most cost-effective alternative. Glasnet is on the Internet. For a Russian account, contact Glasnet in Moscow at 217-6173, fax 216-6033.

Infocom, in the US, phone Infonet at 800-766-8737
This Russo-Finnish joint venture has been much lower profile than Sprint or Sovam and a bit pricier as well. It links you into the large Infonet network (and to Compuserve, see above). Not as widespread a service in North America; in Europe, call directory assistance for the local affiliate company. For a Russian account, contact Infocom JV at Kamergerskiy per. 4, ph. 925-1235, fax 200-3219.

Telex and Email Transliteration	
А	A
Б	B
В	V
Г	G
Д	D
Е	YE
Ё	YO
Ж	ZH
З	Z
И	I
К	K
Л	L
М	M
Н	N
О	O
П	P
Р	R
С	S
Т	T
У	U
Ф	F
Х	KH
Ц	TS
Ч	CH
Ш	SH
Щ	SHCH
Ы	Y
Э	E
Ю	YU
Я	YA

MCI Mail, 1150 17th Street NW, Suite 800, Washington, DC 20036, phone (800) 444-6245

A very user-friendly atmosphere and cost-effective on the US or European side, but, like Compuserve, a bit pricey on the Russian end, since traffic goes through the VNIIPAS host. For a Russian account, contact Sovam Teleport in Moscow (see note on Compuserve above).

Sovam Teleport, 3278 Sacramento St., San Francisco, CA 94115, phone 800-257-5107, fax 415-931-2885

The Email provider which provides the best service value. Your Russian partner can access the system and pay in rubles, and you pay a reasonable fee for access in the US. Delivery is nearly immediate and the system also supports fax, telex capabilities and binary file transfer. The company is also developing a range of database services which users can access on-line. For a Russian account (access numbers in Moscow, St. Petersburg, Kiev, Vladivostok, Riga, Minsk and more – see City Guide, chapter 4), as well as via any US or European city (via Telenet servers). Contact Sovam in Moscow at ph. 229-9663.

Relcom, In Moscow, Ovchinnikovskaya nab. 6, ph. 231-2129, 231-6395, fax 198-9510.

This is the largest domestic Russian/CIS telecommunications network, founded originally, as was the case with Internet in the US, for academic purposes. It has since gone commercial and is expected to grow by leaps and bounds by virtue of its new alliance with the largest commodities exchange in Russia, the RCME. It operates with some delay, but can provide access to Internet, Bitnet, MCI, Compuserve, and other Email services.

Sovset, c/o Comtex, 4900 Seminary Road, Suite 800, Alexandria, VA 22311, ph. (703) 820-2000.

Primarily a network of bulletin boards for academics, this is nonetheless the network for slavophiles. Accessible worldwide through Bitnet, Internet and Telenet, this is also accessible from Moscow by using the VNIIPAS or Sprint hosts (see above). Cost effective, but a bit less user-friendly interface.

SprintNet, 12490 Sunrise Valley Drive, Reston, VA 22096, ph. (800) 736-1130; in Northern Europe: Norton House, Kingsland Business Park, Basingstoke RG24 OPL, England; in France: Z.A. De Courtaboeuf, Miniparc Du Verger, 1 Rue De Terre Neuve, 91967 Les Ulis Cedex B

Sprint offers a nice user interface for an additional fee which will help you keep your Email organized (Compuserve also offers a similar system). Prices are reasonable on the US and European end, but high on the Russian end ($45 per hr.). The best selling point

is that this system, which has the usual fax, telex and database/news service access capabilities, sits on the world's largest data network, making international access easier. For a Russian account (access numbers in dozens of cities of the former USSR) contact Sprint in Moscow at (095) 201-6890.

TELEX

As noted above, one of the main ways to communicate from all points of Russia and the Commonwealth is by telex. Sending telexes can be inexpensive and simple. You can send telexes from almost any post office in any city or town in Russia. And if you have Email back at your home office, this may be a viable way to communicate quickly. Use the table on the previous page for sending Russian language telexes from the West. A US company, ANSAT, can install bi-lingual telex terminals, ph. 202-483-0400.

Shipping to/from Russia

AIR MAIL

The Russian mail system is slow, unreliable and not very safe. It's fine for personal letters, but don't send anything of value by the post. Use one of the alternatives listed under Express Mail below (indeed, it is still technically illegal to send certain items of value, like stamps, lottery tickets, checks, cash, stock certificates and photographic negatives by mail into Russia). You may send, by airmail, goods as gifts to Russians that are valued at <$200, although, as noted above, it is not recommended to send anything of value by mail.

The cost of a domestic letter is low by international standards (R200 at the time of publication). An international letter cost R700 at the time of publication, an international parcel (<10 kg) cost R110,000.

EXPRESS MAIL & COURIER SERVICES

A number of Western companies, either independently or through joint ventures, now provide express letter and package service to and from Russia. Typical delivery time (to Moscow or St. Petersburg) is 2-4 days to and from the US and 1-3 days to and from Europe. Delivery to outlying cities takes somewhat longer. For pick up or contact numbers, see the Yellow Pages in our *Where in Moscow* or *Where in St. Petersburg*. DHL and TNT deliver to the largest number of cities in the CIS, followed by Annandale, and then Fedex.

The following companies are currently serving the major CIS and Baltic cities (subject to change without notice, this information is correct at the time of printing). Prices fluctuate greatly according to the city being delivered to. The basic price for a one pound package of documents to Moscow (from the US) is indicated as a benchmark. Other cities often carry a surcharge. Call the carrier for more information. For an excellent summary of express mail services to the Russian Far East, contact the publishers of *Russian Far East Update* at ph. 206-447-2668. Prices below do not include duties or taxes.

Express Mail Services

Airborne Express, ph. 703-802-3812; $69
Alaska Airlines (to/from Russian Far East), ph. 800-426-0333; $40
Annandale Express (out of NY), ph. 703-591-2477; $38
Federal Express, ph. 800-247-4747; $68
DHL, ph. 800-225-5345; UK: 81-890-9393; $71
Emery Worldwide, ph. 800-323-4685; $65
TNT Skypack, ph. 800-558-5555; UK: 81-561-2345; $78.50
UPS, see local phone directories for 800 numbers; $65

National mail services, such as US Postal Service and Royal Mail also provide express mail services to Moscow and some major cities, usually using the Russian mail service for outlying cities. Most all air carriers serving Russia also offer air cargo or air freight services. You may need to use a freight forwarder for such services, however (see section following).

For express mail services *within* Russia, in addition to the companies listed above, a less-expensive, though widely-employed alternative is to pay a train car conductor to put your package in their compartment, for pick up at the other end of the line by a colleague who meets the train (you call your friend and tell them the train car and train that the packet is arriving on). This used to be safer than it currently is, with crime on the trains increasing, but is still a good alternative for non-valuable items.

Courier Services

Post International: Twice-weekly courier service between New York and Moscow. For $50-70 per month, clients may send up to a pound of printed matter into and out of Moscow each week. Additional material costs $10/lb. Contact Post International in Moscow at 200-0927 or 200-2848.

PX Post: Offers a twice-weekly mail service between Moscow and the UK Outgoing mail is sent by airmail from the UK. You can send/receive as little or as much mail as you like, but you can get lower mail rates by agreeing to send and receive a total of $10 worth of mail each week (about 1/2 pound of total traffic). For more information, contact PX Post in Moscow at 956-2230, fax 956-2231.

Russia Direct Couriers: Offers hand-to-hand service, anywhere in Russia or the CIS, ph. 413-367-2853, fax 413-367-2810. One pound: $237.50

Russia House, Ltd.: Operates a weekly courier between Moscow and London, on a pay as you go basis. Cost is £40 for up to three kilos, in the UK, call 71-439-1271.

AIR/SEA CARGO

For heavier shipments, it is more cost effective to send via air or sea freight. Air freight can be as quick as an express courier (after documentation and upon delivery to the point of departure), and becomes cost effective at weights of 20-25 pounds. Sea freight will take 3-4 weeks and can be subject to significant unloading delays at destination points, and is only suitable for

MOSCOW'S
ONLY CHOICE
FOR INTERNATIONAL MAIL

RCMI, Inc.

Business Start-Up &
Market Entry in Russia

I. Strategy Planning and Market Entry

Business Plans

Project Analysis

Legal & Tax Updates

Competition Surveys

Market Analysis

II. Tax, Banking, Currency Conversion

Russian & International Taxation

Russian & International Accounting

Treaties & Tax Reduction

Local Banking Considerations

Currency Conversion

III. Company Registration and Visa Support

Joint Stock Companies

Limited Partnerships

Representative Offices

Non-Profit Organizations

Offshore Registration

Multi-Entry Visas

IV. Translation, Travel, Secretarial Services

Phone, Fax, Moscow Address

Translation Projects

Secretarial Services

Domestic Air & Rail Tickets

Logistics & Travel Coordination

Staffing Issues

IN THE U.S.:

19000 MacArthur Blvd., Suite 400
Irvine, CA 92715
(714) 476-7850
(714) 540-7108
Internet: <rcmi@igc.apc.org>

IN MOSCOW:

15 Ulitsa Chekhova
Moscow, Russia 103006
Tel +(7095) 209-98-14
Fax +(7095) 209-13-98
Glasnet: <rcmi@glas.apc.org>

containerloads. Most any freight forwarder can arrange all documentation and shipping services for you, by air or land. And there are thousands of freight forwarders. Be sure to check a forwarder out thoroughly before committing your shipment to their care.

You will need to have an Air Waybill for air express or air freight shipments, plus a pro forma commercial invoice listing the contents of the shipment, their weight and the number of pieces. The latter should also state the total value of the shipment, and you may need to state the cost of shipping. There is, at the time of publication, a 15% duty on the total value of most all shipments into Russia, including on the cost of shipping.

Below is a list of just a few freight forwarding and shipping companies who are known to have a good deal of experience shipping to Russia. The European companies listed can truck in shipments, thus sending by sea for transshipment by one of these shippers is a good way to avoid current port delays. This listing does not constitute an endorsement of any kind.

US Shippers and Freight Forwarders

Air-Sea Forwarders, PO Box 90637, Los Angeles, CA 90009, phone 213-776-1611, fax 310-216-2625

Baltic Shipping Company, c/o Rice, Unruh, Reynolds Co., 29 Broadway, Room 1315, New York, NY 10006, ph. 212-943-2350, fax 212-363-5032

Corporate Forwarding, Stamford Landing, 102 Southfield Ave., Stamford, CT 06902, ph. 203-353-1441, fax 203-353-1497

Danzas Corp., 3650 - 131st Ave, SE, Newport Towers, Suite 700, Bellevue, WA 98006, ph. 800-426-5962, 206-649-9339, fax 206-649-4940 (call this office for the office closest to you)

Finn Container Cargo Services, Inc., 3000 Weslayn, Suite 200, Houston, TX 77027, ph. 713-961-5200, fax 713-961-4088

Radix Group, Intl., Building 75, North Hangar Road, JFK Int'l Airport, Jamaica, NY 11430, ph. 718-917-4800, fax 718-917-6509

Schenkers, 150 Albany Ave., Freeport, NY 11520, for air freight: ph. 516-377-3006, fax 516-377-3076, for sea freight: phone 201-434-5500.

Sea-Land Service, Inc., 379 Thornall St., 5th Floor, Edison, NJ 08837, ph. 800-753-2500

Stalco Forwarding Services, 254 W. 35th St., 16th floor, New York, NY 10001, ph. 212-736-1960, fax 212-594-9588

Shippers Outside the US

John Nurminen Oy, Pasilankatu 2, SF 00240, Helsinki, Finland, ph. (0) 015-071, fax (0) 0145-614

Scan Cargo Transport a/s, 44 Fabriksparken, Dk 2600 Glostrop, Denmark, ph. (424) 535-11, telex 331-63

Sovfracht, ul. Rozhdestvenka 1/4, Moscow, Russia 103759, ph. (095) 926-1118, fax (095) 230-2640, telex 411168

Sovtransservice GmbH, Wendenstrasse 151, 2000 Hamburg 26, Germany, ph. (40) 251-3126, fax (40) 258-065, telex 211-294

8

Doing Business

This new period in Russian history offers unique opportunities and certain risks for investors. The Russian investment frontier has been open for just over seven years. Thousands of firms and individuals have ventured East (or West, as the case may be) in that time. Some have been wildly successful; most have been sobered; many have failed. This section considers some of the lessons of the past seven years and, at the same time, summarizes some of the unique aspects of the Russian market.

The Russian Style of Business

When it comes to understanding the Russian business culture, it is prudent to remember that the imprint of over 70 years of communist administrative style and practice lays heavy on Russian industry and trade. It is also worth remembering that, while Russia lived some 74 years under communist rule, it has lived over a thousand years under authoritarian and autocratic rule. There are only remote pockets of democratic or free market experience in the whole of Russian and Soviet history.

At times it may be difficult to discern which elements of the present Russian style of business are "Russian" and which are "Soviet." Regardless, there are certainly some distinctive characteristics of the Russian business "style" which are unique.

It should be noted that this is a necessarily cursory review of some of the characteristics of Russian business culture. While there are certainly risks in such generalization, there must be a starting point for understanding potential cultural differences which are bound to arise when doing business in Russia.

RED TAPE

In 1839, the Marquis de Custine, while waiting to enter Russia through St. Petersburg, unnerved by the customs bureaucracy, was consoled by a Russian customs agent who commented that "Russia is the land of useless formalities." In this respect at least, Russia has not changed much in 150 years.

Doing business in Russia means daily taking on a bureaucracy with few equals. Be it in customs clearing, taxation or enterprise registration, red tape binds the economy and society to the point of strangulation. Notaries, auditors, bookkeepers and inspectors hold the business person hostage to an endless procession of stamps, forms and signatures.

But, as in Custine's case, the bureaucrat himself is also long-suffering and will often beat you to the punch in decrying the bureaucracy's injustices and intractability. This rebellion against the system, while working complacently within it, often leads to a frustrated bureaucrat finding himself able to overlook minor infractions for personal gain (in fact, one could argue the system is supported by such outlets for personal gain). But, short of bribery, there is the opportunity to use the latent sympathy of individual bureaucrats to ease a difficult situation. This should not be taken to the extreme, however. Crying outrage most often begets stonewalling.

FORMALISM

The bureaucracy's useless formalities belie a more general formalism in the business sphere which is in stark contrast to the more casual Western business style, in particular the American.

Paper communications are very formulaic and formal (see our *Business Russian*, reviewed in Chapter 1, for samples).

Business is rarely conducted over the phone, and face to face negotiations are the only real forum for decision-making. For this, the Soviet KGB carries much of the blame. But it is also that Russians very much feel that any matter of import should be discussed by looking one another in the eyes.

Even the simplest meetings are termed negotiations (переговоры – *peregovori*) and include a certain protocol all their own. There is the ceremonial exchange of business cards, the rambling speeches, the tea and cookies, and the ever-serious tone implying that issues of great import are being negotiated.

The problem with such meetings, which certainly harken back to the pre-1987 period, is that they take time, too much time. They are rarely productive in a practical sense. But certainly the older management personnel, raised in the communist form of economic management, are more prone to this type of formalism. The younger and newer entrepreneurs tend to eschew such formalities and rightly place a higher value on their time and energies.

SENSE OF TIME

Even the younger, more impatient Russians, however, share with their counterparts among the older management a sense of time and timeliness which differs somewhat from Western business practice.

Being late for business meetings is far from taboo in Russia. In fact it is almost the rule. Punctuality is very rare. Given that, expect meetings to drag on into overtime.

The flip side of this more casual relationship to time is that Russian business people generally have a greater reserve of patience than their Western counterparts. They are likewise more conservative (pessimistic?) about change and schedules for change. Therefore, expect new ideas to be met with a brick wall of skepticism. Expect change to meet with great delays.

Conversely, expect decisions made and commitments believed in to be pursued with incomparable vigor and effort.

MANEUVERING

Every negotiation is an occasion for Machiavellian intrigues, maneuvering and posturing. Rest assured that there is nothing personal in this and great malice is not usually intended. This is just part of the game of business as Russians see it. Not unlike a round of chess.

Whereas Americans and other Western business persons tend to work from the assumption that the result of any negotiation should be a win-win situation, all too often Russian business people are zero-sum thinkers: our side cannot win without putting the other side at a disadvantage.

This is reinforced by a general political and business ethos that implies that, in order to get by, you must deceive the authorities and find loopholes in laws. So far there has been little in Russian business legislation to show such behavior to be unjustified. For now, the sphere of business is one of intrigues and mirrors.

"SVYAZI"

For seven decades, the binding force which held the Soviet economy together was the Communist Party. It was an institutionalized "old boy" network. Doing anything of consequence under the old system required Party approval and patronage. If you didn't have connections (связы – svyazi), you stood little chance of getting anywhere or getting anything done.

While the edifice of both the Soviet Union and the Party has crumbled, the importance of connections in this highly bureaucratic society has not waned. It has just become less institutionalized.

Rare is the occasion when a business meeting will not be a venue for name dropping and claims of uncommon influence (at the highest levels). It is often difficult, if not impossible, to test the veracity of these claims, but the importance of "friends in high places" is not to be overlooked.

The importance of connections and access is heightened by deeply ingrained traditions of patronage and co-optation. Connections and the ability to take care of your friends are real indicators of status, still even more so than the new status symbols of incipient capitalism. But this is not surprising in a society where the economy has always been highly politicized and statist (and founded on scarcity).

CULT OF LARGESSE

Russians are lovers of grand designs and largesse. It is often said that, much as with Texans, this has to do with their geographic disposition, that huge open spaces give rise to expansive thinking. Regardless of the reasons, Russians, like Americans, love to do things in a big way. You only need to look at the Stalinist architecture of Moscow or the feat of St. Petersburg for examples.

The positive connotations of this are ambition and vision (i.e. the Virgin Lands program and the Soviet Space Program). The negative connotations are hastiness and inability to build a proper foundation (Stalin's sinking Palace of Soviets and the poor quality of St. Petersburg water come to mind). And unfortunately, too many of the "first wave" of Russian entrepreneurs are after the fast buck and the big score, erecting empires on sand, trying to be the biggest, rather than the best, trying to do all things, rather than one thing very well. Too few recognize the worth of building lasting value and doing one thing and doing it very well. The solution is merely a matter of channeling innate ambition and vision, which, some have postulated, will be the manner of the coming "second wave" of Russian entrepreneurs.

EGALITARIANISM

Any Western investor who begins an enterprise in Russia and takes on a significant number of employees will soon notice some real differences between Russian workplace mentality and that in the West. Russian workers (particularly the older ones) typically expect a much higher level of support and non-wage compensation. This is very much a result of a scarcity economy and of uncertainty (and of course of the big-brother socialism which gave birth to such an economy).

As well, Russian workers seek higher levels of workplace democracy. This is a legacy of socialist trade unions (which are yet a force to be reckoned with in Russia) and of the Russian *mir* (мир) or village, where decisions were made consensually and supported unanimously.

Stretching from these same roots, Russian workers are much more sensitive than their Western counterparts to wage differentials. From childhood, collectivism has been stressed over individualism and even individual bonuses for individual achievement are much less preferred than group bonuses based on group efforts. Certainly some aspects of this are softening up as "marketization" rocks the society to its core. But old habits die hard.

Choosing a Partner

The present somewhat uncertain times, along with the lessons of the last seven years, recommend a more circumspect and cautious approach to the selection of a partner and the cementing of business relationships.

The process of choosing a partner can be either passive or proactive. The passive approach means working with the first person who comes along who claims expertise and capabilities in your area of interest. A proactive stance means you and the goals and needs you identify drive your search. Only a proactive stance is in your best interests.

If you think that there is an opportunity for your business in Russia, try to step back far enough from the project idea to identify all of the components. What needs to be put in place – from your point of view – for the project to succeed? Identify what you need for real estate, equipment, supplies, personnel and so forth. Ask yourself, when considering a partner, how effectively the Russian organization can provide what is necessary.

Do not choose a partner before you know exactly what your needs are. Do not choose a partner unless they have a proven ability to satisfy those precise needs. Beware the prospective partner who claims to be capable of everything. Doing any *one* thing in Russia is difficult.

Keeping these points in mind, there are some questions you should ask yourself before getting too closely tied with any partner.

WHAT TO ASK ABOUT A PARTNER

- Do your potential partners have any experience in foreign trade or business management?
- Does your potential partner have any valuable political affiliation? And in these uncertain times, is this a help or a hindrance?
- Does your prospective partner want to build General Motors overnight or are they willing to focus, to start slowly and carefully?
- Does your partner measure business/organizational success in the number of bodies employed or by the bottom line? Can they construct a realistic business plan?
- Do the people that work with your prospective partner have good educational backgrounds? Did they achieve their current position by virtue of skill and intelligence or was there some other, less valuable reason? How do they go about selecting and hiring personnel?
- Does your prospective partner have an abundance of young, energetic personnel?
- Does your partner have access to a valuable section of the market you are targeting, or the supplies you will need to provide your service or product?
- Will your partner have a real ownership interest? That is, will the partner be making a commitment or investment and getting a return in a fashion that will motivate people – will there be individual motivation as opposed to merely institutional motivation?
- How is privatization affecting this partner?
- How is this partner coping with the difficult issues currently thwarting honest Russian business: crime, inflation and unclear legal jurisdictions?
- How would you evaluate this partner's respect for important legal issues, such as intellectual property rights, taxation, registration?
- Would you be working with this partner because you like him/her or because you have so far found no one else to work with? Too many people have been unwilling to admit the latter when it is the case and have thus contributed to the high failure rate of joint ventures. Would you work with these people in your home country?

GETTING STARTED

If you have found a partner you feel you can work with, it is most advisable to begin working with your partner on a contract basis, if your type of venture would allow this. You need to develop a framework within which you can test one another's abilities, strengths and weaknesses, while not committing blindly to a long term engagement. If the Western partner is contributing technology, it can be provided on a lease or license basis, as opposed to contributing to the equity or authorized capital or a new joint venture.

Such an arrangement also allows you to get to know the market, the environment, your partner and the problems you will face. When you are fully informed, you can always form a more lasting structure.

The key is to go slowly and not commit more resources than your familiarity with the Russian market can bear. The Russian market is significantly different from any other that it is worth emphasizing the importance of this. The thousands of unexecuted Letters of Intent, and the hundreds of inactive joint ventures are a testimony to the unrealistic expectations and misplaced efforts of thousands of Western and Russian firms.

Recruiting Personnel

Like your search for the right partner, your search for management and other personnel should be proactive: driven by your venture's short and long term goals, not by who you happen to meet, and when. It is easy to be drawn into Russia's ubiquitous old-boy network, hiring friends of friends (which, in and of itself, can create managerial nightmares). While in some cases this may be a desirable alternative, more often than not it leads to "satisficing" in the job search, not going out and looking for the ideal candidate.

Any new venture in Russia has two distinguishable stages as concerns hiring: short-term start-up and long-term sustained activity. The personnel needed for each stage may or may not be the same, depending upon the type and scope of your endeavor. The first task is therefore to identify your needs in each stage and let this frame your recruitment efforts. The most successful ventures have limited strong Western management involvement to the first stage of activity, seeking to train qualified Russian managers to lead for growth in the second stage.

Among Russians, Western companies and joint ventures are seen as highly-preferred work situations by virtue of the higher compensation, better working conditions and potential access to foreign travel that they offer. On the surface, this would seem to offer prospects of hiring Russia's "best and brightest." But the reality is that finding good employees is a difficult task in any environment.

Advertising: Many foreign firms have found advertisement in local Russian papers an efficient way to find prospective employees. It is relatively inexpensive and effective, since there tend to be single, dominant newspapers in a municipality. Be warned, however, that if you are not careful in using highly-specific job descriptions, you could be inundated with responses. If you are seeking personnel without foreign language skills, these media may be your best bet. But if language skills are a must, you will want to focus advertising efforts on the locally-published media for expatriates and English language speakers (if such exists), such as the *Moscow Times* or *Moscow Tribune* in Moscow or the *St. Petersburg Press* in that city. See also the *Marketing, Media & Advertising Directory*, abstracted in Chapter 1.

Executive search firms: Local and internationally-based executive search services (for the latter, see the list in Chapter 1) are also beginning to operate in Russia. Some can offer background checks, which one would be hard-pressed to conduct independently. All can undertake the time-consuming task of pre-screening. A *caveat:* Locally-based firms are new to this line of work. Thus, you must consider how to check the record of those you seek to have doing background checks for you.

The resume and job interview, as employed in the US, are not the general norm in Russia. Consider that, until just a few years ago, in the absence of a private sector, jobs were "filled" and employees "placed" by government bodies and institutes. Little recruiting *per se* took place. Job expertise was generally assumed based on one's passage through an institute. The resume was the individual's labor book (трудовая книжка – *trudovaya knizhka*), which followed him or her from job to job and which recorded demerits and promotions. Most importantly, since no one was spending their own money and since labor was relatively cheap, hiring was not seen as a critical procedure to spend time on (vs., say, acquiring production supplies).

What all this means is that Russia has long lacked a sophisticated, competitive labor market. The norms in place are not likely those that will provide you with any guidance in making hiring decisions. If you want resumes, you will have to inform applicants of how to formulate them. Some firms have found therefore, that, even for senior positions, having applicants fill in a form is the most effective means of generating the right types of information. Likewise, effective, challenging interviews need to be built up to through a series of screening interviews.

Pay scales: In deciding what to pay management and employees, be careful to use local standards for your benchmark, not your company's standards at home or in other countries. Talk to other locally-active Western and Russian business people to become educated on generalized expectations and what the market is demanding (the *Russian Employee Compensation Report,* a semi-annual publication, can also be a useful guide, see Chapter 1). Finally, look to ways to build in protections for employees against inflation and social welfare concerns that are mounting with the breakdown of Russian institutions. Become familiar with Russian labor law and the expectations it has bred (see Chapter 9).

Russian vs. Western managers: Eventually you will run up against the issue of whether to hire Russian or expatriate personnel for management positions. The fact is that finding the best qualified candidate is less and less a case of finding the right nationality. In a recent study published by the Harvard Business School, researchers found that the most successful joint ventures in Russia have "put local managers in charge and delegated radically." There is a limitless supply of qualified Russian managers who seek a productive work environment, something the Soviet system rarely allowed. As the Harvard interviews showed, Russian managers are more able to quickly adapt to Russia's fast-changing legal and regulatory environment; they have no cultural or linguistic barriers to overcome; they are better at turning seemingly intractable problems to the venture's advantage; and, if given the material wherewithal, have demonstrated commitments to quality and service matching any Western counterpart.

This said, successful joint ventures and foreign companies have found it prudent to invest in the management or technical experience of expatriates in the earliest stages of a venture's start-up. Here the focus is on getting the enterprise off on the right foot, in accordance with the foreign company's expectations, and beginning a process of the transfer of know-how. Experience has also shown that foreign companies are wise to construct water-tight systems of financial control from the outset, based on Western accounting standards and norms.

Business Etiquette

Good etiquette is, in most cases, a matter of simple common sense. The following guidelines for the business traveler (which also certainly can be extended to the independent traveler) to Russia should help you adjust to some of the cultural difficulties you may encounter.

DRESS

Most Russian business people have high expectations of Western business people. You will be judged immediately by the way you dress. Dress conservatively and well. Shoes are especially important, as is a nice hat in winter. Women should wear a hat or scarf if visiting an orthodox church. For dinners at someone's house, dress casually.

In winter, dress in layers. Buildings are usually overly-warm inside and you will want to be able to adjust flexibly. Take your overcoat off in public places (most restaurants, museums, etc. have a place to check your coat).

DISCRETION

Few people are as critical of Russia as Russians. But do not mistake their remarks as an invitation for your criticisms. Russians are also very proud, and justly so, of their country. It may at times be easy to criticize Russia for its inefficiency. But it is a mistake to focus on the present problems and suffering, while overlooking the achievements of Russian and non-Russian cultures and the economic and social potential of these peoples.

MEETINGS

Allow extra time to be on time. Getting places takes a long time (and is subject to innumerable mishaps). While being on time may often not seem too important to your Russian contacts, it should always be very important to you.

Shake everyone's hand firmly when your greet them.

Defer to the senior official to lead the meeting, and wait to be given the floor. Be firm and polite at all times; don't be pushed. Try to get an agenda worked out before the meeting gets started or too far along.

Accept cookies and tea when offered. Tolerate smoking in meetings if you don't smoke (if you are completely intolerant of smoking, doing business in Russia is not for you). Ask first before lighting up to smoke and share your cigarettes generously.

A good translator avoids a thousand headaches. Do all you can to test your translator out in informal situations before you enter into formal situations. A simultaneous translator can be more efficient, but distracting.

BACKGROUND

When preparing for meetings, know who you are meeting with, how important this person is, what his/her background is, etc. Remember, this is a culture which is based on patronage and status. Before a meeting starts, know who everyone in the room is and why they are there — you will thus avoid stepping on egos. And be sure they know who you are and why you are there (and not someone else).

Know something about the company, association or department these people work in/for. As anywhere in the world, you will flatter people by showing them that what they do is known about by someone they previously did not know. You will also impress your hosts with your seriousness about working with them.

COMMUNICATION

Never underestimate the importance of written communications in Russia. The country runs on paper (and rubber stamps). Do not commit something to writing lightly. Retain any written records. When in doubt, notarize.

Written communication is formulaic and formal. Be sure you address the addressee formally. For letters in English, follow good Western business correspondence etiquette. Always type letters. Consult a knowledgeable Russian on writing any letter in Russian.

Fax your letters if your contact has a fax (which is now becoming more common), or send it by telex, which is ubiquitous in the former USSR. Use these as your main means of communication. Don't rely on the mail. Faxes and telexes will get the most reliable and timely responses – but also send copies through the mail. You can set up telex capability (and fax for that matter) on your PC with a modem (see Chapter 7, *Communications*).

GIFTS

There are three types of gifts. The first is the token gift you should bring along to hand out to business contacts. These souvenirs (lighters, pens, solar calculators with your logo on them) are essential and may be part of what is expected, particularly at New Year's.

The second type of gift is favors. There are things you will be able to provide that no one else can, that are either unavailable or unattainable in Russia. These run the whole gamut and you should try whenever you feel it is right to do all you can to help – you will rarely regret it.

The final type of gift is the bribe. Some would call this a bargain for exchange: computers for access to apartments, VCR's for car registration, computers for an office lease, etc. Often these are unavoidable "given current conditions." Still, try to resist the argument that "this is how things are done here," if only because this is a cost of doing business that is impossible to write off legally. If the arrangement is a *quid pro quo*, try to get your quo before handing over the quid. The best general slogan for doing business in Russia is: Believe it when you see it. Understand that you are engaged in trade (торговля – *torgovlya*), and if you do not get what was promised, you probably have no recourse.

BUSINESS CARDS

There is a ritual exchange of business cards at any business meeting or negotiation. Do not underestimate the importance of this event. Your business card may be all the information your Russian partner has on you. Make sure your cards say what you want to say about you and your firm – try to have them in Russian. See Chapter 1 for a list of companies that specialize in typesetting and printing bilingual, two-sided cards.

MONEY

You are bound to find yourself, while in Russia, in situations which involve significant hard currency outlays and yet your Russian counterpart will not have a hard currency expense account. What starts out as generosity can easily turn into exploitation. Think this issue out ahead of time and do not be extravagant unless this is the image you want to convey. Know where you are going, know what it costs (what currency), and know who is going to pay.

AFTER WORK

While it is sometimes frowned upon to conduct business outside normal working hours, your host will often feel the need to take you out on the town, have a reception, etc. Feel free to discuss business insofar as your host takes the lead. But be better prepared at these times to show an interest in and knowledge of Russia, its history, politics, arts, and culture. Show yourself not to be all business.

Many foreign business people are not accustomed to consuming hard liquor (i.e. vodka and cognac) in the quantities and frequency which is accepted at dinners and receptions in Russia. Don't go overboard in your desire to fit in. Russian hospitality has a well-deserved reputation around the world. But know how and when to say no. If you need an out, be the designated driver.

CUSTOMS AND SUPERSTITIONS

Russian culture is steeped in superstition. Some aspects apply, quite seriously, to business. Russians will joke about these superstitions, but deep down they will also take these things very seriously. As well, there are some customs and points of etiquette which you should adhere to. Both customs and superstitions are listed below (you may judge for yourself which they are). You will avoid potentially embarrassing situations and/or show yourself to be knowledgeable about things Russian by noting these.

- Never shake hands over a threshold: it will lead to an argument.
- Don't whistle indoors: you will blow your money away.
- Take off your shoes when visiting a home and your hat when indoors. Take off your suit coat in meetings only after asking if it is acceptable.
- Russia is still a very male-chauvinist society. Women in business should always dress conservatively or will end up being thought below their position. Women are not expected to pay for themselves or to be assertive in social situations.
- Always bring flowers or wine when invited to a Russian's home. Always bring an odd number of flowers; even numbers are for funerals.
- Russian personal space is much smaller than what is usual in the US or Europe. Expect more physical contact.
- Be careful when refusing food or drink when visiting friends; they will likely take it as a slight.
- Never pour wine back-handed. It is considered an insult to the person for whom you are pouring.
- Never gesture with your thumb between your first two fingers: this is an obscene gesture.
- Never put your feet up on furniture or show the soles of your feet when sitting: it is considered very rude.
- If you call someone on the phone and they don't recognize your voice, it means you will soon be rich.
- "Rough" language is frowned upon in "educated society."
- A black cat crossing your path is a bad omen taken very seriously.
- Never light a cigarette from a candle: it will bring bad luck.
- Before going on a long trip, sit down for a few minutes to collect your thoughts: your trip will go better.
- Be careful complementing something in a host's home; they may try to give it to you.
- Do not sit at the corner of a table: you will end up single.
- If you leave something behind when departing Russia, it is a good sign, it means you will be back.

TOLERANCE

You will probably meet with many situations in Russia which you would normally consider "intolerable." Tolerate them. Be flexible. If you want to be doing business in a comfortable atmosphere, your way, you should be doing business elsewhere.

9

Russian Business Law

The Investment Climate

The figures do not misrepresent Russian reality: double-digit declines in GDP since 1991, double-digit *monthly* inflation, double-digit declines in industrial production over the past two years. Truly, the Russian economy is deep in the black tunnel of reform. Standard economic indicators that would sack any Western government will be the norm for the next several years.

So why invest in Russia? Are there not better, safer and wiser places to invest?

Why indeed. Russia will long be feeling the after-effects of communism, which thoroughly abused the spirits and minds of the population to the point of despondent and reactionary dependency on the powers that be. Economies can bounce back rather quickly from adversity. But attitudes and mindsets take a bit longer.

Then there is the crumbling infrastructure. Phone systems pre-date the revolution (of 1917). Storage and warehousing facilities are insufficient for basic merchandising and trade. Poorly-maintained and rarely-paved roads make for transportation nightmares. Hospitals, schools and public institutions are sorely under-funded and over-burdened.

Clearly, investing in Russia is not for the faint-hearted or shallow-pocketed. The risks of investment are great. And these risks only begin with the nature and state of the Russian economy. Crime and corruption are growing, as one would expect in a "transitional" economy. Unfathomable red tape and excessive regulations and taxes beset even the most profitable and best-informed ventures.

But, as the maxim goes, without risk, there is no opportunity. And, in Russia, opportunity abounds.

Begin with the outward signs. Despite admittedly bleak statistics, the Russian economy is on the rebound. Monthly inflation rates are slowly declining. Credit emissions from the Central Bank (a prime culprit of inflation)were being gradually limited through 1993 (although there is the fear that this will be reversed in 1994). And most importantly: private enterprise is swiftly gaining ground. Nearly one-half of all Russians now work in the private sector, vs. just 5% five years ago.

Continue with the political and social climate. While there may be some disputing the speed and content of economic reforms (as the December

1993 parliamentary elections attest), it is clear that a consensus has formed around the direction and goals of reform: toward a pluralistic, democratic market economy. Real wages of workers have increased by a factor of three in the past year and a factor of eight in the past two years. While prices are on the rise, store shelves are full in major cities and the average Russian now knows that, though times are tough, the hard-working and enterprising person can get what they need to take care of their family and even get ahead.

Conclude with the opportunities created by Russia's natural resources. From oil and gas to rarer industrial and precious metals and minerals, Russia possesses a significant portion of available world supplies. But Russia's most under-rated natural resource is its workforce. Very highly-educated and very inexpensive by Western standards, the Russian workforce can, with properly-focused investments and incentive, provide distinct comparative advantages in basic manufacturing, mining and refining industries. Moreover, this workforce is grossly under-employed, eagerly awaiting investments that will make proper use of their capabilities. A survey by the International Labor Organization showed that, in many larger factories, 20% of the labor force is superfluous.

Russia is in the midst of the most ambitious and far-reaching economic transition ever undertaken. Anywhere. An entire industrialized economy, employing some 60 million persons, is being wrenched from the clutches of mendacious bureaucrats and ceded to workers, managers and entrepreneurs. It is the largest sell-off of assets in history. As such, it has entailed a massive decentralization of economic decision-making that, by necessity almost, has ground the Russian economy to a halt.

But there are signs that recovery is underway:

Privatization is on a fast track. Over 80,000 enterprises have been privatized in the past two years, with 500-1000 new sell-offs each month. It is forecasted that, by the end of 1994, privately-held companies will have turned the tables on the state sector and will comprise over 80% of all industrial output. This privatization, combined with legalization of land ownership (and a recent loosening of the resale procedures by President Yeltsin) means that, for the first time in 70 years, all manner of real assets in Russia can be bought and sold freely by foreign (and domestic) investors.

Capital is accumulating and trade is on the rise. Foreign and domestic hard currency holdings (liquid assets) of Russian individuals and companies has been estimated at some $200 bn. Some $3-4 bn in cash hard currency transactions are already taking place inside Russia each year. Russia is expected to show a trade surplus of over $20 bn in 1993 and imports from the West (now financed by private traders, not state ministries), are growing geometrically.

Ruble convertibility. What was previously cited as the greatest hindrance to expanded trade with Russia, the inconvertibility of the ruble, has become a non-issue. While the ruble is not traded on international currency markets, it is now fully convertible within Russia, either into foreign currencies at the twice-weekly currency auctions, or into readily-exportable commodities.

Legislative predictability. The investment climate has been made more predictable with a recent presidential decree protecting enterprises through the grandfathering of business legislation and assertion of central government preeminence in foreign investment legislation. Important intellectual property legislation was also passed in late 1993. Still, much remains to be accomplished. Bureaucratic hindrances to enterprise registration, legislative uncertainty and the comparatively high rates of enterprise taxation are still matters of great concern (indeed, the afore-mentioned decree hints at future tax benefits for some foreign investments).

In the final analysis, it is legal and regulatory developments that will drive or destroy reform in Russia. Certainly Russian Central Bank monetary policy, privatization efforts, foreign aid and political reform will play significant supporting roles. But without a predictable, coherent and consistent legal environment, business people, be they Russian or foreign, will not make the long-term investments in infrastructure and manufacturing that are required to reinvigorate the Russian economy.

With this in mind, what follows is a summary of Russian legal acts relating to the most important aspects of business, trade and investment. Continual "adjustments" in this area are expected. While this summary can serve as a thorough introduction, for detailed and current appraisals of the legal climate, readers should subscribe to some of the legal periodical publications reviewed in Chapter 1 and seek competent legal counsel (some Western law firms with offices in Moscow are also listed in Chapter 1).

Russian Foreign Investment Law

On July 4, 1991, the Russian law, *On Foreign Investment Activity in the RSFSR*, was passed. It, along with the law, *On Enterprises and Entrepreneurial Activity*, is the cornerstone of legal norms regulating investment activity in Russia. A recent (September 27, 1993) presidential decree strengthened central government control over foreign investment legislation, established a three-year grandfathering norm for all such legislation, and called for amendments to the July 4, 1991 law so as to encourage foreign investment in priority sectors (through tax benefits), ensure equal status of foreign participants in privatization, and allow for mortgaging of land and real estate as guarantees of investment. As such, the decree reaffirms the general trend toward liberalization of Russian foreign investment legislation, begun in earnest with the collapse of the USSR at the end of 1991. This said, Russian foreign investment legislation, as of January 1994, had the following characteristics.

EQUAL TREATMENT

The key statement is in Article 6 of the July 1991 law, *On Foreign Investment Activity in the RSFSR*: "The legal regime of foreign investments and investment activity may not be less favorable than the regime for the property, proprietary rights, and investment activity of legal entities and citizens of the RSFSR (Russia), with the exceptions stipulated by the present law."

The law puts foreign investors on an even footing with Russian business persons, granting the right to purchase shares in existing joint stock companies and privatizing state and municipal enterprises, to acquire various types of property and rights, including land and mineral use rights. It asserts, as is the case with all related Russian legislation, the primacy of the ruble for such transactions.

The September 27, 1993 presidential decree, *On Improving Work with Foreign Investment*, further requires changes in government legal acts to ensure "the creation for foreign investors of equal conditions with Russian investors for participation in the privatization of state and municipal enterprises."

TYPES OF INVESTMENT

Three types of *equity investment* are open to foreign investors as regards the establishment of enterprises: joint ventures, fully owned subsidiaries, and affiliates (also known as branches). Two other forms of business activity *not involving direct equity investment* are also allowed: private (unregistered) business activity, and a representation. The procedures for establishing each and the laws that govern them are enumerated below.

The law explicitly allows resident investors and companies to maintain ruble accounts in Russia. Such monies, provided they are obtained from earnings within Russia, may be used to buy hard currency at auctions, to reinvest in the economy, and to buy shares in Russian companies, although foreign investors cannot use rubles to buy shares or securities if those rubles are acquired at rates lower than the MICE rate (see Chapter 5). There are some restrictions on the hard currency operations of any enterprise, and foreign representations (and non-resident investors) have some further restrictions on their ruble operations.

Certain activities (insurance, banking, brokering) require licenses. Otherwise, foreign investors can engage in any activity stated in their enterprise's statute, or which is not disallowed by existing legislation.

INVESTMENT VEHICLES

Joint Ventures

Russia does not have a law on joint ventures. The Russian law, *On Foreign Investment Activity in the RSFSR*, however, defines a joint venture as any registered Russian enterprise with foreign equity investment. Thus a joint venture is any type of Russian enterprise which has a foreign investor, including an individual, irregardless of whether that investor was a founder or has purchased shares in an existing enterprise.

The implication is that *there are now few specific tax or other advantages accorded joint ventures* (yet the September 1993 presidential decree hints that such advantages may be in the offing). The registration, activity and taxation of joint ventures is the same as for 100% Russian-owned enterprises, with but a few exceptions. These generally relate to import of equity contributions, foreign employees, avoidance of double-taxation, dividend repatriation and the like. What follows therefore is a review of the different types of Russian enterprises. Where a particular aspect of their activity is or may be different when foreign investors are involved, this is noted.

There are four types of Russian private enterprises (some have sub-types):
- joint stock company (open, closed)
- partnership (limited liability, full, mixed)
- private enterprise
- individual labor activity

In addition, any of the first three of these enterprises may be classified as a "small enterprise," which, among other things, may enjoy some tax benefits.

Joint Stock Companies

At the end of 1990, the Russian republic passed a joint stock company law which made it possible for the first time to found a company whose ownership was divided into transferable shares and which had liability limited to the extent of its assets.

The law allows for *open* and *closed* joint stock companies. For all intents and purposes, both types are treated identically under the legislation. Two important distinctions set the two types of entities apart, however.

First, shares in an *open* joint stock company can be sold or ceded to third persons with few restrictions. In a *closed* joint stock company, the founders retain preeminent right over the disposition of shares; a shareholder may not sell or transfer his/her shares in the enterprise to a third person without the permission of other shareholders.

Second, the minimum statutory capital of the two types of companies is different. *Open* joint stock companies must have a minimum statutory capital of 50,000 rubles; for *closed* joint stock companies it is 10,000 rubles.

CREATION AND REGISTRATION

- Companies may be founded by one or more participants, be they enterprises, establishments and organizations, state authorities or individual citizens. Article 11 explicitly allows foreign citizens and companies to be founders. Companies are established and operate on the basis of a Charter and a Founders' Agreement.

- The Charter (устав – *ustav*) is the fundamental document. It sets out the legal name, address and type of enterprise being created, as well as the goals and objectives of its activity. It defines the management bodies and the procedures for their decision making (including a listing of decisions wholly within the competence of the board), the procedures for profit distribution and recovery of damages, and conditions for the organization and liquidation of the enterprise.

- The Founders' Agreement (учредительный договор – *uchreditelny dogovor*) is just that, a written agreement between the founders. In addition to reiterating the basic information about the enterprise, it enumerates the investments each founder is to make and how they are to be made, how this may affect distribution of profits, and how a founder may withdraw from the corporation.

• Article 34 of the law, *On Enterprises and Entrepreneurial Activity* and Article 7 of the law, *On Joint Stock Companies*, state that, to register an enterprise, you must submit the following documents to the registration chamber (палата – *palata*) within 30 days of the enterprise's founding meeting:

❶ a notarized and certified **application** for the company's registration, which includes the company name, location, its objectives and the main types of activity of the company, the liability of the shareholders, the amount of statutory capital, the names and legal addresses of the founders and their citizenship, and the number of shares acquired by them (application forms are available at registration chambers);

❷ a notarized and certified copy of the company's **Charter**;

❸ a notarized and certified **minutes of the founding meeting** (unless the company has just one founder);

❹ proof that the enterprise's **registration fee** has been paid.

In reality, the following documents are also required:

❶ a copy of the **Founders' Agreement** (both this and the Charter should be supplied in multiple copies, usually six each);

❷ two copies of a notarized and certified guarantee **letter from the landlord**, attesting to the company's right to use the space at its intended legal address (a rental agreement may also be attached) – there are different forms this letter must take if the legal address is to be an apartment vs. a non-residential space;

❸ *in the case of a joint venture*, **documents attesting to the liquidity of the foreign investor** (ability to make the specific capital contributions) issued by the investor's bank or another financial institution (with certified translations of said documentation into Russian);

❹ *in the case of a joint venture*, an **extract from the trade register** from the country of the foreign investor's origin, proving the legal status of the investor's company according to local law; if the foreign investor is an individual, then this means documents proving the right of the individual to conduct business activity in the country of his/her residence or citizenship (with certified translation into Russian);

❺ in cases where potentially harmful production processes are to be carried out, or in the oil and gas spheres, and particularly *in the case of joint ventures* in either case, an *expertiz* (examination) must be carried out by the responsible state authorities.

Other considerations:

• If the establishment capital fund of a *joint venture* is to exceed 100 million rubles, the venture's registration must have the prior approval of the Russian Council of Ministers. *Note:* The US-Russian Bilateral Investment

Treaty required Russia to raise this ceiling for US companies, to $56 mn prior to August 1993.

- In all cases, a *joint venture* is registered with the Ministry of Finance after being registered with the local registration chamber.

- A joint stock company may be established by the conversion of a state enterprise (i.e. through privatization), but this requires a joint decision of the employees and the appropriately empowered state authority – see the section below on privatization.

- In addition to the right to found a joint stock company, foreign investors have the right, as explicitly stated in this law (Articles 3, 4 and 35) and the law, *On Foreign Investment*, to purchase shares in existing joint stock companies.

When compiling the Charter and Founder's Agreement, some general caveats to the process of drafting these documents should be noted:

- Avoid boiler-plate Charters or Agreements which can in no way account for the unique aspects of your enterprise; do not put anything but the name and type of enterprise on the title page of the documentation (i.e. do not write "small enterprise").

- Do not use the word Russia, Moscow or other geographical designations or words deriving from them without checking first to see if there are associated licensing fees or permissions required (as is the case with Russia and Moscow).

- The doctrine of *ultra vires* is enforced with some strictness in Russia. The company should have a very carefully worded statement of purpose. It should be broad and clear. Explicitly assert the company's purposes and rights in the foundation documents.

- Be very explicit in allocating responsibility, financial and otherwise, between the parties.

- Ownership protection and property rights regarding any inventions or new technology developed by the company should be carefully circumscribed in the documents.

- Set out a clear procedure for board access to enterprise finances including clear, regular procedures for supplying partners with information on profits and losses.

- Draft a clause that limits inspections or audits to specific circumstances or at least regular intervals.

- The reserve funds required by Russian law are the equivalent of costs and taxes that get careful consideration in the West. At a minimum, you should specify the amount of annual appropriations to these funds for each partner so that the cost is precise and predictable.

- Be sure all real estate and property issues (payment for facilities, utilities, pace of renovation, etc.) are explicitly enumerated. Be certain that the founding documents clearly and unequivocally state whether assets contributed by Russian partners (and Westerners for that matter) are to be directly owned by the new enterprise or merely within their purview – assets they have the right to control, but not liquidate.

- Retain significant Western partner input into and/or veto power over hiring and firing management personnel and spending beyond certain thresholds.
- Any employee profit-sharing programs should be included in the charter, with consideration of relevant tax and currency issues.
- Set out the exact dates for distribution of profits and the procedures for making those distributions.
- Draft a clear and unequivocal liquidation clause that allows each partner, at a minimum, to walk away with the equivalent of capital and equipment invested.
- Draft clear arbitration clauses, specifying the procedures for arbitrating disputes either via the Arbitration Court of the Russian Chamber of Commerce or another court. It is also wise to include provisions for execution of arbitration awards within the actual contract and for collection in the event of either partner's insolvency.

SPHERES OF ACTIVITY

- No limits are placed on the areas of economic activity open to joint stock companies, as long as the activity does not violate the laws of Russia or its constitution. Only the government is allowed to engage in certain types of activity (i.e weapon production, tobacco and spirits production, processing of ores and precious metals – see the Russian law, *On Enterprises and Enterprise Activity*). Certain other areas of activity require the approval of the Council of Ministers (e.g. mining, fur, raw materials, timber).

Activity must technically be within the scope of activity defined in the Charter, yet transactions conducted beyond the scope of the Charter are legal insofar as they conform to existing Russian law.

- Joint stock companies have the right to establish subsidiaries in Russia or abroad. Establishing subsidiaries abroad, as well as investing abroad (including making simple bank deposits) requires approval of the Russian Ministry of Finance and/or the Russian Central Bank.
- All Russian enterprises, including joint stock companies, are forbidden from making hard currency settlements with other Russian enterprises, except in currency purchase and sale transactions. Joint stock companies can participate in currency auctions.
- A Russian presidential decree of October 27, 1993 strengthened rights of land ownership, allowing persons with title to land "to sell, bequeath, donate, mortgage, lease and change, and also to transfer land parcels or parts thereof as contribution to the authorized capital of joint stock companies, partnerships and cooperatives, including those with foreign investments."
- In November 1993, the Moscow city government decreed that all foreign firms engaged in several business sectors, from food services to tourism to pharmaceuticals and consumer goods, obtain licenses for such activity from specified agencies. Other cities may have or introduce similar requirements.

LIABILITY

• The resolution invokes limited liability of the partners or founders of the joint stock company in the following manner (Article 8): "Shareholders shall be liable for the Company's obligations within the limits of their personal capital contribution." Yet, "wrongful acts" by company executives may require them to pay compensation for damage caused the company.

• A joint stock company created from the conversion of a state enterprise (i.e. via privatization) assumes the rights, responsibilities and liabilities of the state enterprise.

SHARES AND OWNERSHIP

• Unless specifically stated in the Charter, the sale or transfer of shares in a joint stock company does not require the consent of the company. Joint stock companies can issue registered, bearer, and preference (dividend) shares (up to 10% of total shares in the case of the latter). The minimum value of a share is 10 rubles. Joint stock companies can also issue bonds.

• In closed joint stock companies, participants enjoy priority right to buy shares which another participant wishes to sell or transfer. Further, the participant may cede a share or a part thereof to a third party or to other participants only with the consent of the other participants, unless stated otherwise in the Charter. Shares can be transferred to third parties only if the participant transferring the shares has paid their contribution in full.

• Sales of over 15% of shares of the company to a legal or natural person (who is not a founder) requires the consent of the Ministry of Finance. Sale of more than 50% of shares requires the consent of both the Ministry of Finance and the State Anti-Monopoly Committee.

MANAGEMENT

Russian joint stock companies are to have a management structure not unlike that of Western corporations. Shareholders elect directors, who in turn elect/hire and oversee management. In addition, the company is to form an auditing commission to oversee and audit financial activities of the company.

TAXATION & ACCOUNTING

• Joint stock companies are currently subject to a 32% profits tax. Other taxes also apply (see the section below, *Enterprise Taxation*), among others: the value added tax, mandatory currency sales (which is, in effect a tax), property tax, advertising tax, social welfare and road taxes.

• In the absence of a tax treaty to the contrary, *in joint stock companies which are joint ventures*, the Western partner(s) will be subject to a 15% transfer tax on any dividends transferred to the Western partner(s)' domicile. The new US-Russia tax treaty sets a maximum transfer tax rate on dividends of 10% (5% if the US company's equity share exceeds 10%).

• A joint stock company must maintain its books on model forms prepared by the Ministry of Finance, have its bookkeeping done by accountants directed by the Accountant General and file statistical reports in accordance with "established procedure." The good news is that Russian accounting standards are approaching internationally-accepted accounting standards, which means, in the case of Russian companies with foreign investment, keeping only one set of books to satisfy both partners.

• Imported equipment and supplies for production are exempt from customs, tariffs or taxation. Office supplies are not.

LABOR LAWS

• Under current Russian legislation, all labor issues of import in joint stock companies are to be decided in the process of negotiation of collective and/or individual labor contracts. But the legacy of Soviet labor law still imbues this process with certain expectations and realities. See the section on Labor Law below.

• Employees who are foreign nationals work under the same labor laws as Russian employees and must pay the same income tax rates. All income taxes on all forms of income (rubles or hard currency) are payable in rubles. These taxes can be as high as 30% on net income (see the section on Individual Taxation below).

Partnerships

Russian law allows the formation of partnerships (товарищество – *tovarishchestvo*) as either legal entities or as temporary, task-oriented commercial arrangements. Partnerships can be between individuals or legal entities (companies) or a combination of both. The law defines two types of partnerships: general and mixed. Some experts have said the law allows for limited liability partnerships, but in elaboration have been unable to demonstrate any differences between such partnerships and closed joint stock companies. A foreign citizen or foreign company can enter into a partnership as would a Russian individual or company. The resulting entity, however, would be a joint venture and require additional registration procedures.

• A *general partnership* (полное товарищество – *polnoye tovarishchestvo*) is not a legal entity and therefore does not need to be registered in the manner of joint stock companies. It must, however, be registered in the Unified State Register of Enterprises. To effect this, it must submit a copy of its Partner's Agreement to the regional statistical bureau, and fill out an application indicating the location, type, and spheres of activity of the partnership as well as other information. The name of the partnership should be unique and include the name of at least one of the partners.

A general partnership entails no limitation of liability on the partners, and shares of ownership and profit are set in the Agreement. Profits and dividends taken out of the partnership by a partner are taxed as individual income (or in the case of companies that are partners, profit taxes).

• A *mixed partnership* (смешанное товарищество – *smeshannoe tovarishchestvo*) combines the features of a general partnership with the option of allowing outside investors who do not take part in day-to-day administration. Such investors' liability is limited to the level of their investment, while the liability of other, full partners is not limited, yet they are not liable for other activities of the investor. A mixed partnership is a legal entity and therefore must register according to the procedures indicated above for joint stock companies, and must pay enterprise, profit and other taxes.

Private Enterprises

The Russian law, *On Enterprises and Enterprise Activity* (Article 8) defines this type of enterprise as a "private (family) enterprise." As such, it is an enterprise "constituting the property solely of a private citizen or held in common by members of his or her family..." A private enterprise can be founded with assets owned by an individual or by an individual's acquisition of assets through the privatization of state or municipally-owned enterprises. The enterprise should have a unique name which includes the name of the founder of the enterprise. The registration procedure for a private enterprise is essentially the same as that indicated above for joint stock companies.

A private enterprise has the advantage of limiting the liability of its owner to the extent of his/her investment in the company. As well, a private enterprise may hire employees and carry out commercial activity as stipulated in its Charter. As a legal entity and an enterprise, it is subject to enterprise taxation. Further, revenues drawn from the company by the owner are subject to the income tax. A foreign citizen can found a private enterprise.

Individual Labor Activity

Essentially, this entails self-employment, as a private contractor or private entrepreneur. Registration procedures require only a "patent" for conduct of individual labor activity (индивидуальная трудовая деятельность – *individualnaya trudovaya deyatelnost*). Income taxes are paid on earned income, and entrepreneurs must only pay a VAT on their activity if their total annual income is anticipated to exceed 500,000 rubles. It allows the individual to obtain a bank account, credit and legal registration for business activity, as well as conclude any type of civil agreement allowed by law. A private entrepreneur cannot hire labor.

Small Enterprises

A small enterprise is a sub-classification of joint stock companies, partnerships or other legal entities. It is not a separate type of legal entity unto itself. The label merely denotes the scale of the enterprise. A small enterprise does, however, enjoy certain tax benefits.

SIZE

• Depending upon the sphere of economic activity in which an enterprise engages, restrictions are placed on the number of employees which may be employed by the enterprise and still be designated as *small*. If the enterprise engages in several activities, that activity which is responsible for the largest volume of goods or services provided is the operative sphere of activity. These limits are: Industry and construction – up to 200 people; Science and scientific activities – up to 100 people; Other branches of industry – up to 50 people; Non-manufacturing – up to 25 people; Retail sales – up to 15 people.

• Autonomous republics and localities may also place limits on the amount of total revenue which small enterprises of various sectors may earn and still be classified as small enterprises. Similarly, they may designate minimum numbers of employees for small enterprises.

TAXATION

• Certain types of small enterprises are wholly exempt from taxation during their first two years of operation. This applies to small enterprises engaged in agricultural production and processing of farm produce, consumer goods production, construction, maintenance/construction, building materials production, and to small innovation enterprises. Small enterprises engaged in other activities must pay only 25% of their normal tax rate in their first year of operation and 50% in the second year.

• Profits which are allocated to construction, modernization, retooling and renovation of fixed assets or training and retraining of personnel are tax exempt in an amount equal to 10% of the investment in fixed assets.

• All small enterprises must pay the full tax rate after two full years of operation (see section below, *Enterprise Taxation*). If a small enterprise ceases operations before it has been in existence for three years, it is liable for the full measure of taxes for the entire period of its operation.

Wholly-owned Subsidiaries

The Russian law, *On Foreign Investment Activity in the RSFSR* and some Soviet legislation which preceded it, laid a groundwork for legalizing registration and operation of 100% foreign-owned companies in Russia. On the surface, organization and registration of such companies is made to appear no more difficult than for Russian enterprises (which is, in fact, far from simple). As such, this is fast becoming the preferred mode of direct foreign investment in Russia.

CREATION AND REGISTRATION

Typically, foreign companies are forming wholly-owned subsidiaries in Russia as joint stock companies, according to the procedures outlined above for such entities. But this does not mean that wholly-owned subsidiaries cannot be founded as other legal Russian enterprise types. In terms of the documentation required for registration, the law essentially treats wholly-owned subsidiaries as it does joint ventures. In any case, *in addition to the registration material and documents specified for the particular enterprise type,* the foreign company/investor must submit the following materials to the Ministry of Finance (via the registration chamber – *palata* – representing it):

❶ **documents attesting to the liquidity of the foreign investor**, issued by the investor's bank or other financial/credit institution (with certified translations into Russian);

❷ an **extract from the trade register** from the country of the foreign investor's origin, proving the legal status of the investor's company according to local law (with a certified translation into Russian);

❸ an *expertiz* (examination) of the project in those cases required by law (when the investment targets certain "sensitive" areas and when investments are of a significant size).

Typically, temporary registration of such an enterprise can be achieved within one week from submission of the above documents. To achieve permanent registration, the enterprise must, within 30 days, open a bank account, deposit 50% of the charter capital therein, obtain a company seal (stamp), and register at the regional taxation inspectorate (and for import/export codes at the State Statistics Committee if desired). Proof of these actions is submitted to the registration chamber, which will issue a permanent registration certificate, which is then submitted to the State Committee on Foreign Investment.

TAXATION & ACCOUNTING

Wholly-owned subsidiaries are treated, for taxation purposes, as any other enterprise registered in Russia and therefore subject to a 32% profits tax from the date of their founding. Other taxes also apply (see the section below, *Enterprise Taxation*).

Wholly-owned subsidiaries are subject to Russian accounting rules (see notes above under joint stock companies). In addition, subsidiaries must submit an annual audit of their financial operations.

OTHER CONSIDERATIONS

In all respects, a wholly-owned subsidiary operates according to Russian law and is a Russian enterprise. It therefore is subject to the same restrictions and rights with regard to property ownership, labor laws, etc. as Russian enterprises. Certain advantages may be available for creation of such enterprises in Free Economic Zones.

Affiliates

Also known as a branch, the affiliate (филиал–*filial*) is something of a legal orphan. While the Russian law, *On Foreign Investment* clearly established the right of foreign firms to found affiliates in Russia, in actual practice, foreign firms have found that local registration chambers do not routinely know how to register such entities.

REGISTRATION

For creation of an affiliate of a foreign company, the following documentation must be submitted to the registration chamber (*palata*):

❶ a **declaration**, signed by the director of the foreign firm which seeks to create the affiliate, with a request to carry out its registration;

❷ a notarized and certified **copy of the decision** of the competent management organ of the enterprise to create the affiliate;

❸ two notarized and certified copies of the **Regulations** of the affiliate;

❹ notarized and certified copy of the **establishment documents** and certificate of registration of the enterprise creating the affiliate;

❺ an **extract from the trade register** from the country of the foreign investor's origin, proving the legal status of the investor's company according to local law (with a certified translation into Russian);

❻ an *expertiz* (examination) in those cases required by law;

❼ a **letter of guarantee** from the landlord of the premises where the affiliate is to be located.

SPHERES OF ACTIVITY

The affiliate of a Western company may legally act in the company's name in Russia. While the affiliate's Regulations are to delineate its spheres of activity, its activities are somewhat circumscribed by the fact that *it would be a foreign legal entity.* While, for instance, it could negotiate and conclude hard currency contracts with Russian entities, repatriate the earnings and fees from such contracts (considering appropriate taxation), appoint agents, licensees and distributors, it could not contract for the sale of goods or services in *rubles* to Russian legal entities.

FINANCIAL ACTIVITY

While an affiliate would be able to open ruble and hard currency bank accounts, it would be allowed to earn rubles only from dividends or distributions from Russian enterprises in which it had a ruble-denominated equity investment. It would be able to obtain local credit and enter into contractual arrangements in the name of its head office, insofar as it had the appropriate authority, granted in its Regulations, to do so. It would be able to transfer abroad currency revenues earned in Russia (and be able to open foreign bank accounts without Russsina Central Bank approval), and would not be required to sell 50% of currency earnings. In short, *an affiliate is treated in all financial matters as a foreign legal entity.* Further, as an extension of the parent company, its financial liability is inseparable from its parent organization.

TAXATION

An affiliate would be subject to the 32% profits tax on profits directly attributable to its commercial activity on Russian soil. In most instances, however, only the transfer tax on dividends applies (i.e. to repatriation of dividends earned from equity investments in joint ventures or other enterprises). Other taxes also apply (see the section below, *Enterprise Taxation*).

SCOTT–EUROPEAN CORPORATION

FOR 20 YEARS, SPECIALISTS IN SALES AND MARKETING IN RUSSIA AND THE COMMONWEALTH, WITH A MOSCOW STAFF OF OVER 50 PROFESSIONALS, HEADQUARTERED IN THE WORLD TRADE CENTER, MOSCOW

SERVICES OFFERED

MANUFACTURER'S REPRESENTATIVE

We have traditionally provided representation and consultation services to a wide range of Western manufacturers.

HOSPITAL/MEDICAL EQUIPMENT & PHARMACEUTICALS SUPPLIER

We act as distributor, dealer or agent for a wide range of medical/hospital equipment and pharmaceuticals. We can plan and supply a complete, multi-disciplinary hospital. We also supply individual units of equipment and various supplies to clinics and hospitals across the Commonwealth. We own and operate a Russian company which provides high-quality technical service to medical devices of any manufacturer.

CONSTRUCTION, MINING, AND OILFIELD EQUIPMENT SUPPLIER

We own and operate one of the first successful dealerships for construction equipment in Russia. We act as sales agent and distributor for a wide range of equipment for the oilfields and the open-cast mines.

INVESTMENT ADVISING/INVESTMENT MANAGEMENT

We are one of the few Western firms to successfully master the complexities of working within local joint-ventures. We offer to share our experience and knowledge of the market to assist in finding suitable investment targets and partners in manufacturing ventures.

In the CIS:
12 Krasnopresneneskaya nab. Suite 502
Rosinpred
Moscow 123610
Ph. (095) 253-1094 • Fax (095) 253-9382
Telex 411813 REPR SU

In the United States:
58 East State Street
Montpelier
Vermont 05602 USA
Ph. (802) 223-0262 • Fax (802) 223-0265
Telex 5101011983

6 easy ways to make doing business in Moscow well worth the trip.

❶

Fax Service-Globus your Moscow itinerary,
language requirements and visa support needs

❷

Let Service-Globus make or confirm
your hotel reservations

❸

Step off the plane and be greeted by an
experienced Service-Globus interpreter

❹

Check out a free copy of the Business Survival Guide
while your personal Service-Globus driver
delivers you to your hotel or meeting

❺

Get right to work in well-equipped
meeting sites pre-arranged by Service-Globus
to meet all your requirements

❻

Say goodbye at the airport
to your Service-Globus interpreter
after a productive, hassle-free stay

Call for information about our *very* reasonable rates.

MOSCOW 109004 BOLSHAYA KOMMUNISTICHESKAYA 1/5
7(095) 298-6146   FAX 7(095) 298-6149

SHEREMETYEVO AIRPORT OFFICES
7(095) 578-7534   FAX 7(095)578-4650

Representations

This entity, also known as an accredited office, is a holdover from the Soviet era, established in the late 1970s, to allow for the maintenance of a local presence for companies doing business with Soviet ministries and enterprises. Its usefulness is, in most instances, dissolving, and most foreign representations are seeking to reformulate their presence into a wholly-owned subsidiary or affiliate. Still, the notion of an accredited office does bestow immediate credibility on a firm, as it carries with it explicit governmental approval of the firm's activities in Russia. It also allows one to more easily obtain a multiple-entry visa, and, at least in the case of press accreditation, allows the dubious benefit of internal air travel for ruble fares.

REGISTRATION

Registration of a representation is done through the Accreditation Service of the Russian Chamber of Commerce and Industry, or the Ministry of Foreign Trade or the Russian Agency for International Cooperation and Development. The foreign company must submit the following documentation to the Service:

❶ a written application;

❷ a notarized copy of the company's Charter;

❸ a notarized copy of the company's Articles of Incorporation or similarly valid documentation concerning the nature of the company and its activity;

❹ a notarized extract from the trade register from the country of the foreign investor's origin, proving the legal status of the investor's company according to local law (with a certified translation into Russian) or a copy of the company's registration certificate;

❺ a notarized document issued by the company's bank, attesting to the liquidity and payment capabilities of the company (with a certified translation into Russian);

❻ a power of attorney giving the representative effecting the accreditation the authority to act on the company's behalf;

❼ a least two letters of support from Russian companies with whom your company has done business in the past.

Registration, at the time of publication, costs $1000 and may be renewed for up to three years. Upon accreditation, the company receives a Permission Certificate for opening an accredited representation in Russia.

SPHERES OF ACTIVITY

A representation, since it is not a Russian legal entity, is not allowed to engage in commercial activity (it was originally conceived to be like an embassy of the foreign company in the USSR) and may not hold bank accounts in Russia except for financial operations directly related to operation of its office. It may do business only on behalf of its parent company.

Revenues from the representation's activity in Russia (i.e. sales of the company's output) must be transferred directly to the foreign bank accounts of the parent company.

TAXATION

Many representations are non-taxable, since some intergovernmental agreements specify that certain types of activity which are not directly commercial are not taxable. Russian law, however, specifies that, in cases where a company's net profits from operations are not readily ascertainable, it shall be liable for taxes equal to 25% of its total costs of operation.

Private Business Activity

Russian law allows prospective investors to operate without legal status for a time while exploring the market and/or while managing the processes of registration, partner-search or negotiation. It does not entail the status of a legal entity, and does not allow hiring of staff (with the exception that foreign companies can contract with Russian individuals for the provision of services) or acquisition of legal premises (with the exception that private foreign citizens can both rent and purchase apartments from Russian citizens and companies). Taxation is entailed (and appropriate registration required), if a "base of operations" is established – at the rate set for Russian enterprises, and in any case for certain types of Russian-sourced income (i.e. rental income, licensing fees and interest).

Choosing the Appropriate Investment Vehicle

The type of investment vehicle appropriate for a particular venture is dependent upon the range of activities foreseen and the level of one's commitment to the Russian market.

The broadest range of commercial activity is allowed to "Russian" companies, be they jointly-owned by Russian and foreign entities, or wholly-owned subsidiaries of a foreign entity. Affiliates, representations and private business activity all have serious restrictions placed on the range of activities which they can undertake. And there are few tax benefits to *not* establishing such a Russian company. A Russian company, however, has the disadvantage of not being allowed to freely establish bank accounts, affiliates or investments overseas.

Choosing between a joint venture and a wholly-owned subsidiary depends primarily on the level of control and involvement (and of course, dividends) the foreign investor seeks from the investment in Russia. That the registration of joint ventures is declining and the registration of wholly-owned subsidiaries is on the rise is some indication that foreign investors are seeking a larger measure of control over their investments in Russia, something the law did not previously allow.

A joint venture or wholly-owned subsidiary is most often founded on the basis of a joint stock company. The obvious advantage of this being that joint stock companies limit investors' liability and allow a fairly free transfer of shares. But joint ventures and wholly-owned subsidiaries can also be founded with or on the basis of partnerships or individual enterprises. Both the latter may, in fact, be better-suited for initial, small-scale investments or investments by individuals.

The affiliate may be best for operating a local representation of a foreign company and for making direct equity investments in Russian companies and either re-investing revenues earned or repatriating them. But, as this means of investment is somewhat untested to date, it could be said to be a bit riskier and more prone to unforeseen regulatory developments. And, since this type of investment vehicle has real limits to the type of activity which it can undertake, it is likely best for initial forays into the marketplace.

The representation, as noted above, offers few real advantages to the investor, now that real direct foreign investment is possible. The opening up of the Russian economy has, in a sense, caused the representation to outlive its usefulness, except for those entities not engaged in strictly commercial activity, such as press agencies or aid organizations.

Leasing an Office

If you are not relying on your Russian partners to provide office space for your venture, you will need to deal with this issue directly. The real estate market in Russia is, as yet, immature and over-priced, particularly in Moscow and St. Petersburg. Due to a lack of suitable commercial space, over one-fourth of all Russian companies are housed in converted apartments.

There are first-class office buildings being renovated and built in Moscow and St. Petersburg, although never enough to meet demand, and usually at prices only Fortune 500 companies would consider paying. Assuming that purchase of real estate is not the intention (see *Privatization* section below), this leaves the option of leasing from a Russian landlord. The following guidelines will help structure a safe lease. In any event, lean on the advice of an experienced Western lawyer based in Russia before signing any deal.

• Question one is who owns the property for lease. If it is owned by a state enterprise, that enterprise cannot sign a lease. Only the committee that is overseeing or will oversee the enterprise's privatization can do this.

• If the property to be leased is owned by either an individual or a company, it may be leased directly. Get proof of ownership at the outset of any discussions. An individual or company owns property (i.e. an apartment) if they have privatized it (ask to see the privatization certificate). If you are dealing with a company, be certain the person you are dealing with is properly empowered to lease this property on the company's behalf. Be sure any lease agreement is examined by your lawyer and fully notarized.

• If the person seeking to lease you the property does not own it, you must find out who does. Usually the property will be under lease or grant from a city or regional committee for property administration. With this body's approval, your future landlord can sublease the property to you.

• Rent payable to a Russian landlord must be paid in rubles, by bank transfer. The VAT applies to rental payments. The landlord must pay taxes on rental income. If a landlord is a Western company or has a legal right to have a foreign bank account, the rent can be paid in foreign currency. The many individuals and companies currently renting office or apartment space from Russians for cash foreign currency do so illegally and have no redress should the landlord demand a change in rental terms.

• Commercial space should be inspected meticulously before rental. Ask to see the *tekhnicheskiy passport* for the space, which will help address zoning and use questions. If the space is a historical building, is being used for social welfare purposes, or requires capital repair, have your lawyer look into potential associated complications and additional approvals that might become necessary for you to use the space as planned.

Privatization

There has never in history been an effort to privatize state-owned assets on the scale of that now being undertaken in Russia. No significant private economic activity has existed in Russia for over 60 years. This means there is no capital market to absorb massive divestment of state assets and no store of business knowledge with which to profitably manage new privatized enterprises. Nevertheless, privatization of the over 200,000 state-owned enterprises has taken center stage in the economic reform effort. And since there is no precedent upon which to base policy, the handful of ministers and deputy ministers overseeing the effort rely on sheer force of will and continual *ad hoc* adjustments to push the program forward.

The most significant recent alteration in course came in June of 1992, when President Boris Yeltsin issued a decree establishing a system of vouchers, and later investment funds, which was to form the foundation for a paper market. The immediate intent was to jump-start the privatization process, which had become bogged down for lack of any sense of urgency. The presidential decree required state-owned enterprises to choose a manner of privatization (from among three choices) before year's end. It further required vouchers to be distributed to all citizens by year's end, and required their redemption before the end of 1993 (subsequently extended into 1994). As of the end of 1993, about half of all vouchers remained in circulation, and about one-third of all larger enterprises and 60% of small shops and restaurants had been privatized. Twelve of 89 regions in Russia have not been participating in the federal privatization program.

ENTERPRISE PRIVATIZATION

Enterprise work forces remain at the center of the privatization effort. Enterprise employees enjoy preeminent rights in both choosing the manner of privatization and, consequently, their share of ownership in the newly privatized enterprise. The first stage of any privatization foresees employees buying shares at nominal value.

But the voucher system (which replaced a convoluted and complicated system of privatization accounts for citizens) also entails a system of direct auctions for the remaining enterprise capital (20-60%) not assumed by enterprise employees. Vouchers – each citizen received a single voucher, with a face value of 10,000 rubles – are the singular currency in these auctions.

Three options: The amount of shares available for purchase by auction are determined by the amount of shares purchased or obtained by enterprise workers and management during the period of closed subscription prior to open auctions. Three privatization options are open to large enterprises being transformed into joint stock companies.

❶ *Limited control:* In the first variant, workers and management receive 25% of non-voting shares free. Workers may also purchase up to 10% of voting shares at a 30% discount off the face value and management may buy an additional 5% of shares at face value. In this variant, therefore, outside investors can obtain from 60-75% of common stock through subsequent auctions.

❷ *Majority interest:* In the second variant, workers and management purchase, at 1.7 times the nominal price, 51% of common stock, with the balance for sale via auctions or other competitive means.

❸ *Employee bail-out:* In the third variant, rarely adopted, a group of employees may exercise the right to take control of the enterprise, pledging to make it profitable within one year. They are given an option on 20% of enterprise shares, for sale at face value, but must put up personal assets as collateral, equaling a minimum of 200 times the current average monthly wage. Thus, through this variant, potentially 80% of shares could become available through auctions.

In any case, final say on the amount of overall shares for sale by various means for vouchers is granted by the relevant councils of people's deputies and dealt with on a case-by-case basis.

The investment fund system, to aggregate vouchers and invest them broadly in privatizing enterprises, has only begun to develop. As was the case with the birth of Russian commercial banking and commodity exchanges, there has been a sudden proliferation of such funds, and no system exists for verifying their claims or assessing their activity.

As mentioned, the privatization options enumerated above apply to larger state and municipal enterprises (those with over 1000 workers or assets in excess of 50 mn rubles on January 1, 1992) that are being transformed into open joint stock companies. Smaller enterprises (less than 200 workers or less than 1 mn rubles in assets), particularly those in the service and retail spheres, are being privatized directly through auctions and tenders. Already over 70,000 small enterprises have been privatized in this manner.

Small scale enterprise privatization via auction stipulates some safety nets for employees of the enterprise. Employees may purchase shares in their own enterprises at 30% under the face value. If the enterprise is sold via tender and if conditions are attached to the sale, employees are potentially allowed a bonus of 20% of the final purchase price (or 15 times the monthly minimum wage each). If no conditions are attached to the sale of an enterprise and it goes on the auction block, employees may receive up to 30%

of the final purchase price (or up to 20 times the minimum monthly wage each) as a bonus.

PRIVATIZATION AND FOREIGN INVESTMENT

Given the present situation, there are a number of ways in which an interested investor can take advantage of the privatization process to obtain ownership of or shares in a Russian enterprise:

- Purchase, through negotiation, the assets of a bankrupt enterprise;
- Purchase vouchers from Russian citizens and partake in auctions or invest them in investment funds;
- Negotiate directly with small and medium-sized enterprises privatizing through direct sale (vs. a changeover to a joint stock company) for investment and ownership of a portion or all of the enterprise;
- Purchase shares of investment funds which manage the purchase, sale and investment of vouchers;
- Purchase shares of privatizing enterprises for cash;
- Purchase enterprise shares obtained through privatization by employees and management;
- Negotiate directly for purchase of enterprises already privatized, to re-register as a joint stock company with foreign investment or a wholly-owned subsidiary (in either case the new entity replaces the old);
- Found a joint venture (joint stock company) with an enterprise that has privatized (in this case the privatized enterprise continues to function separately).

HOUSING PRIVATIZATION

Privatization of housing has not been put on the fast track, as has been the case with enterprises. Still, some progress is occurring on this front as well. The plan for privatization of housing entails granting free to all Russian citizens a specified amount of housing space. Space above this norm (and which is part of the housing a person already occupies) may be purchased at an established rate. Similarly, citizens will receive compensation from the state for any unused portion of their quotas. At present, the state plans to allot $18m^2$ of space to each individual, plus an additional $9m^2$ to each family (the average amount of living space for all Russians is $16.5m^2$).

Local councils are to set up privatization commissions to inspect and appraise privatized property, which is, obviously, a huge and daunting task. All of this, of course, does not exclude the conduct of housing auctions, which are already occurring. Foreign individuals are allowed to rent, lease or buy privatized apartments. Similarly, properly registered firms with foreign investment may acquire real estate in this manner.

Foreign Trade

The rules and regulations governing foreign trade activity by Russian enterprises (including joint ventures) were changed dramatically by a November 15, 1991, Russian Presidential decree, *On the Liberalization of*

Foreign Economic Activity in the Russian Federation. The decree, which took effect January 1, 1992, lifted nearly all previous restrictions on foreign trade activity, while at the same time banned the use of foreign currency on Russian territory (this latter was subsequently amended and finally brought into force on January 1, 1994). The November decree and subsequent amendments and additions by other legal acts form the essential legal framework for the conduct of foreign trade in and with Russia:

- all types of foreign trade activity, including barter, are permitted;
- all enterprises registered in accordance with the Russian law, *On Enterprises and Enterprise Activity* and the law, *On Foreign Investment Activity in the RSFSR*, may conduct import/export activity directly. Further, no special authorization or registration documents need to be submitted to the Ministry of Foreign Economic Relations or any State Licensing Committee (although there is still the need to show a customs official proof of valid registration of the enterprise, and the enterprise must be entered in the State Register of Enterprises, see below). Importers are required to show proof of a hard currency bank account when importing according to contracts valuated in currency;
- the November decree lifted all *taxes* on import and export activity. Export *duties* remain on many goods (excluding those produced by joint ventures with over 30% foreign ownership), however, and, from January 1, 1992 (Resolution #91), are evaluated in ECUs, and payable in rubles at the market rate of exchange as set at the MICE. In late 1992 import duties were also imposed at a *minimum* 5% of contract value, and increased to 15% in early 1993. Also effective from early 1993, the Russian government retroactively imposed the VAT (at 23% on almost all goods) on all imports, valued in currency and payable in rubles at the current rate of exchange;
- licensing of and quotas on imports and exports are almost wholly abolished; now just some 5% of export items and 3% of import items are subject to licensing or quotas. The main items subject to quotas and licenses are goods of strategic importance, i.e. raw materials. Firms with greater than 30% foreign ownership are not subject to licensing on the goods they produce. Both general and single-use licenses are available; both are non-transferable and issued by the Ministry of Foreign Economic Relations;
- all fixed currency ↔ ruble exchange rates are abolished in the Russian Federation. Banks may buy and sell rubles from foreign and Russian citizens at independently set rates; citizens are not required to prove the sources of any hard currency and have unlimited right of purchase and sale of rubles. Foreign citizens and companies may take part in currency auctions only via legally-registered Russian companies (including joint ventures);
- hard-currency settlements between Russian enterprises is forbidden, except those involving currency ↔ ruble exchanges. Foreign legal entities (i.e. non-Russian entities, including affiliates of foreign companies) may not conclude contracts with Russian enterprises for payment in rubles;
- the USSR law, *On Currency Operations* has been abolished, as has the USSR Customs Tariff and Customs Code. However, since June 1992, by presidential decree, all enterprises, irregardless of their form of ownership

(i.e. including joint ventures) are now required to sell 50% of hard currency earnings (minus costs of transportation) within 14 days of receipt of revenues. Enterprises with over 30% foreign ownership may sell the entire 50% on the free market (see below, *Enterprise Taxation*).

CUSTOMS

While foreign trade has been greatly simplified since the Soviet period, this does not obviate certain customs formalities. These are outlined below.

Documentation and Registration

• To conduct foreign trade, an enterprise must be entered into the State Register of Enterprises. For enterprises with foreign investment, the list is maintained, and proof of entry is issued by, the Main Administration for Registration of Enterprises with Foreign Investment. After receiving a certificate of registration as an enterprise, such companies should seek registration with the Agency for International Cooperation and Development (in Moscow at Georgievskiy per. 2). The paperwork required is: a notarized copy of certification of registration and of the Charter and Agreement; a certificate from Goskomstat attesting to assignment of registration codes; a certificate from one's bank attesting that an account has been opened and that 50% of establishment capital has been deposited. Registration is to take 21 days.

• To receive goods and property at customs and to officially register a shipment, the following documents are required (either the official recipient or a fully-empowered representative may present them):

❶ customs shipping declaration;

❷ permission of specified government organs, if the goods or property falls under the control of these organs;

❸ documents affirming payment for the customs procedure and, where necessary, for customs duties and taxes;

❹ other documents indicated in the declaration;

❺ a copy of the enterprise's establishment documents as proof of registration, if not already on file. Bank account certification may also be requested.

• Customs institutions may, as an exception, allow customs registration without a declaration. This is with the understanding that such a declaration will be presented within 15 days after customs registration. In such an instance, the declarant must affirm in writing that the declaration will be presented in the specified time period.

• Registration for export of "strategically important" goods and raw materials is done through the Ministry of Foreign Economic Relations (MFER). Strict quotas and licensing procedures apply. Firms seeking independent registration for such export activity must submit to MFER the following documentation: a notarized copy of the enterprise Charter and Agreement; a copy of the certificate attesting to registration as a legal enterprise; proof of the enterprise's maintenance of ruble and currency accounts in a Russian bank, together with a recommendation letter from the bank, attesting to the liquidity of the enterprise; a financial report of the company for the previous year and, if required, audit documentation proving the validity of the report; a list of contracts fulfilled in the previous year dealing with the concerned group of goods and indicating the basic terms of said contracts.

Where to Receive Imported Goods

• Two main customs points are used in Moscow. Items shipped into Russia by air transit Sheremetevo II customs terminal. Goods arriving by truck typically transit Butovo customs point (on the Southern outskirts of the city). Goods arriving by train can be claimed at the train station. There are customs agents at all stations where goods can arrive from abroad. Declarations for train arrivals must be processed at Oktyabrskaya Tovarnaya Stantsiya, located at Komsomolskaya ploshchad. Private customs clearing houses and customs storage warehouses have been springing up as well, and these may prove more efficient means of receiving goods (see the Yellow Pages in our *Where in Moscow*); in fact, they can broker all customs formalities on your behalf.

• In St. Petersburg, goods arriving by air transit Pulkovo customs terminal, those arriving by boat or truck transit Central Customs. For more detailed information see our *Where in St. Petersburg*.

• Under current rules, goods and property can also be declared and cleared through customs:

❶ at the declarant's place of business, under the condition that the declarant assumes the costs of bringing the customs official to the site. The declarant may also request the assistance of the customs office in setting up an inspection committee (expert) or designation of a customs representative (see section below on *akt*);

❷ at the location of the customs office, whereby goods or property should be shipped to/received at that office;

❸ at other locations agreed upon with the customs office having jurisdiction for the declarant's region, provided other options are not possible.

The akt of Receipt

• When equipment arrives in Russia on contract, the opening of the shipment should be witnessed by an expert (or inspection committee) from customs or the Russian Chamber of Commerce. If the equipment arrives in unsatisfactory condition, the recipient will thereby be protected by a certified statement (*akt*) which will be jointly signed by the expert and the recipient, who will be able to take recourse for compensation with the party sending and/or shipping the equipment. A similar procedure is to be followed in the event damaged goods are received.

• For accounting and inventory purposes in a joint venture or other enterprise registered on Russian soil, any shipment received must be certified by an *akt*. This means drawing up a list of the items received, their quantity, and their value, and having the person who received the goods sign the list.

Processing Fees

- Processing fees for customs clearing are 0.1% of the contract value payable in rubles, plus 0.05% payable in the currency of the contract.
- No payment for processing is required if:

❶ the total price of declared goods and property is less than 2000 rubles;

❷ property previously imported or exported on a temporary basis is being returned from whence it came;

❸ the goods or property are to be used for the official purposes of diplomatic or consulate representations of foreign states resident in Russia, of international intergovernmental organizations and the representatives of foreign governments which work in them, or of other international organizations which enjoy duty-free treatment on Russian territory;

❹ a preliminary declaration is presented for shipments made upon a State writ;

❺ the goods are part of equipment under assembly and if a general declaration covering such goods has been previously filed. If such property subsequently becomes the object of a purchase, sale or barter and is re-declared as such, payment for customs processing follows the procedures specified above.

How to Pay for Processing Fees, Taxes and Duties

- Payment can be made in advance or at the time of customs clearing (if at a customs point such as Sheremetevo II or Butovo). If made in advance, payment should be made by bank transfer to the account of the Russian State Customs Committee. Ruble payments for duties and taxes can be paid to the account of the customs office through which goods are being cleared. The document which, for the bank's purposes, serves as the basis for payment, is the filled-in customs declaration. Proof of payment should accompany the declaration when it is presented at customs.
- Payment can also be made at the customs point, in cash. In general, payment should be made before customs will release the goods or property. Yet an organization or enterprise can present a guarantee letter (*garantiynoye pismo*) with the proper certification as proof that proper payment will be made.

FREE ECONOMIC ZONES (FEZS)

As a mechanism for encouraging foreign investment in targeted regions and industries, Russia has established Free Economic Zones (FEZs) in certain cities, regions and oblasts. Among these are St. Petersburg, Vyborg, Kemerovo, Novgorod and Nakhodka (see Chapter 1 for a complete list). The specific "privileged terms" for foreign investment and foreign trade are different for each FEZ (a general Russian law governing Free Economic Zones has yet to be passed), but all have certain elements in common.

- **Taxation is reduced**. In some cases, special tax holidays are extended to joint ventures; in others, caps are placed on the tax burden enterprises will have to bear (thus limiting some uncertainty). Generally, profits invested back into the FEZ's development are not taxed.

- **Import and export duties and taxes are reduced or eliminated.** In general, there are promises of "easing" the process of foreign trade, and quotas and licensing requirements are removed.
- **Local authorities are vested with greater authority** to register enterprises, set tax rates and terms of lease.

Labor Laws

The Russian law *On Enterprises and Enterprise Activity* significantly loosens state control over enterprise labor policy. It recognizes that the impending break-up of state enterprises creates new imperatives to allow private companies to set their own labor policies, within certain parameters. The law designates that collective and/or individual labor contracts are the primary basis for regulating labor-management relations, workers' rights, vacation time, etc., and may be valid for up to five years.

This said, it bears noting that the RSFSR Labor Code (1983) is still technically in effect and, supposedly, has juridical weight greater than any individual or collective labor contract. The Labor Code. as a relic of the Soviet era, is significantly more "pro-labor" than is the currently accepted norm. In fact, recent court rulings have overruled the Labor Code, in favor of independently-negotiated labor contracts on issues of employee hiring and firing. The reasoning has been that the higher compensation inherent in such contracts sufficiently counterbalances any less advantageous working conditions (i.e. greater uncertainty) that the contracts might offer vs. what the Labor Code specifies.

The norms and expectations of Russian workers carried over from the Soviet period are still of great relevance, however, aside from the fact that they may be codified in the Labor Code.

- It is illegal to discriminate against employees or applicants on the basis of sex, race, nationality, or religious beliefs.
- The right to strike is not forbidden, nor is it allowed.
- Employees are expected, for the most part, to work a 41 hour, five or six day week. There are exceptions for teenagers and people employed at hazardous jobs; in fact persons under 18 years of age cannot be employed in "hard labor."
- An individual can be hired for a trial period (as specified in a labor contract), during or at the end of which they may be fired with or without cause or reason.
- There are seven holidays recognized as Russian national holidays when no one is expected to work. These are January 1-2, January 7, March 8, May 1-2 and May 9, June 12, November 7. Other regional or city holidays may also be celebrated. If a holiday falls on Tuesday, Monday is also a holiday and the previous Saturday is a workday. In addition, industrial, office and professional workers are entitled to at least 24 working days of leave (*otpusk*) per year with pay based on average salary for the past year.

- Jobs are typically classified according to skill grades and wage categories. Workers can be employed hourly or on a piece-work basis. Time-and-a-half is paid for overtime and double time for holidays.
- Management is expected to ensure occupational safety and health. It must satisfy the requirements of building codes. The facilities must meet with the approval of the state sanitary and technical supervisor, the trade union "technical inspectorate," the fire marshal, the trade union committee of the enterprise and any ministry or organization that may oversee the enterprise.
- Special clothing, instruction and safety equipment, as well as medical exams, are required in certain job categories. The enterprise is financially liable for disabilities to employees "arising from the performance of their duties."
- Female workers are afforded somewhat greater protection than males. For example, pregnant women and women with children under the age of one may not work at night (unless it is especially necessary). Pregnant women are guaranteed 112 days maternity leave with pay (140 days in the event of an abnormal birth). They may take up to a year with partial pay for child care.
- At least 2-3 days are to be given to workers getting married; 1-2 days for paternity leave; 2-3 days for a death in the family. There are, similarly, added protections for teenage labor. Special incentives often exist, such as a shortened work day, to encourage employees to continue with their education.
- Labor disputes in larger enterprises (where a labor union is present) are resolved, generally, before one of three tribunals:
- ❶ Labor dispute commissions are set up at the enterprise to hammer out differences internally.
- ❷ If the commission fails, the dispute is taken to a trade union committee with authority to overrule the commission.
- ❸ Either management or labor may appeal the trade union committee decision to district (or town) court.
- Cases of theft or property damage go straight to district court. Regarding theft, it should be noted that a doctrine similar to *respondeat superior* carries a special significance. Lost supplies or illegal use of equipment such as photocopiers may be the responsibility of the employer. Theft is very common. One way to avoid it is through adequate compensation and benefits. In some cases, employees' contracts can include a clause whereby they are individually or collectively liable for lost supplies. Joint ventures may also want to investigate insurance coverage for this problem or consider some sort of hold-back provision such as in construction contracts to cover losses.
- A labor contract in a large enterprise (with a labor union presence) often cannot be cancelled unilaterally by management. Cancellation is done only with the consent of the employees' trade union. If management wrongfully dismisses or transfers an employee, the management is personally liable for the damage sustained. Generally, employees in such enterprises cannot be unwillingly transferred to different jobs or different locations.
- While employment contracts are not required by law, if one is signed with an employee subsequent to their beginning work, the contract has

retroactive force. The term for a labor contract must be either less than 5 years or indefinite in term. It must indicate the employee's salary, and the scope and duration of work to be performed.

- Although the Labor Code says a place of work can keep an employee from leaving for two months in order to find a replacement, a worker is, in reality, free to leave at will. Likewise, the limits on a manager's ability to fire employees are much less strict than the written laws lead one to believe. One source on labor codes says that one acceptable reason for letting a worker go is "discrepancies of a worker in fulfilling his duties." The worker must be given one month's written notice.

- The following are generally accepted reasons for immediate firing of employees: liquidation or bankruptcy of an enterprise; drunkenness on the job; unauthorized absence from work or absence due to certain illnesses for more than four months; embezzlement; failure to perform; unqualified for the position; the company is rehiring an employee who was on leave and who previously held the position in question.

- A percentage of the income of large enterprises is typically earmarked for the cultural and sports activities of the trade union/employees. The enterprise also sets aside funds for all employees' "social insurance" (aside from the taxes in this area). These funds are used for disability, maternity leave, pensions, as well as medical treatment and dietary supplements.

Legal Status of Foreign Nationals

No new Russian legislation has been passed to date regulating the status of foreign nationals in Russia. Therefore, until this happens, by default Soviet legislation still applies. Yet even Soviet law on the status of foreign nationals is not a monument to precision.

- Foreign nationals in Russia are supposed to "enjoy the same rights and bear the same duties as citizens of [Russia] unless otherwise laid down in acts of [Russian] legislation." (Part 1 of Article 3, law, *On Foreign Nationals*). All of the labor laws are fully applicable to foreigners. This includes wages, taxation, contracts, leisure time and so forth. Likewise, the provision for maternity leave and other benefits are applicable. In reality, as noted above, labor contracts govern these and other benefits.

- Foreign nationals who are permanent residents have the right, on the basis of and in the manner prescribed for Russian citizens, to receive accommodation in state and socially owned houses and in cooperative houses. Foreigners (excepting diplomatic personnel) further have the right to pay for accommodation in rubles.

- Resident foreigners are required to register with the local UVIR (visa registration) office within 72 hours of arrival.

- Foreign nationals who are permanent residents are entitled to the same free medical care as Russian citizens. Temporary residents are entitled to medical care as may be prescribed from time to time.

• Foreign nationals, temporary and permanent, must pay taxes (see section below, *Personal Taxation*), but are likewise entitled to pensions and other forms of social security.

• Foreign nationals have the same educational rights as Russian citizens. And, of course, they face similar obligations. They cannot vote, join political parties, and are not required to serve in the military.

• Foreign nationals may have their period of stay reduced if there are "no longer any grounds" for the stay. The period of stay may also be reduced for a violation of the law. It follows that, if the offense is serious enough, the period of stay can be extended. A foreign national's departure from Russia may be postponed until the fulfillment by him or her of property obligations to Russian citizens, organizations or the state.

• Foreign businesses in Russia should become familiar with the basic provisions of visa, customs and currency regulations (see Chapter 2, *Visa and Customs*), and should be certain their employees do the same. Employees in Russia should be briefed on criminal law, housing law, and the court system.

• When traveling in Russia, a foreign national should always have his passport with himself/herself. For instance it is illegal to board a domestic flight without a passport; purchase of train tickets and boarding trains now also require display of some form of photo identification.

Personal Taxation

Businesses that are considering an investment in Russia need to consider a myriad of personal and enterprise tax issues and absolutely must have legal advice on these questions. This section on personal taxation, and the following one on enterprise taxation, can serve as an introduction to these issues but cannot replace the advice of a competent lawyer or accountant (see Chapter 1 for a list of firms active in Russia).

• On December 7, 1991, the Russian law, *On Income Taxes on Natural Persons* was passed, with significant consequences for the individual taxpayer. Tax rates are based on annual income and affect income received on or after January 1, 1992. Every citizen who receives income outside of enterprises which deduct taxes from salaries shall be required, prior to April 1 of each year, to make a declaration at their local tax organ of revenues actually received and to provide adequate documentation of same.

• The main changes wrought by the new tax law are that there are fewer types of individuals free of the income tax, and, of particular note to foreign workers being paid by joint ventures in hard currency, the highest marginal tax rate is 30%.

• Salaries earned in hard currency must be valuated in rubles at the commercial rate. Taxes are payable in rubles or in hard currency via any Sberbank which handles currency operations (a 1% commission is charged). Thus, at the current commercial ruble rate, a foreigner earning greater than the equivalent of $1500-2000 per year must pay a 30% tax on most all income. It therefore makes sense for any joint venture or subsidiary or representation to work out a mechanism whereby the foreign national is paid his or her salary in the home country, if such can be done in a manner that is legal and acceptable (i.e. through a trust held in escrow).

• Income tax is not due on money spent obtaining housing or a *dacha* or payment of financing for same. Up to 500 times the minimum Russian salary level (R50,000 at time of publication) earned from sales of such property is also non-taxable. There is no tax on income from sales of personal items (i.e. a car or other durables), provided the total such income does not exceed 50 times the minimum Russian salary level.

• A foreigner expecting to earn income in Russia and who will be resident in Russia more than 183 days in a calendar year, must submit a declaration within one month of entering Russia of the amount he/she anticipates earning. Taxes for the year are thus estimated and made payable in three equal parts of 25% of the estimated sum, on May 15, August 15, and November 15. A final declaration (and payment), with any changes, is to be made by March 1 of the following year. No declaration is required if one anticipates earning an annual within the lowest (12%) tax bracket, the ceiling for which was raised to one million rubles in mid-1993.

• Non-permanent residents (less than 183 days) earning income based on business (i.e. rental income, royalties, licenses) occurring in Russia are subject to a 20% income tax.

• Income for a private company is considered to be income of the individual owning the company and is taxed as such. This requires a separate declaration from the one mentioned above.

• Taxable income is defined in the law as: wages and salaries, including fees, *per diem* and other compensations for living in Russia, compensation for education of children, for food, and for family members brought on vacation. Not included as part of taxable income are: payments for social insurance and pensions (made by the employer), compensation for rental of living quarters and a car necessary for business purposes, compensation for business trips.

• All Soviet international tax agreements are still in effect until renegotiation with the separate states. All reflect similar treatment. Wages and other personal income that are earned by a person in one contracting state are not subject to taxation in the other state as long as (1) the person is not present in the other state for more than 183 days in any given calendar year, (2) the person's wages/salary are paid by the home office and not the local base of operations, and (3) the employer is not a resident legal entity.

The USSR [Russian] treaties with Sweden, Cyprus, Finland and the United Kingdom provide that technical specialists resident in one contracting state will not be taxed in the other so long as they are not present in the other for more than 365 days in any two year period. It should be noted that, in some treaties, the tax treatment depends on the residency of the employer. To avoid double taxation the taxpayer must declare tax payments made in other countries.

Enterprise Taxation

There are over two dozen different types of federal and local taxes which may be levied on an enterprise, from customs taxes to property taxes to profits and VAT taxes. Only the most general and significant taxes are reviewed below. For a full understanding of tax obligations, consult a competent tax attorney or accountant (see Chapter 1 for a list of qualified law and accounting firms).

PROFITS TAX

All Russian enterprises, irrespective of their form of ownership (including foreign) are subject to a profits tax of 32%. This is calculated based on total revenues, minus expenses, excepting wages. This rate jumps to 45% for brokerage firms, trading services and middlemen, and to 70% for auctions, casinos, video/audio rental companies and companies offering video games. Taxes are payable on world-wide income of the enterprise, unless a double taxation treaty applies. Estimated taxes are to be paid quarterly with a final return due March 15.

A number of profits tax breaks can be sought. Specifically, companies will enjoy a deduction from taxable profits of: 30% of total monies spent on environmental protection measures; 100% of the sum invested in health care centers, retirement homes, pre-schools, pioneer camps, cultural and sports centers, educational institutions and housing projects which are on the enterprise's balance sheet; 100% of the sum donated to certain charities; 100% of the sum devoted to agricultural and food processing improvements, to technical re-equipping and improvements in the oil and gas, medical/pharmaceutical and consumer goods spheres; 100% of donations to ecological, humanitarian, health, religious and other social organizations, but not more than 2% of overall profits in this case. This said, such deductions cannot eliminate more than 50% of an enterprise's profits tax burden.

Small enterprises are eligible for certain tax holidays during the first two years of their operation. See the section above in this chapter, *Small Enterprises.*

Enterprises whose primary activity is as a religious or social organization, as a creative union or humanitarian fund, if properly registered as such, are freed from payment of the profits tax.

Losses can be carried over for five years to diminish profits and the consequential tax burden.

The profits tax can be reduced by up to 50% for enterprises in which more than 50% of the workers are disabled and/or 70% of the employees are pensioners.

VALUE ADDED TAX

On December 6, 1991, the Russian Parliament passed a value added tax (VAT) law which set the tax rate at 28% (21.88% for goods with regulated prices) of the sales price or contract value of goods and services. The rate has since been lowered to 20% (10% for some food items, children's clothing, medicine and medical equipment) and recently increased to 23%. The amount of the tax is to be included in the price of goods sold, and the enterprise is to pay the government the amount of tax collected from goods sold, minus the amount it payed to suppliers (who also include the tax in their sales price). This VAT does not apply to exports, but it does apply to imports (levied on the sum of the imports' value, plus any excise taxes and duties). The VAT does not apply to rent (for offices or housing) paid by foreign citizens or companies (if there is a reciprocal tax treaty to this effect).

Enterprises must pay the VAT three times monthly if their average monthly payment would exceed 100,000 rubles, monthly if the payment would be 50-100,000 rubles, and quarterly if less than 50,000 rubles. Persons involved in individual labor activity only pay a VAT on income earned in excess of 500,000 rubles.

EXCISE TAX

The sale of liquor, beer, caviar, luxury seafoods, chocolate, tobacco, cars, tires, jewelry, diamonds, furs, high-quality porcelain and cut glass, rugs and carpets and natural leather garments is taxed with an excise tax. The tax does not apply to goods sold outside the Commonwealth (i.e. exported abroad). The rates are set by the Russian government and vary by the type of product (e.g. furs are taxed at 10-35%, leather 35%, vodka 80%, cars 35-70%).

EXCESS WAGES TAX

Enterprises, including joint ventures, which pay out a total amount in salaries that exceeds the minimum wage (currently about $50) by more than four times, must pay a 50% tax on the amount over and above twice the norm.

EXPORT AND IMPORT TARIFFS

Export tariffs are established on natural resources, produce, agricultural products and arms. Two tariff rates are set. The first is the basic level of tariffs and varies depending on the item in question. The second is the level for goods which do not fall under the terms of mandatory currency sales (i.e. barter operations or non-currency operations), or *which are produced by* wholly-owned subsidiaries of foreign firms or joint ventures with at least 30% foreign ownership (which also are not subject to mandatory currency sales). The tariff on this second level is 50% above the basic level. The export tariff is valued in ECU, but paid in rubles at the current rate of exchange.

The import tariff is set at between 5-150% of the import value of the goods and applies mainly to excised items like alcohol (150%), cigarettes (100%) and cars (35-70%). The tariff is doubled for goods originating in countries with which Russia does not have most favored nation status. Food and agricultural goods are no longer free of import tariffs. Tariffs are denominated in ECU and payable in rubles at the current rate of exchange.

SOCIAL INSURANCE TAXES

Pension Fund: The amount payable to the national pension fund is based on total expenditures on worker salaries (including temporary contract labor or subcontractor labor). For enterprises, the amount due is 28% of paid salaries; for agricultural enterprises the tax is 20.6%. Persons engaged in individual labor activity, lawyers and some other activities must pay 5% of total revenues to the fund. 26% of author's honoraria paid must be paid to the pension fund. Employees pay 1% of their salary to the fund.

Social insurance fund: Beginning in 1993, all enterprises must pay a tax valued at 5.4% of all salaries to this fund.

Unemployment fund: An additional 2% of salaries must be paid to this fund.

Health Insurance fund: A tax to this fund is levied at 3.6% of all salary payments.

In sum, therefore, your typical enterprise will be required to pay, for each 100 rubles of salary to an employee, an additional 39 rubles to various social insurance funds.

CURRENCY EARNINGS TAX

Russian enterprises are required to sell to the Russian State Bank a set amount of all hard currency earnings from exporting (if that amount exceeds $500), excluding any costs of transport. Presently, Russian enterprises, including those with foreign investment, must sell 50% of such earnings through the centralized currency exchange, or banks participating in the exchange.

Wholly-owned subsidiaries of foreign firms and joint ventures with more than 30% foreign ownership are exempted from this requirement for goods of their own production. For other export operations, they are entitled to sell their currency through licensed commercial banks (whose rates are better than on the currency exchange). In any case, the sales must occur within 7 days of receipt of revenues.

There is no mandatory sale of currency obtained through its purchase on the currency exchange. Therefore, rubles gained from sales of currency that was earned through exports can be used to re-purchase currency on the exchange, and that currency may be repatriated or used as the enterprise sees fit. The difference in the amount of currency before and after this transaction, therefore, should be considered a tax on doing business in currency.

There is also no mandatory sale of currency which: (a) is part of an investment in the establishment fund of an enterprise; (b) is earned as a dividend from equity participation in an enterprise; (c) is earned from the sale of securities; (d) is part of credits borrowed or is part of payments for credits loaned; or (e) is received for humanitarian purposes.

OTHER MISCELLANEOUS TAXES

• Banking and securities companies are subject to a 0.5% tax on issuance of securities; the buyer of such securities must also pay a 0.1% tax on the value of said securities.

• Resale of some items, such as cars and computers, is subject to a resale tax of 10% or higher.

• A tax on advertising is levied at up 5% of the value of advertising services; payment is quarterly.

• There is a vehicle tax of 20% of the cost of the vehicle before VAT.

• A roads tax is assessed on all enterprises, valued at 0.4% of sales in production enterprises and 0.03% of the turnover of trading, supply and distribution enterprises.

• A property tax on enterprise assets, levied at up to 1% of the assessed value of those assets. Certain tax breaks are extended for social investments and account is given for reinvestment and depreciation. A land tax is assessed at 10 rubles per hectare and, for private farming plots, 1000 rubles per m^2.

• Capital gains are taxed at the same rate as corporate profits (32%) or individual income (up to 40%), depending on the recipient.

• There is a 6% tax on income from international transport services.

• There is a 25% tax on insurance activity and a 30% tax on banking activity (reduced to 18-20% for some dividends). These are in place of the enterprise profits tax.

• Local governments (i.e the Moscow City Government) impose taxes on buildings, motor vehicles, land, and any number of other objects. They are also increasingly introducing miscellaneous fees on certain types of trade and business activity.

• There is an investment tax credit law which can take some of the sting out of the above-mentioned laws, allowing a 10% tax deferment for 5 years on the total value of certain internal enterprise capital investments, with a ceiling of 50% of the total taxable amount. This law also allows privatizing enterprises to receive up to a 50% credit on profit taxes for interest paid on bank credit.

• Firms engaging in retail trade in Moscow (other cities should be expected to follow suit) must pay significant annual registration fees of 50 times the minimum monthly salary level; the fee is just 12.5 times this level for trade in non-excised food items. There are discounts for dealing in multiple items.

WITHHOLDING (TRANSFER) TAXES

There is a 15% transfer tax on the dividends a foreign partner repatriates from investments in Russia. This withholding tax will not be imposed if it conflicts with one of Russia's double taxation treaties (which, in most cases, are the Soviet treaties). In the absence of an applicable treaty, the Ministry of Finance has the authority to waive this tax for a specific period of time or to reduce the rate. The Ministry of Finance is supposed to use this authority to encourage particular industries (medical equipment, high technology, consumer goods).

The US-Russia Treaty for Avoidance of Double Taxation of Income places a maximum 10% tax rate on dividends, at source (5% for investors with >10% ownership or voting stock in a company).

Treaty shopping (i.e. founding a joint venture using a subsidiary company registered in a third country) can provide access to more favorable provisions in other double taxation treaties. Several of these treaties (Austria, Cyprus and Finland, for example) provide that a distribution of profits and dividends are exempt from taxation in the country from which the dividends are remitted. Thus, dividends remitted by a Russian joint venture to a Finnish company would be free of the 15% transfer tax.

Of course, the big problem is whether or not these dividends can be remitted without incurring similar or even larger taxes in the other country. It obviously does not do any good to avoid a 15% transfer tax in Russia only to discover a 25% corporate tax in Austria.

Under the Cyprus-[Russia] Tax Treaty, dividends paid to a resident of Cyprus by a resident of Russia are not subject to taxation in Russia. Furthermore, it appears that under Cypriot law the income of companies that derive their income exclusively from sources outside Cyprus are subject to an income tax of only 4.25% and shareholders receiving a dividend from such a company are not subject to any tax.

It may also be advantageous to structure a deal in terms of licensing tangible or intangible assets to a Russian partner in exchange for royalties. Under the terms of the US-Russia treaty (and those of Russia with other states), royalties of this type may be taxable only in one's home country, as is the case with interest payments.

In any event, in the case of withholding taxes, as with all aspects of Russian business law, rely on the research and advice of a competent and informed lawyer to guide your decisions. Russian tax and business law is constantly changing and this chapter, and indeed any printed source on Russian law, can at best be accurate up to the moment of its publication, and thus should serve mostly as a thorough introduction to the murky waters of Russian commercial law.

Index

Sources for facts on page 1: #1. *Rossiyskiye Vesti,* 6/26/93; #2. *Kommersant,* 6/16/93; #3. *Business MN,* 7/4/93; #4. *Moscow Times,* 9/1/93; #5. *Argumenti i Fakti,* January 1994, #1; #6-7. *Moscow Times,* 11/11/93; #8-9. *LA Times Magazine,* 1/16/94; #10. US Department of Commerce, 12/93; #11. *NYT,* 12/10/93; #12-13. *NYT,* 11/29/93; #14. *NYT,* 12/1/93; #15-16. *NYT,* 11/26/93; #17. *NYT,* 11/10/93; #18-19. *Moscow Times,* 11/11/93; #20-23. *LA Times Magazine,* 1/16/94; 24. *NYT,* 11/30/93

H

You can go to Moscow or St. Petersburg without these...

...of course you can also go fishing without rod or reel.

Nobody Covers Russia Better

Business & Travel Guides

Russia Survival Guide
The essential guide to doing business in the new Russia, now in its 4th edition. (March 1994, $18.50)

Where in Moscow
Essential directories and color city street map, now in its third edition. (March 1994, $13.50)

Where in St. Petersburg
Essential directories and color city street map, updated and now in its 2nd edition. (March 1994, $13.50)

Language

Business Russian
The practical Russian you need to know for doing business in Russia. (May 1993, $16)

Maps

New Moscow City Map & Guide
A meticulously-accurate color map of the capital city. (March 1994, $6.95)

New St. Petersburg City Map & Guide
The first new Western city map of St. Petersburg in decades. (April 1993, $6.95)

Travel Information

Russian Travel Monthly
What to read to keep up-to-date on the latest business and independent travel news. (Monthly, $36/yr.)

Reference Information

Russian News Abstracts
Indexed abstracts of over 1900 key articles from the Russian press during 1993 (1992 volume also avail.). (April 1994, $48)

Legal Information

Business Legal Materials: Russia
A monthly listing of current Russian legal acts related to trade and investment. (Monthly, $225/yr)

Russian Business Legal Materials: 1992
A comprehensive, indexed listing of over 800 Russian laws related to foreign trade with, and investment in, Russia. (February 1994, $68)

Access Russia Catalogue

Be sure to also ask for a copy of *Access Russia,* our catalogue of over 130 publications on Russia by over 40 US and European publishers.

For more information, or to place an order, contact:

Russian Information Services, Inc.

89 Main St., Box 2
Montpelier, VT 05602
ph. (802) 223-4955
fax (802) 223-6105

B. Kondratyevskiy per. 4
Moscow, Russia
ph./fax (095) 254-9275